Edifying AI Self-Driving Cars

Practical Advances in Artificial Intelligence and Machine Learning

Dr. Lance B. Eliot, MBA, PhD

ISBN: 978-1-73-630316-0

DEDICATION

To my incredible daughter, Lauren, and my incredible son, Michael.

Forest fortuna adiuvat (from the Latin; good fortune favors the brave).

CONTENTS

ACKNOWLEDGMENTS

I have been the beneficiary of advice and counsel by many friends, colleagues, family, investors, and many others. I want to thank everyone that has aided me throughout my career. I write from the heart and the head, having experienced first-hand what it means to have others around you that support you during the good times and the tough times.

To Warren Bennis, one of my doctoral advisors and ultimately a colleague, I offer my deepest thanks and appreciation, especially for his calm and insightful wisdom and support.

To Mark Stevens and his generous efforts toward funding and supporting the USC Stevens Center for Innovation.

To Lloyd Greif and the USC Lloyd Greif Center for Entrepreneurial Studies for their ongoing encouragement of founders and entrepreneurs.

To Peter Drucker, William Wang, Aaron Levie, Peter Kim, Jon Kraft, Cindy Crawford, Jenny Ming, Steve Milligan, Chis Underwood, Frank Gehry, Buzz Aldrin, Steve Forbes, Bill Thompson, Dave Dillon, Alan Fuerstman, Larry Ellison, Jim Sinegal, John Sperling, Mark Stevenson, Anand Nallathambi, Thomas Barrack, Jr., and many other innovators and leaders that I have met and gained mightily from doing so.

Thanks to Ed Trainor, Kevin Anderson, James Hickey, Wendell Jones, Ken Harris, DuWayne Peterson, Mike Brown, Jim Thornton, Abhi Beniwal, Al Biland, John Nomura, Eliot Weinman, John Desmond, and many others for their unwavering support during my career.

And most of all thanks as always to Lauren and Michael, for their ongoing support and for having seen me writing and heard much of this material during the many months involved in writing it. To their patience and willingness to listen.

INTRODUCTION

This is a book that provides the newest innovations and the latest Artificial Intelligence (AI) advances about the emerging nature of AI-based autonomous self-driving driverless cars. Via recent advances in Artificial Intelligence (AI) and Machine Learning (ML), we are nearing the day when vehicles can control themselves and will not require and nor rely upon human intervention to perform their driving tasks (or, that <u>allow</u> for human intervention, but only *require* human intervention in very limited ways).

Similar to my other related books, which I describe in a moment and list the chapters in the Appendix A of this book, I am particularly focused on those advances that pertain to self-driving cars. The phrase "autonomous vehicles" is often used to refer to any kind of vehicle, whether it is ground-based or in the air or sea, and whether it is a cargo hauling trailer truck or a conventional passenger car. Though the aspects described in this book are certainly applicable to all kinds of autonomous vehicles, I am focused more so here on cars.

For this book, I am going to borrow my introduction from those companion books, since it does a good job of laying out the landscape of self-driving cars and my overall viewpoints on the topic.

INTRODUCTION TO SELF-DRIVING CARS

This is a book about self-driving cars. Someday in the future, we'll all have self-driving cars and this book will perhaps seem antiquated, but right now, we are at the forefront of the self-driving car wave. Daily news bombards us with flashes of new announcements by one car maker or another and leaves the impression that within the next few weeks or maybe months that the self-driving car will be here. A casual non-technical reader would assume from these news flashes that in we must be on the cusp of a true self-driving car.

We are still quite a distance from having a true self-driving car. A true self-driving car is akin to a moonshot. In the same manner that getting us to the moon was an incredible feat, likewise, is achieving a true self-driving car. Anybody that suggests or even brashly states that the true self-driving car is nearly here should be viewed with great skepticism. Indeed, you'll see that I often tend to use the word "hogwash" or "crock" when I assess much of the decidedly ***fake news*** about self-driving cars.

Indeed, I've been writing a popular blog post about self-driving cars and hitting hard on those that try to wave their hands and pretend that we are on the imminent verge of true self-driving cars. For many years, I've been known as the AI Insider. Besides writing about AI, I also develop AI software. I do what I describe. It also gives me insights into what others that are doing AI are really doing versus what it is said they are doing.

Many faithful readers had asked me to pull together my insightful short essays and put them into another book, which you are now holding.

For those of you that have been reading my essays over the years, this collection not only puts them together into one handy package, I also updated the essays and added new material. For those of you that are new to the topic of self-driving cars and AI, I hope you find these essays approachable and informative. I also tend to have a writing style with a bit of a voice, and so you'll see that I am times have a wry sense of humor and poke at conformity.

As a former professor and founder of an AI research lab, I for many years wrote in the formal language of academic writing. I published in referred journals and served as an editor for several AI journals. This writing here is not of the nature, and I have adopted a different and more informal style for these essays. That being said, I also do mention from time-to-time more rigorous material on AI and encourage you all to dig into those deeper and more formal materials if so interested.

For those of you that are reading this book and have a penchant for writing code, you might consider taking a look at the open-source code available for self-driving cars. This is a handy place to start learning how to develop AI for self-driving cars. There are also many new educational courses spring forth. There is a growing body of those wanting to learn about and develop self-driving cars, and a growing body of colleges, labs, and other avenues by which you can learn about self-driving cars.

This book will provide a foundation of aspects that I think will get you ready for those kinds of more advanced training opportunities. If you've already taken those classes, you'll likely find these essays especially interesting as they offer a perspective that I am betting few other instructors or faculty offered to you. These are challenging essays that ask you to think beyond the conventional about self-driving cars.

THE MOTHER OF ALL AI PROJECTS

In June 2017, Apple CEO Tim Cook came out and finally admitted that Apple has been working on a self-driving car. As you'll see in my essays, Apple was enmeshed in secrecy about their self-driving car efforts. We have only been able to read the tea leaves and guess at what Apple has been up to. The notion of an iCar has been floating for quite a while, and self-driving engineers and researchers have been signing tight-lipped Non-Disclosure Agreements (NDA's) to work on projects at Apple that were as shrouded in mystery as any military invasion plans might be.

Tim Cook said something that many others in the Artificial Intelligence (AI) field have been saying, namely, the creation of a self-driving car has got to be the mother of all AI projects. In other words, it is in fact a tremendous moonshot for AI. If a self-driving car can be crafted and the AI works as we hope, it means that we have made incredible strides with AI and that therefore it opens many other worlds of potential breakthrough accomplishments that AI can solve.

Is this hyperbole? Am I just trying to make AI seem like a miracle worker and so provide self-aggrandizing statements for those of us writing the AI software for self-driving cars? No, it is not hyperbole. Developing a true self-driving car is really, really, really hard to do. Let me take a moment to explain why. As a side note, I realize that the Apple CEO is known for at times uttering hyperbole, and he had previously said for example that the year 2012 was "the mother of all years," and he had said that the release of iOS 10 was "the mother of all releases" – all of which does suggest he likes to use the handy "mother of" expression. But, I assure you, in terms of true self-driving cars, he has hit the nail on the head. For sure.

When you think about a moonshot and how we got to the moon, there are some identifiable characteristics and those same aspects can be applied to creating a true self-driving car. You'll notice that I keep putting the word "true" in front of the self-driving car expression. I do so because as per my essay about the various levels of self-driving cars, there are some self-driving cars that are only somewhat of a self-driving car. The somewhat versions are ones that require a human driver to be ready to intervene. In my view, that's not a true self-driving car. A true self-driving car is one that requires no human driver intervention at all. It is a car that can entirely undertake via automation the driving task without any human driver needed. This is the essence of what is known as a Level 5 self-driving car. We are currently at the Level 2 and Level 3 mark, and not yet at Level 5.

Getting to the moon involved aspects such as having big stretch goals, incremental progress, experimentation, innovation, and so on. Let's review how this applied to the moonshot of the bygone era, and how it applies to the self-driving car moonshot of today.

Big Stretch Goal

Trying to take a human and deliver the human to the moon, and bring them back, safely, was an extremely large stretch goal at the time. No one knew whether it could be done. The technology wasn't available yet. The cost was huge. The determination would need to be fierce. Etc. To reach a Level 5 self-driving car is going to be the same. It is a big stretch goal. We can readily get to the Level 3, and we are able to see the Level 4 just up ahead, but a Level 5 is still an unknown as to if it is doable. It should eventually be doable and in the same way that we thought we'd eventually get to the moon, but when it will occur is a different story.

Incremental Progress

Getting to the moon did not happen overnight in one fell swoop. It took years and years of incremental progress to get there. Likewise, for self-driving cars. Google has famously been striving to get to the Level 5, and pretty much been willing to forgo dealing with the intervening levels, but most of the other self-driving car makers are doing the incremental route. Let's get a good Level 2 and a somewhat Level 3 going. Then, let's improve the Level 3 and get a somewhat Level 4 going. Then, let's improve the Level 4 and finally arrive at a Level 5. This seems to be the prevalent way that we are going to achieve the true self-driving car.

Experimentation

You likely know that there were various experiments involved in perfecting the approach and technology to get to the moon. As per making incremental progress, we first tried to see if we could get a rocket to go into space and safety return, then put a monkey in there, then with a human, then we went all the way to the moon but didn't land, and finally we arrived at the mission that actually landed on the moon.

Self-driving cars are the same way. We are doing simulations of self-driving cars. We do testing of self-driving cars on private land under controlled situations.

We do testing of self-driving cars on public roadways, often having to meet regulatory requirements including for example having an engineer or equivalent in the car to take over the controls if needed. And so on. Experiments big and small are needed to figure out what works and what doesn't.

Innovation

There are already some advances in AI that are allowing us to progress toward self-driving cars. We are going to need even more advances. Innovation in all aspects of technology are going to be required to achieve a true self-driving car. By no means do we already have everything in-hand that we need to get there. Expect new inventions and new approaches, new algorithms, etc.

Setbacks

Most of the pundits are avoiding talking about potential setbacks in the progress toward self-driving cars. Getting to the moon involved many setbacks, some of which you never have heard of and were buried at the time so as to not dampen enthusiasm and funding for getting to the moon. A recurring theme in many of my included essays is that there are going to be setbacks as we try to arrive at a true self-driving car. Take a deep breath and be ready. I just hope the setbacks don't completely stop progress. I am sure that it will cause progress to alter in a manner that we've not yet seen in the self-driving car field. I liken the self-driving car of today to the excitement everyone had for Uber when it first got going. Today, we have a different view of Uber and with each passing day there are more regulations to the ride sharing business and more concerns raised. The darling child only stays a darling until finally that child acts up. It will happen the same with self-driving cars.

SELF-DRIVING CARS CHALLENGES

But what exactly makes things so hard to have a true self-driving car, you might be asking. You have seen cruise control for years and years. You've lately seen cars that can do parallel parking. You've seen YouTube videos of Tesla drivers that put their hands out the window as their car zooms along the highway, and seen to therefore be in a self-driving car. Aren't we just needing to put a few more sensors onto a car and then we'll have in-hand a true self-driving car? Nope.

Consider for a moment the nature of the driving task. We don't just let anyone at any age drive a car. Worldwide, most countries won't license a driver until the age of 18, though many do allow a learner's permit at the age of 15 or 16. Some suggest that a younger age would be physically too small to reach the controls of the car. Though this might be the case, we could easily adjust the controls to allow for younger aged and thus smaller stature. It's not their physical size that matters. It's their cognitive development that matters.

To drive a car, you need to be able to reason about the car, what the car can and cannot do. You need to know how to operate the car. You need to know about how other cars on the road drive. You need to know what is allowed in driving such as speed limits and driving within marked lanes. You need to be able to react to situations and be able to avoid getting into accidents. You need to ascertain when to hit your brakes, when to steer clear of a pedestrian, and how to keep from ramming that motorcyclist that just cut you off.

Many of us had taken courses on driving. We studied about driving and took driver training. We had to take a test and pass it to be able to drive. The point being that though most adults take the driving task for granted, and we often "mindlessly" drive our cars, there is a significant amount of cognitive effort that goes into driving a car. After a while, it becomes second nature. You don't especially think about how you drive, you just do it. But, if you watch a novice driver, say a teenager learning to drive, you suddenly realize that there is a lot more complexity to it than we seem to realize.

Furthermore, driving is a very serious task. I recall when my daughter and son first learned to drive. They are both very conscientious people. They wanted to make sure that whatever they did, they did well, and that they did not harm anyone. Every day, when you get into a car, it is probably around 4,000 pounds of hefty metal and plastics (about two tons), and it is a lethal weapon. Think about it. You drive down the street in an object that weighs two tons and with the engine it can accelerate and ram into anything you want to hit. The damage a car can inflict is very scary. Both my children were surprised that they were being given the right to maneuver this monster of a beast that could cause tremendous harm entirely by merely letting go of the steering wheel for a moment or taking your eyes off the road.

In fact, in the United States alone there are about 40,000 deaths per year by auto accidents, which is more than 100 per day. Given that there are about 263 million cars in the United States, I am actually more amazed that the number of fatalities is not a lot higher.

During my morning commute, I look at all the thousands of cars on the freeway around me, and I think that if all of them decided to go zombie and drive in a crazy maniac way, there would be many people dead. Somehow, incredibly, each day, most people drive relatively safely. To me, that's a miracle right there. Getting millions and millions of people to be safe and sane when behind the wheel of a two-ton mobile object, it's a feat that we as a society should admire with pride.

So, hopefully you are in agreement that the driving task requires a great deal of cognition. You don't' need to be especially smart to drive a car, and we've done quite a bit to make car driving viable for even the average dolt. There isn't an IQ test that you need to take to drive a car. If you can read and write, and pass a test, you pretty much can legally drive a car. There are of course some that drive a car and are not legally permitted to do so, plus there are private areas such as farms where drivers are young, but for public roadways in the United States, you can be generally of average intelligence (or less) and be able to legally drive.

This though makes it seem like the cognitive effort must not be much. If the cognitive effort was truly hard, wouldn't we only have Einstein's that could drive a car? We have made sure to keep the driving task as simple as we can, by making the controls easy and relatively standardized, and by having roads that are relatively standardized, and so on. It is as though Disneyland has put their Autopia into the real-world, by us all as a society agreeing that roads will be a certain way, and we'll all abide by the various rules of driving.

A modest cognitive task by a human is still something that stymies AI. You certainly know that AI has been able to beat chess players and be good at other kinds of games. This type of narrow cognition is not what car driving is about. Car driving is much wider. It requires knowledge about the world, which a chess playing AI system does not need to know. The cognitive aspects of driving are on the one hand seemingly simple, but at the same time require layer upon layer of knowledge about cars, people, roads, rules, and a myriad of other "common sense" aspects. We don't have any AI systems today that have that same kind of breadth and depth of awareness and knowledge.

As revealed in my essays, the self-driving car of today is using trickery to do particular tasks. It is all very narrow in operation. Plus, it currently assumes that a human driver is ready to intervene. It is like a child that we have taught to stack blocks, but we are needed to be right there in case the child stacks them too high and they begin to fall over.

AI of today is brittle, it is narrow, and it does not approach the cognitive abilities of humans. This is why the true self-driving car is somewhere out in the future.

Another aspect to the driving task is that it is not solely a mind exercise. You do need to use your senses to drive. You use your eyes as vision sensors to see the road ahead. You vision capability is like a streaming video, which your brain needs to continually analyze as you drive. Where is the road? Is there a pedestrian in the way? Is there another car ahead of you? Your senses are relying a flood of info to your brain. Self-driving cars are trying to do the same, by using cameras, radar, ultrasound, and lasers. This is an attempt at mimicking how humans have senses and sensory apparatus.

Thus, the driving task is mental and physical. You use your senses, you use your arms and legs to manipulate the controls of the car, and you use your brain to assess the sensory info and direct your limbs to act upon the controls of the car. This all happens instantly. If you've ever perhaps gotten something in your eye and only had one eye available to drive with, you suddenly realize how dependent upon vision you are. If you have a broken foot with a cast, you suddenly realize how hard it is to control the brake pedal and the accelerator. If you've taken medication and your brain is maybe sluggish, you suddenly realize how much mental strain is required to drive a car.

An AI system that plays chess only needs to be focused on playing chess. The physical aspects aren't important because usually a human moves the chess pieces or the chessboard is shown on an electronic display. Using AI for a more life-and-death task such as analyzing MRI images of patients, this again does not require physical capabilities and instead is done by examining images of bits.

Driving a car is a true life-and-death task. It is a use of AI that can easily and at any moment produce death. For those colleagues of mine that are developing this AI, as am I, we need to keep in mind the somber aspects of this. We are producing software that will have in its virtual hands the lives of the occupants of the car, and the lives of those in other nearby cars, and the lives of nearby pedestrians, etc. Chess is not usually a life-or-death matter.

Driving is all around us. Cars are everywhere. Most of today's AI applications involve only a small number of people. Or, they are behind the scenes and we as humans have other recourse if the AI messes up. AI that is driving a car at 80 miles per hour on a highway had better not mess up. The consequences are grave.

Multiply this by the number of cars, if we could put magically self-driving into every car in the USA, we'd have AI running in the 263 million cars. That's a lot of AI spread around. This is AI on a massive scale that we are not doing today and that offers both promise and potential peril.

There are some that want AI for self-driving cars because they envision a world without any car accidents. They envision a world in which there is no car congestion and all cars cooperate with each other. These are wonderful utopian visions.

They are also very misleading. The adoption of self-driving cars is going to be incremental and not overnight. We cannot economically just junk all existing cars. Nor are we going to be able to affordably retrofit existing cars. It is more likely that self-driving cars will be built into new cars and that over many years of gradual replacement of existing cars that we'll see the mix of self-driving cars become substantial in the real-world.

In these essays, I have tried to offer technological insights without being overly technical in my description, and also blended the business, societal, and economic aspects too. Technologists need to consider the non-technological impacts of what they do. Non-technologists should be aware of what is being developed.

We all need to work together to collectively be prepared for the enormous disruption and transformative aspects of true self-driving cars.

WHAT THIS BOOK PROVIDES

What does this book provide to you? It introduces many of the key elements about self-driving cars and does so with an AI based perspective. I weave together technical and non-technical aspects, readily going from being concerned about the cognitive capabilities of the driving task and how the technology is embodying this into self-driving cars, and in the next breath I discuss the societal and economic aspects.

They are all intertwined because that's the way reality is. You cannot separate out the technology per se, and instead must consider it within the milieu of what is being invented and innovated, and do so with a mindset towards the contemporary mores and culture that shape what we are doing and what we hope to do.

WHY THIS BOOK

I wrote this book to try and bring to the public view many aspects about self-driving cars that nobody seems to be discussing.

For business leaders that are either involved in making self-driving cars or that are going to leverage self-driving cars, I hope that this book will enlighten you as to the risks involved and ways in which you should be strategizing about how to deal with those risks.

For entrepreneurs, startups and other businesses that want to enter into the self-driving car market that is emerging, I hope this book sparks your interest in doing so, and provides some sense of what might be prudent to pursue.

For researchers that study self-driving cars, I hope this book spurs your interest in the risks and safety issues of self-driving cars, and also nudges you toward conducting research on those aspects.

For students in computer science or related disciplines, I hope this book will provide you with interesting and new ideas and material, for which you might conduct research or provide some career direction insights for you.

For AI companies and high-tech companies pursuing self-driving cars, this book will hopefully broaden your view beyond just the mere coding and development needed to make self-driving cars.

For all readers, I hope that you will find the material in this book to be stimulating. Some of it will be repetitive of things you already know. But I am pretty sure that you'll also find various eureka moments whereby you'll discover a new technique or approach that you had not earlier thought of. I am also betting that there will be material that forces you to rethink some of your current practices.

I am not saying you will suddenly have an epiphany and change what you are doing. I do think though that you will reconsider or perhaps revisit what you are doing.

For anyone choosing to use this book for teaching purposes, please take a look at my suggestions for doing so, as described in the Appendix. I have found the material handy in courses that I have taught, and likewise other faculty have told me that they have found the material handy, in some cases as extended readings and in other instances as a core part of their course (depending on the nature of the class).

In my writing for this book, I have tried carefully to blend both the practitioner and the academic styles of writing.

It is not as abstract as is typical academic journal writing, but at the same time offers depth by going into the nuances and trade-offs of various practices.

The word "deep" is in vogue today, meaning getting deeply into a subject or topic, and so is the word "unpack" which means to tease out the underlying aspects of a subject or topic. I have sought to offer material that addresses an issue or topic by going relatively deeply into it and make sure that it is well unpacked.

In any book about AI, it is difficult to use our everyday words without having some of them be misinterpreted. Specifically, it is easy to anthropomorphize AI. When I say that an AI system "knows" something, I do not want you to construe that the AI system has sentience and "knows" in the same way that humans do. They aren't that way, as yet. I have tried to use quotes around such words from time-to-time to emphasize that the words I am using should not be misinterpreted to ascribe true human intelligence to the AI systems that we know of today. If I used quotes around all such words, the book would be very difficult to read, and so I am doing so judiciously. Please keep that in mind as you read the material, thanks.

Some of the material is time-based in terms of covering underway activities, and though some of it might decay, nonetheless I believe you'll find the material useful and informative.

COMPANION BOOKS BY DR. ELIOT

1. **"Introduction to Driverless Self-Driving Cars"** by Dr. Lance Eliot
2. **"Innovation and Thought Leadership on Self-Driving Driverless Cars"**
3. **"Advances in AI and Autonomous Vehicles: Cybernetic Self-Driving Cars"**
4. **"Self-Driving Cars: The Mother of All AI Projects"** by Dr. Lance Eliot
5. **"New Advances in AI Autonomous Driverless Self-Driving Cars"**
6. **"AV Driverless Self-Driving Cars & AI"** by Dr. Lance Eliot and Michael B. Eliot
7. **"Transformative Artificial Intelligence Driverless Self-Driving Cars"**
8. **"Disruptive Artificial Intelligence and Driverless Self-Driving Cars"**
9. "**State-of-the-Art AI Driverless Self-Driving Cars**" by Dr. Lance Eliot
10. "**Top Trends in AI Self-Driving Cars**" by Dr. Lance Eliot
11. **"AI Innovations and Self-Driving Cars"** by Dr. Lance Eliot
12. **"Crucial Advances for AI Driverless Cars"** by Dr. Lance Eliot
13. **"Sociotechnical Insights and AI Driverless Cars**" by Dr. Lance Eliot.
14. **"Pioneering Advances for AI Driverless Cars"** by Dr. Lance Eliot
15. **"Leading Edge Trends for AI Driverless Cars"** by Dr. Lance Eliot
16. **"The Cutting Edge of AI Autonomous Cars"** by Dr. Lance Eliot
17. **"The Next Wave of AI Self-Driving Cars"** by Dr. Lance Eliot
18. **"Revolutionary Innovations of AI Driverless Cars"** by Dr. Lance Eliot
19. **"AI Self-Driving Cars Breakthroughs"** by Dr. Lance Eliot
20. **"Trailblazing Trends for AI Self-Driving Cars"** by Dr. Lance Eliot
21. **"Ingenious Strides for AI Driverless Cars"** by Dr. Lance Eliot
22. **"AI Self-Driving Cars Inventiveness"** by Dr. Lance Eliot
23. **"Visionary Secrets of AI Driverless Cars"** by Dr. Lance Eliot
24. **"Spearheading AI Self-Driving Cars"** by Dr. Lance Eliot
25. **"Spurring AI Self-Driving Cars"** by Dr. Lance Eliot
26. **"Avant-Garde AI Driverless Cars"** by Dr. Lance Eliot
27. **"AI Self-Driving Cars Evolvement"** by Dr. Lance Eliot
28. **"AI Driverless Cars Chrysalis"** by Dr. Lance Eliot
29. **"Boosting AI Autonomous Cars"** by Dr. Lance Eliot
30. **"AI Self-Driving Cars Trendsetting"** by Dr. Lance Eliot
31. **"AI Autonomous Cars Forefront"** by Dr. Lance Eliot
32. **"AI Autonomous Cars Emergence"** by Dr. Lance Eliot
33. **"AI Autonomous Cars Progress"** by Dr. Lance Eliot
34. **"AI Self-Driving Cars Prognosis"** by Dr. Lance Eliot
35. **"AI Self-Driving Cars Momentum"** by Dr. Lance Eliot
36. **"AI Self-Driving Cars Headway"** by Dr. Lance Eliot
37. **"AI Self-Driving Cars Vicissitude"** by Dr. Lance Eliot
38. **"AI Self-Driving Cars Autonomy"** by Dr. Lance Eliot
39. **"AI Driverless Cars Transmutation"** by Dr. Lance Eliot
40. **"AI Driverless Cars Potentiality"** by Dr. Lance Eliot
41. **"AI Driverless Cars Realities"** by Dr. Lance Eliot
42. **"AI Self-Driving Cars Materiality"** by Dr. Lance Eliot
43. **"AI Self-Driving Cars Accordance"** by Dr. Lance Eliot
44. **"AI Self-Driving Cars Equanimity"** by Dr. Lance Eliot
45. **"AI Self-Driving Cars Divulgement"** by Dr. Lance Eliot
46. **"AI Self-Driving Cars Consonance"** by Dr. Lance Eliot
47. **"Revelatory AI Self-Driving Cars"** by Dr. Lance Eliot
48. **"Edifying AI Self-Driving Cars"** by Dr. Lance Eliot

These books are available on Amazon and at other major global booksellers.

CHAPTER 1

ELIOT FRAMEWORK FOR AI SELF-DRIVING CARS

This chapter is a core foundational aspect for understanding AI self-driving cars and I have used this same chapter in several of my other books to introduce the reader to essential elements of this field. Once you've read this chapter, you'll be prepared to read the rest of the material since the foundational essence of the components of autonomous AI driverless self-driving cars will have been established for you.

When I give presentations about self-driving cars and teach classes on the topic, I have found it helpful to provide a framework around which the various key elements of self-driving cars can be understood and organized (see diagram at the end of this chapter). The framework needs to be simple enough to convey the overarching elements, but at the same time not so simple that it belies the true complexity of self-driving cars. As such, I am going to describe the framework here and try to offer in a thousand words (or more!) what the framework diagram itself intends to portray.

The core elements on the diagram are numbered for ease of reference. The numbering does not suggest any kind of prioritization of the elements. Each element is crucial. Each element has a purpose, and otherwise would not be included in the framework. For some self-driving cars, a particular element might be more important or somehow distinguished in comparison to other self-driving cars.

You could even use the framework to rate a particular self-driving car, doing so by gauging how well it performs in each of the elements of the framework. I will describe each of the elements, one at a time. After doing so, I'll discuss aspects that illustrate how the elements interact and perform during the overall effort of a self-driving car.

At the AI Self-Driving Car Institute, we use the framework to keep track of what we are working on, and how we are developing software that fills in what is needed to achieve Level 5 self-driving cars.

D-01: Sensor Capture

Let's start with the one element that often gets the most attention in the press about self-driving cars, namely, the sensory devices for a self-driving car.

On the framework, the box labeled as D-01 indicates "Sensor Capture" and refers to the processes of the self-driving car that involve collecting data from the myriad of sensors that are used for a self-driving car. The types of devices typically involved are listed, such as the use of mono cameras, stereo cameras, LIDAR devices, radar systems, ultrasonic devices, GPS, IMU, and so on.

These devices are tasked with obtaining data about the status of the self-driving car and the world around it. Some of the devices are continually providing updates, while others of the devices await an indication by the self-driving car that the device is supposed to collect data. The data might be first transformed in some fashion by the device itself, or it might instead be fed directly into the sensor capture as raw data. At that point, it might be up to the sensor capture processes to do transformations on the data. This all varies depending upon the nature of the devices being used and how the devices were designed and developed.

D-02: Sensor Fusion

Imagine that your eyeballs receive visual images, your nose receives odors, your ears receive sounds, and in essence each of your distinct sensory devices is getting some form of input. The input befits the nature of the device. Likewise, for a self-driving car, the cameras provide visual images, the radar returns radar reflections, and so on. Each device provides the data as befits what the device does.

At some point, using the analogy to humans, you need to merge together what your eyes see, what your nose smells, what your ears hear, and piece it all together into a larger sense of what the world is all about and what is happening around you. Sensor fusion is the action of taking the singular aspects from each of the devices and putting them together into a larger puzzle.

Sensor fusion is a tough task. There are some devices that might not be working at the time of the sensor capture. Or, there might some devices that are unable to report well what they have detected. Again, using a human analogy, suppose you are in a dark room and so your eyes cannot see much. At that point, you might need to rely more so on your ears and what you hear. The same is true for a self-driving car. If the cameras are obscured due to snow and sleet, it might be that the radar can provide a greater indication of what the external conditions consist of.

In the case of a self-driving car, there can be a plethora of such sensory devices. Each is reporting what it can. Each might have its difficulties. Each might have its limitations, such as how far ahead it can detect an object. All of these limitations need to be considered during the sensor fusion task.

D-03: Virtual World Model

For humans, we presumably keep in our minds a model of the world around us when we are driving a car. In your mind, you know that the car is going at say 60 miles per hour and that you are on a freeway.

You have a model in your mind that your car is surrounded by other cars, and that there are lanes to the freeway. Your model is not only based on what you can see, hear, etc., but also what you know about the nature of the world. You know that at any moment that car ahead of you can smash on its brakes, or the car behind you can ram into your car, or that the truck in the next lane might swerve into your lane.

The AI of the self-driving car needs to have a virtual world model, which it then keeps updated with whatever it is receiving from the sensor fusion, which received its input from the sensor capture.

D-04: System Action Plan

By having a virtual world model, the AI of the self-driving car is able to keep track of where the car is and what is happening around the car. In addition, the AI needs to determine what to do next. Should the self-driving car hit its brakes? Should the self-driving car stay in its lane or swerve into the lane to the left? Should the self-driving car accelerate or slow down?

A system action plan needs to be prepared by the AI of the self-driving car. The action plan specifies what actions should be taken. The actions need to pertain to the status of the virtual world model. Plus, the actions need to be realizable.

This realizability means that the AI cannot just assert that the self-driving car should suddenly sprout wings and fly. Instead, the AI must be bound by whatever the self-driving car can actually do, such as coming to a halt in a distance of X feet at a speed of Y miles per hour, rather than perhaps asserting that the self-driving car come to a halt in 0 feet as though it could instantaneously come to a stop while it is in motion.

D-05: Controls Activation

The system action plan is implemented by activating the controls of the car to act according to what the plan stipulates.

This might mean that the accelerator control is commanded to increase the speed of the car. Or, the steering control is commanded to turn the steering wheel 30 degrees to the left or right.

One question arises as to whether or not the controls respond as they are commanded to do. In other words, suppose the AI has commanded the accelerator to increase, but for some reason it does not do so. Or, maybe it tries to do so, but the speed of the car does not increase.

The controls activation feeds back into the virtual world model, and simultaneously the virtual world model is getting updated from the sensors, the sensor capture, and the sensor fusion. This allows the AI to ascertain what has taken place as a result of the controls being commanded to take some kind of action.

By the way, please keep in mind that though the diagram seems to have a linear progression to it, the reality is that these are all aspects of the self-driving car that are happening in parallel and simultaneously. The sensors are capturing data, meanwhile the sensor fusion is taking place, meanwhile the virtual model is being updated, meanwhile the system action plan is being formulated and reformulated, meanwhile the controls are being activated.

This is the same as a human being that is driving a car. They are eyeballing the road, meanwhile they are fusing in their mind the sights, sounds, etc., meanwhile their mind is updating their model of the world around them, meanwhile they are formulating an action plan of what to do, and meanwhile they are pushing their foot onto the pedals and steering the car. In the normal course of driving a car, you are doing all of these at once. I mention this so that when you look at the diagram, you will think of the boxes as processes that are all happening at the same time, and not as though only one happens and then the next.

They are shown diagrammatically in a simplistic manner to help comprehend what is taking place. You though should also realize that they are working in parallel and simultaneous with each other. This is a tough aspect in that the inter-element communications involve latency and other aspects that must be taken into account. There can be delays in one element updating and then sharing its latest status with other elements.

D-06: Automobile & CAN

Contemporary cars use various automotive electronics and a Controller Area Network (CAN) to serve as the components that underlie the driving aspects of a car.

There are Electronic Control Units (ECU's) which control subsystems of the car, such as the engine, the brakes, the doors, the windows, and so on.

The elements D-01, D-02, D-03, D-04, D-05 are layered on top of the D-06, and must be aware of the nature of what the D-06 is able to do and not do.

D-07: In-Car Commands

Humans are going to be occupants in self-driving cars. In a Level 5 self-driving car, there must be some form of communication that takes place between the humans and the self-driving car. For example, I go into a self-driving car and tell it that I want to be driven over to Disneyland, and along the way I want to stop at In-and-Out Burger. The self-driving car now parses what I've said and tries to then establish a means to carry out my wishes.

In-car commands can happen at any time during a driving journey. Though my example was about an in-car command when I first got into my self-driving car, it could be that while the self-driving car is carrying out the journey that I change my mind. Perhaps after getting stuck in traffic, I tell the self-driving car to forget about getting the burgers and just head straight over to the theme park. The self-driving car needs to be alert to in-car commands throughout the journey.

D-08: V2X Communications

We will ultimately have self-driving cars communicating with each other, doing so via V2V (Vehicle-to-Vehicle) communications. We will also have self-driving cars that communicate with the roadways and other aspects of the transportation infrastructure, doing so via V2I (Vehicle-to-Infrastructure).

The variety of ways in which a self-driving car will be communicating with other cars and infrastructure is being called V2X, whereby the letter X means whatever else we identify as something that a car should or would want to communicate with.

The V2X communications will be taking place simultaneous with everything else on the diagram, and those other elements will need to incorporate whatever it gleans from those V2X communications.

D-09: Deep Learning

The use of Deep Learning permeates all other aspects of the self-driving car. The AI of the self-driving car will be using deep learning to do a better job at the systems action plan, and at the control's activation, and at the sensor fusion, and so on.

Currently, the use of artificial neural networks is the most prevalent form of deep learning. Based on large swaths of data, the neural networks attempt to "learn" from the data and therefore direct the efforts of the self-driving car accordingly.

D-10: Tactical AI

Tactical AI is the element of dealing with the moment-to-moment driving of the self-driving car. Is the self-driving car staying in its lane of the freeway? Is the car responding appropriately to the controls commands? Are the sensory devices working?

For human drivers, the tactical equivalent can be seen when you watch a novice driver such as a teenager that is first driving. They are focused on the mechanics of the driving task, keeping their eye on the road while also trying to properly control the car.

D-11: Strategic AI

The Strategic AI aspects of a self-driving car are dealing with the larger picture of what the self-driving car is trying to do. If I had asked that the self-driving car take me to Disneyland, there is an overall journey map that needs to be kept and maintained.

There is an interaction between the Strategic AI and the Tactical AI. The Strategic AI is wanting to keep on the mission of the driving, while the Tactical AI is focused on the particulars underway in the driving effort.

If the Tactical AI seems to wander away from the overarching mission, the Strategic AI wants to see why and get things back on track. If the Tactical AI realizes that there is something amiss on the self-driving car, it needs to alert the Strategic AI accordingly and have an adjustment to the overarching mission that is underway.

D-12: Self-Aware AI

Very few of the self-driving cars being developed are including a Self-Aware AI element, which we at the Cybernetic Self-Driving Car Institute believe is crucial to Level 5 self-driving cars.

The Self-Aware AI element is intended to watch over itself, in the sense that the AI is making sure that the AI is working as intended. Suppose you had a human driving a car, and they were starting to drive erratically. Hopefully, their own self-awareness would make them realize they themselves are driving poorly, such as perhaps starting to fall asleep after having been driving for hours on end. If you had a passenger in the car, they might be able to alert the driver if the driver is starting to do something amiss.

This is exactly what the Self-Aware AI element tries to do, it becomes the overseer of the AI, and tries to detect when the AI has become faulty or confused, and then find ways to overcome the issue.

D-13: Economic

The economic aspects of a self-driving car are not per se a technology aspect of a self-driving car, but the economics do indeed impact the nature of a self-driving car. For example, the cost of outfitting a self-driving car with every kind of possible sensory device is prohibitive, and so choices need to be made about which devices are used. And, for those sensory devices chosen, whether they would have a full set of features or a more limited set of features.

We are going to have self-driving cars that are at the low-end of a consumer cost point, and others at the high-end of a consumer cost point. You cannot expect that the self-driving car at the low-end is going to be as robust as the one at the high-end.

I realize that many of the self-driving car pundits are acting as though all self-driving cars will be the same, but they won't be. Just like anything else, we are going to have self-driving cars that have a range of capabilities. Some will be better than others. Some will be safer than others. This is the way of the real-world, and so we need to be thinking about the economics aspects when considering the nature of self-driving cars.

D-14: Societal

This component encompasses the societal aspects of AI which also impacts the technology of self-driving cars. For example, the famous Trolley Problem involves what choices should a self-driving car make when faced with life-and-death matters. If the self-driving car is about to either hit a child standing in the roadway, or instead ram into a tree at the side of the road and possibly kill the humans in the self-driving car, which choice should be made?

We need to keep in mind the societal aspects will underlie the AI of the self-driving car. Whether we are aware of it explicitly or not, the AI will have embedded into it various societal assumptions.

D-15: Innovation

I included the notion of innovation into the framework because we can anticipate that whatever a self-driving car consists of, it will continue to be innovated over time. The self-driving cars coming out in the next several years will undoubtedly be different and less innovative than the versions that come out in ten years hence, and so on.

Framework Overall

For those of you that want to learn about self-driving cars, you can potentially pick a particular element and become specialized in that aspect. Some engineers are focusing on the sensory devices. Some engineers focus on the controls activation. And so on. There are specialties in each of the elements.

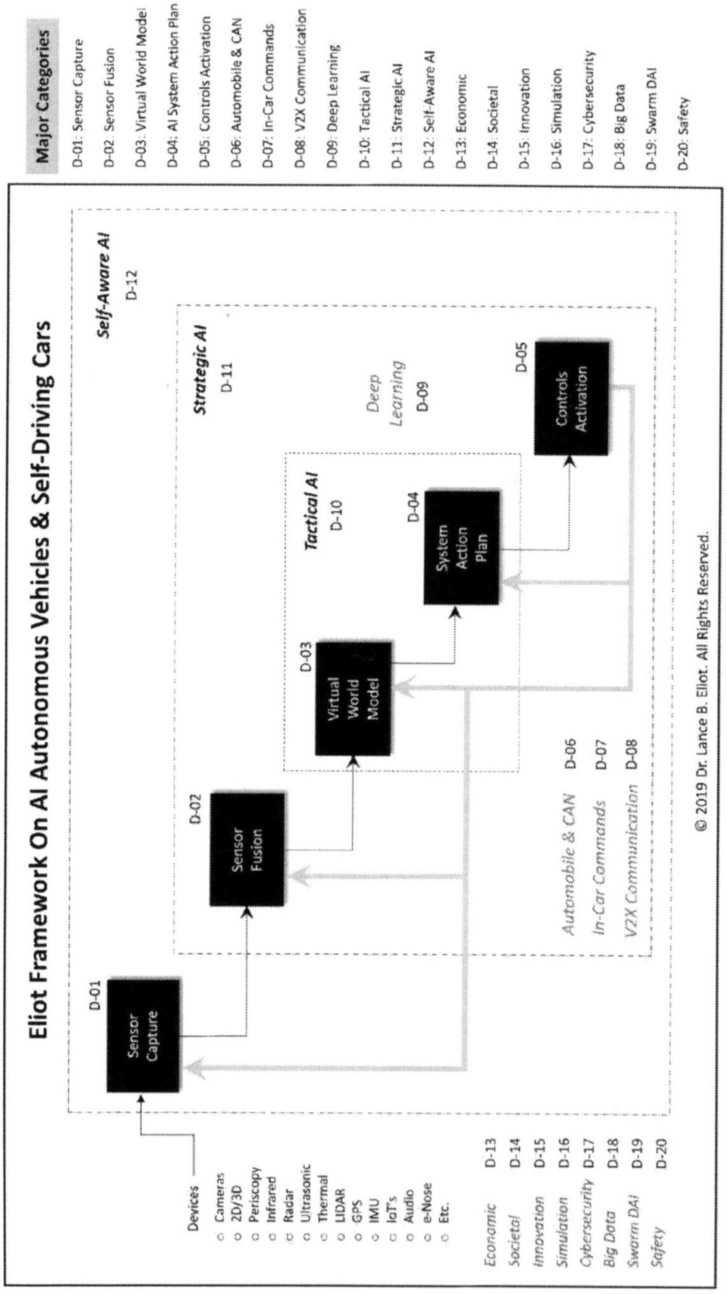
Eliot Framework On AI Autonomous Vehicles & Self-Driving Cars
Major Categories
D-01: Sensor Capture
D-02: Sensor Fusion
D-03: Virtual World Model
D-04: AI System Action Plan
D-05: Controls Activation
D-06: Automobile & CAN
D-07: In-Car Commands
D-08: V2X Communication
D-09: Deep Learning
D-10: Tactical AI
D-11: Strategic AI
D-12: Self-Aware AI
D-13: Economic
D-14: Societal
D-15: Innovation
D-16: Simulation
D-17: Cybersecurity
D-18: Big Data
D-19: Swarm DAI
D-20: Safety
Self-Aware AI
D-12
Strategic AI
D-11
Tactical AI
D-10
Deep Learning
D-09
Sensor Capture
D-01
Sensor Fusion
D-02
Virtual World Model
D-03
System Action Plan
D-04
Controls Activation
D-05
Devices
Cameras
2D/3D
Periscopy
Infrared
Radar
Ultrasonic
Thermal
LIDAR
GPS
IMU
IoT's
Audio
e-Nose
Etc.
Automobile & CAN D-06
In-Car Commands D-07
V2X Communication D-08
Economic D-13
Societal D-14
Innovation D-15
Simulation D-16
Cybersecurity D-17
Big Data D-18
Swarm DAI D-19
Safety D-20
© 2019 Dr. Lance B. Eliot. All Rights Reserved.

CHAPTER 2
STEERING WHEELS AND SELF-DRIVING CARS

There is an elephant in the room, but it seems as though nobody is noticing it.

In the ongoing push toward the fielding of self-driving cars, there is a crucial safety-related factor that has not gotten much attention and will regrettably and predictably become a sorrowful point and a colossal problem that will readily undermine and impede ongoing progress for self-driving cars.

The matter inadvertently and indirectly came up in the recently seen series of tweets between Elon Musk and Waymo that had to do with Waymo's announcement of removing the back-up human drivers in their Phoenix-area self-driving showcase.

The notable significance of this announcement is that Waymo's self-driving cars will proceed apace with their driving efforts, carrying human passengers, but do so without any human driver on-board (there is customarily a back-up or safety driver that sits in the driver's seat, monitoring the AI-based driving, and remains presumably attentive to intervene in the driving task if the self-driving system seems to have faltered or otherwise appears to be unable to handle a driving situation).

Many would say that this is a gutsy move by Waymo.

Some emphasize that this abundantly demonstrates the faith and belief that Waymo must have about the autonomous capability of their devised self-driving system and represents an important step forward for them and the entire self-driving industry.

Imagine though the potential backlash if this giant leap ends-up with a self-driving car crash or incident that involves injuries or possibly even fatalities. Undoubtedly, the news coverage would be massive, likely rousing the public and giving added fodder to regulators that might seek to slowdown such roadway tryouts. The spillover effect would not simply be a blackeye for Waymo, it would seemingly put the entire realm of self-driving into the doghouse.

You might at first glance be assuming that the facet about safety that I am alluding to must be about the omission of a back-up or safety driver from the vehicle.

Nope, that's not the elephant per se (one might suggest that removing the back-up driver is the obvious 600-pound gorilla that clearly resides at the front-and-center of the brouhaha and cannot be missed from being seen).

The unseen or unnoticed elephant within all of this Musk-versus-Waymo twitter storm can be stated in two simple words: *Steering Wheel.*

In today's column, I'll explain why there is an unrealized danger associated with the everyday commonplace steering wheel and how it is potentially going to trip-up the self-driving cars amongst nearly all the entities underway on these state-of-the-art self-driving endeavors.

It is *the* story within the story, as it were.

Tweets Aplenty And Self-Driving Maneuvering

Let's start with the spat between Elon Musk and Waymo.

The tweet dustup that took place involved Elon Musk commenting about Waymo's announcement by stating this (his October 8, 2020 tweet): "Waymo is impressive, but a highly specialized solution. The Tesla approach is a general solution. The latest build is capable of zero intervention drives. Will release limited beta in a few weeks."

For those of you that don't perchance have a decoder ring to ferret out the insider lingo embedded in that tweet, Musk was essentially claiming in the first part of his tweet that since Waymo is focused on particular locales, in this instance the Phoenix area, this aspect might ergo be construed by some as a "highly specialized" approach. In short, Musk has generally been a critic of relying upon detailed digital pre-mapping of an area for use by a self-driving car, and among those that vehemently contend that such maps are an unnecessary crutch.

As a brief explanation, some argue for AI-based driving systems that should be able to drive *without* the aid of specially created digital maps, which one could assert is akin to how humans drive. Namely, a human driver does not need detailed maps per se to drive around and can readily drive in an area that the human has never driven before, being able to drive just fine. The argument goes that if self-driving cars are reliant upon pre-constructed detailed digital maps it means that the AI won't be able to drive in places that have not already been subjected to that kind of specialized and deep mapping.

Thus, those self-driving cars are not "generalized" for driving and are dependent upon a pre-mapping effort, potentially limiting where that particular AI-based driving system can do its driving (a counter-argument is that inevitably such detailed digital maps will be prevalent, plus there is an argument made that driving with such maps is likely to be a safer means of driving than without such maps being available).

Self-driving cars are at times deployed by defining an Operational Design Domain (ODD), meaning that the vehicle has been established by the maker to be able to operate within a specific domain such as a given geographic boundary, along with perhaps weather-related stipulations such as not operating in say snow, and possible indications of time of day operation for only daylight hours, etc. This is considered part-and-parcel of Level 4 self-driving cars.

Returning to Musk's tweet, some would say that he has once again proffered his usual brashness and boldness by claiming that the Tesla approach will be a generalized solution, and will be "capable of zero intervention" during the act of driving the vehicle (meaning that there is no need for a human driver, neither a back-up driver and nor any driver of any ilk).

In another tweet on that same day, Musk indicated: "Our new system is capable of driving in locations we never seen even once" (the wording written in a typical tweet-oriented shorthand manner).

All told, he has continued to make promises about this upcoming "limited beta" that has both whetted the appetite to see what he has, and also garnered a great deal of criticism by industry pundits for as yet being unproven and essentially construed as a vaporware kind of claim, for the moment.

Shortly after Musk's tweets, Waymo responded with this tweet: "Yep, we specialize in zero intervention driving. Check out our steering wheel labels."

A picture was included with the tweet and showed a steering wheel that had on its hub an indication of "Please keep your hands off the wheel" and an indication stating "The Waymo Driver is in control at all times."

Waymo refers to their AI-based driving system as the *Waymo Driver*, and are known for indicating that they are not in the business of making self-driving cars per se and clarify that they are in the business of making AI-based driving systems, suggesting that they ultimately will be able to port the AI capability to whatever suitable self-driving equipped cars might eventually emerge.

It seems relatively apparent that the Waymo tweet was a retort to Musk about potentially trying to lay claim to Tesla being the only game in town that is going to be able to do "zero intervention" driving. Waymo was seemingly trying to set the record straight and point out that they are in the active midst of going the zero-intervention path right now.

In so doing, they added a bit of icing on the cake that is what I am suggesting is the elephant in the room, perhaps done without a realization of doing so and otherwise just offering an eye-catching rejoinder.

Eye-catching but in another way for those that are in the know.

Time to shift gears and look directly at the elephant.

The Steering Wheel Conundrum

I think we can all agree that a steering wheel is quite an important thing.

In the early days of cars, they experimented with using tillers for the steering and gradually gave way to the use of a steering wheel instead. The steering wheels were purposely made large to ease the burden when trying to turn the wheels of the car. This was before power steering emerged. Inexorably, the steering wheel became a relatively standardized piece of equipment and in so doing made it simpler for people to drive cars. You can imagine the issues we would have today if there were dozens of different ways to steer a car and you had to figure out each idiosyncratic approach whenever you rented a car or bought a new car.

Federal regulations provide a very detailed specification about the steering wheels of cars that are used in the United States. The Department of Transportation (DOT) and the National Highway Traffic Safety Administration (NHTSA) are integral to devising and updating the Federal Motor Vehicle Safety Standards, including those rules and regulations governing the ordinary steering wheel.

In short, essentially, a car must have a steering wheel and it must meet the stated regulations.

I doubt that any of you would be surprised at such a revelation and it seems extraordinarily perfunctory. Yes, that is perhaps the case, though you need to add a new twist to the whole topic, consisting of the advent of the self-driving car.

Should a self-driving car have a steering wheel?

One ardent viewpoint is that a true self-driving car should not have a steering wheel, and nor have any driving controls such as the accelerator and nor brake pedal. The notion is that if you include the driving controls, you are basically telling passengers that they potentially can drive the car. But the foundational assumption about a

Level 4 and Level 5 self-driving car is that the AI is supposed to be doing the driving. Indeed, if you believe that the 40,000 annual car crash fatalities and the 2.5 million related injuries will be reduced or possibly reach zero (I've continued to exhort that zero fatalities are a zero chance), via the advent of self-driving cars, you would likewise fervently argue that this well justifies that there should not be any human driving allowed within self-driving cars.

Meanwhile, here's the rub.

For those crafting self-driving tech, right now, do you put your AI-enabled driving system into a car that doesn't have a steering wheel or do you put it into a car that does have a steering wheel?

The future is supposed to include self-driving cars that have no steering wheel in the vehicle. Existing federal regulations though generally prevent the use of a car on public roadways that lack a steering wheel. To try and allow for exceptions in the case of efforts to develop self-driving cars, an exemption can be applied for. I've covered for example the GM Cruise's Origin which has no steering wheel, and Nuro's R2 that doesn't have a steering wheel.

There have been repeated calls by those in the self-driving car realm to have the regulations changed to more readily accept and assume that a car does not have to have a steering wheel. Thus, rather than having to apply for an exemption (usually a somewhat lengthy, complicated, and some assert overly arduous process), the new norm would be that cars can optionally have a steering wheel, rather than the mandated aspect of a steering wheel having to be present.

It is perhaps obvious to state that nearly all cars today have a steering wheel and if you want to try out your AI-enabled driving system it would be a lot easier to do so on a conventional car that has the usual driving controls, rather than creating the futuristic self-driving cars that will slowly and gradually emerge.

Plus, another advantage of a conventional car with a steering wheel is that you can readily make use of human back-up drivers. By augmenting a conventional car with the self-driving sensors and other gear, you can still easily ensure that a human driver can command the vehicle. A true self-driving car that is made without the steering and other driving controls would seemingly preclude the use of a human back-up driver (though, some elaborate designs allow for a steering wheel and pedals that "disappear" from view when not needed, allowing therefore for human driving at times).

Welcome to the quagmire.

The reason this is a quagmire is that putting AI-based self-driving into a conventional car with an everyday steering wheel means that there is a possibility of the two-drivers-at-once scenario.

Let's unpack that.

Suppose that a conventional car is being used for self-driving purposes and has been augmented with self-driving tech and sensors such as video cameras, radar, LIDAR, and so on. Assume that the driver's seat is blocked out for use by any passengers. Passengers can sit in the front passenger seat or sit in the back seats of the vehicle.

There is nothing more amazing than to witness the steering wheel moving to-and-fro while you are seated as a passenger in such a self-driving car. It seems as though an ethereal hand is on the steering and a ghostlike apparition must be seated in the driver's seat, moving the steering wheel mysteriously and mystically. Some view this was rapt attention, others watch with great trepidation and hope that the steering is being done appropriately.

The problem arises if the passenger or passengers were to suddenly decide to make use of the steering wheel.

Your first thought might be that nobody would ever do such a thing, especially if there are clearly displayed signs inside the vehicle that warns to not touch the steering wheel. Certainly, everyone will abide by this decree and realize the seriousness of failing to accede to the stern indication.

Do people obey the signs at national parks that firmly warn "Do

NOT feed the animals" or do they violate this frequently and at times end-up getting run down by an angered wild animal?

We all know how human behavior can be. People disobey signs. People do stupid things. People get themselves into trouble when they even sometimes are clueless about the trouble that they face.

Imagine a self-driving car that has an adult and a toddler in the vehicle. The adult is looking intently at their smartphone and not especially paying attention to the child. The toddler quietly slips into the blocked-off driver's seat and starts to play with the steering wheel, doing so under the thinking that it is simply a toy and it would be joyous to steer a real car.

Here's another example.

Teenagers pile into a self-driving car for a trip to a school party. A teen seated in the front seat wants to show off to their buddies. The teenager reaches over to the steering wheel and gives it a huge tug, aiming to make the self-driving car do a sudden swerve, figuring this will be uproariously funny and really get the goat of the others in the car.

Yet another example.

A person that after work went to a bar and had one too many drinks is astute enough to request a self-driving car to give them a lift home (better than them getting behind the wheel of a car while in a drunken stupor). Once inside the self-driving car, and while intoxicated, the passenger watches in fascination as the steering wheel is rotating left and right. Without any sober thinking, the passenger reaches from the backseat and grabs the steering wheel, curious to see what will happen.

One more example, and then I think it will have been sufficient altogether in showcasing how people might opt to use a steering wheel despite being inside a self-driving car.

Someone inside a self-driving car is fearful of how the AI is driving. Based on this fear, they believe that the self-driving car is about to hit another car, so the person reaches out to the steering wheel in hopes of turning the wheels and averting what they believe is an imminent car crash (without knowing what the AI is doing and that perhaps the AI fully realizes that the car ahead needs to be avoided).

The overarching point is that if the steering wheel is still present inside a self-driving car, and assuming that it is functioning and not otherwise disconnected, there is a chance that a human will attempt to use the steering wheel, despite any kind of admonishments to not do so.

Conclusion

You might argue that the AI will detect the untoward steering usage and can opt to ignore it, refusing to relay the steering indications into the actual steering function of the vehicle.

This is not so easily done.

In fact, for so-called self-driving cars that are intended to be dually driven by both AI and by a human, the question arises as to which is right and which is wrong in terms of the steering control commanding. We usually assume that the moment a human acts upon the steering that they are overtly taking over control.

This is the crux of the two-drivers-at-a-time dilemma. You might remember years ago that some specially equipped cars for driver training purposes would have two sets of driving controls, a set of the usual controls in front of the driver's seat, and another added set at the front seat passenger position. The instructor would sit at the second steering wheel and would be able to take over the driving if the newbie learning to drive maybe froze-up or made a bad steering choice. Despite this appearing to be a clever arrangement, you nonetheless always confronted the danger that either party would make a move that would be wrong, or that the one taking over would inadvertently make a wrong move, etc.

As they say, two cooks in the kitchen can lead to some badly cooked meals.

Note that this twofer confronts nearly everyone in this realm, other than those that already are using specialized cars that omit (or completely hide) the steering wheel and the pedals, thus essentially putting only the AI into the true driver's seat and excluding any human driving intervention.

This facet about steering is the hidden multi-ton elephant that is a hand wringing qualm within the self-driving industry, entailing the vexing conundrum about the seemingly mundane and unheralded steering wheel that we see and use every day of our driving lives. You can bet your bottom dollar that all of this will eventually entail some rather ugly legal wrangling, once there are adverse incidents and the lawsuits start getting slung at the automakers, the self-driving tech firms, and the self-driving car fleet operators. Seems nearly inevitable.

Well, let's hope upon hope that we can steer clear of big troubles on all of this and not get trampled by a stampeding elephant.

.

CHAPTER 3
HIT-AND-RUN AND SELF-DRIVING CARS

Please prepare yourself for a driving scenario that we all dread and profusely hope will never occur.

Wham, while driving your car, you strike and kill a pedestrian.

The anguish is unimaginable.

There is no one around as an eyewitness. You had no passengers in your car. Nobody witnessed the catastrophic event other than you.

What do you do next?

Well, similar to most states, here in California there is a legal requirement that a driver involved in a car crash must stop at the scene of the accident, they are to try and ascertain if anyone has been injured, they are to render aid if at all feasible, and they are to remain at the scene.

In addition, the act of rendering aid could potentially encompass trying to protect the injured from additional harm such as blocking traffic might be a potential safety facet depending upon suitable judgment, prudence, and feasibility.

Another variant of rendering aid would be contacting emergency services, such as calling 911, seeking a response by appropriate first responders for medical assistance, fire department assistance, and law enforcement response.

There is also a reporting requirement too. The California Vehicle Code specifies that a written report of a car crash must be made to the California Highway Patrol (CHP) or the local police department if there was any injury or death involved, and must be formally reported within 24 hours of the incident.

Okay, given those legal stipulations, I'll assume that as a driver we would all conform to those indicated steps and in the scenario of the pedestrian fatality would bring the car to a stop, get out to ascertain the status of the pedestrian, render aid if the pedestrian was not already deceased, and proceed to call 911.

Does the lack of eyewitnesses being present alter or adjust how you would proceed?

In theory, the answer is a resounding no, it shouldn't matter in the least that there weren't any (living) witnesses. Legally the requirement stands whether anyone else saw what happened or not. You are still responsible for your driving acts. The weight and force of the law are still upon your shoulders.

Sadly, woefully, sickeningly, there are quite a number of drivers that scoot away and try to escape their legal and moral duty.

We commonly know this as the infamous hit-and-run.

Annually, there are an estimated 750,000 or so hit-and-run incidents in the United States alone, of which, there are about 2,000 resulting in a fatality. Thus, by-and-large, the hit-and-run is an injury-producing calamity and not so much a death generating one, though I am sure we would all assuredly agree that 2,000 deaths are abhorrent and ought to never happen.

Statistics by the National Highway Traffic Safety Administration (NHTSA) suggest that there is a hit-and-run every minute and a half, somewhere across the USA. Those killed in a hit-and-run are predominantly pedestrians or bicyclists, consisting of about 65% of the fatalities.

Many analyses of hit-and-run incidents have provided suggested ways that the malady of such occurrences could potentially be reduced. Some focus on pedestrians and bicyclists, urging that they be more mindful of traffic around them. Others contend that the onus is on the drivers, rather than those getting hit, and urge that drivers need to refrain from driving while distracted, they need to not drive while intoxicated, etc.

Here's an intriguing question to ponder: *Will the advent of AI-based true self-driving cars potentially mitigate or eliminate the hit-and-run phenomena?*

One form of the logic underlying the belief that true self-driving cars will essentially solve the matter is sometimes couched in terms that assert there will never be any car crashes once we have self-driving cars. In a Utopian viewpoint, self-driving cars will always detect others such as even wayward pedestrians, and always avert a collision. The tag line is zero fatalities will arise once we have self-driving cars.

I've repeatedly debunked this false and misleading claim in my column postings.

My response is that zero fatalities has a zero chance of happening.

First, keep in mind that we are not going to have overnight a circumstance of only and exclusively self-driving cars on our roadway and byways. For many years to come, likely decades, we are going to have a mixture of both human-driven cars and self-driving cars. In the U.S. we have about 250 million conventional cars and those are not going to be summarily replaced by self-driving cars. Plus, we do not yet know whether people will be willing to give up their human-driving "rights" (driving is actually a privilege, not a right), and some vehemently insist they will never stop driving until you pry their cold dead hands from the steering wheel.

The point overall is that we will still have all the foibles and issues associated with human-driven cars, meanwhile gradually gaining ground on the mix of self-driving cars entering into the streets. As such, there will still be a human driver instigated and derived hit-and-run morass.

Second, and this is a twist that few seem to be willing to accept, self-driving cars will not be infallible and nor somehow magical in averting all possible car crashes and collisions.

Suppose a child darts out between two parked cars and into the street while a self-driving car is coming along. The stopping distance for a self-driving car is the same in essence as the stopping distance for any car, namely there are physics involved that are the same in either case (yes, I realize that there is the cognitive thinking time by humans about when to jam on the brakes, but I am referring herein to the physical stopping distance once the brakes have been heavily applied).

No matter how proficient the sensors and AI are, a self-driving car will still get into a car crash or collision if the situation precludes the time needed and space needed to perform an evading action. It's a physics thing.

I realize that some dreamers say that the sensors and AI will never get caught off-guard. Malarky. In the use case of the darting child, it is entirely realistic that the child could have been completely hidden from view, and the sensors, therefore, unable to early detect the presence of the child. Once the child was detected, already into the roadway, if the stopping distance doesn't provide for halting the vehicle in time, the child is going to get struck.

That being said, it is certainly hoped that the annual 40,000 car-related fatalities and some 2.5 million car-related crash injuries in this country will be reduced significantly by the advent of self-driving cars. When you carve out the number of drunk driving incidents and so on, the remaining number of potential self-driving car crash scenarios is presumably going to be extremely low. Nonetheless, it will not be zero (it will be some non-zero number, but thankfully and presumably a lot lower than via human driving).

Returning to the core question, you might then assume that the hit-and-run will for sure no longer occur, since even if the self-driving car does on occasion hit someone or something, surely the AI will do the right thing thereafter.

Will it?

We should think carefully about that notion.

Let's start by clarifying what is meant when referring to AI-based true self-driving cars.

Self-Driving Cars And The User Experience

For Level 4 and Level 5 true self-driving vehicles, there won't be a human driver involved in the driving task.

All occupants will be passengers.

The AI is doing the driving.

Despite the rather startling and impressive feat of being able to have the AI drive a car, do not be fooled by news headlines that herald the AI as being sentient or superhuman. Hogwash. The AI of today is not sentient and utterly lacks in (for example) any semblance of common-sense reasoning. AI that is being devised to drive cars is a product of computer programming, including the vaunted Machine Learning (ML) and Deep Learning (DL), which are data reliant pattern-matching algorithms that though quite helpful for the driving task, are not anything reasonably comparable to the human mind.

Why make this point and do so with such flourish and emphasis?

Because the actions of the AI once there is a car crash are wholly dependent upon how the AI has been programmed, and not somehow axiomatic or mystically divined.

If the AI developers and those fielding a self-driving car have not included an explicit provision about a post-crash scenario, the likelihood is that the AI would just keep driving the car, unabated and undeterred. Unless the vehicle is damaged beyond being able to readily proceed, the AI driving system ostensibly would continue the driving journey that is already underway.

In that sense of things, and amid the question of whether a self-driving car could perform a hit-and-run, the answer is a resounding yes, it is quite possible, though we of course would hope that such AI is not being allowed onto our public roadways.

The assumption is that the automakers and self-driving tech makers are all ensuring that the self-driving car and its AI is programmed to cope with a car crash or collision. In which case, the chances of a hit-and-run are slim in the matter of the running part, though as mentioned earlier there is still the oft chance of a hit (albeit, as already stated, presumably a lot less than human-driven instances).

Does this suggest that a hit-and-run will never ever occur via a self-driving car?

Sorry, it does not provide that promise.

Suppose the AI fails to detect that someone or something has been struck. This is presumably a low chance, but nonetheless, there are circumstances whereby a self-driving car could inadvertently get into that predicament. When I say this, I am usually immediately challenged to provide even one scenario that this could occur.

I will provide an example, but it is ghoulish, and I forewarn you to maybe skip the rest of this paragraph accordingly. Imagine a child is laying on the street. They are barely noticeable and depending upon the nature of the street, the weather underway (such as rain or snow), and other factors, it is possible that the sensors might not detect the presence of the child. The self-driving car could proceed and roll over the figure, not detecting that anything especially untoward has occurred. Perhaps an unlikely situation, but it could happen.

You cannot assume that the sensors are all-knowing and all-detecting. State-of-the-art sensors are impressive, and by-and-large redundancy is being built into self-driving cars, and yet this does not produce an always perfect system. Realize too that whatever data the sensors collect still has to be examined by the AI driving system and interpreted, which adds another layer of uncertainty into being able to always and unerringly avoid car crashes and collisions.

Generally, the AI is being programmed that once a car crash happens, assuming that the AI detects as such, the AI will attempt to bring the self-driving car to a safe stop. The AI then will contact the fleet operator to alert as to the arising situation.

Some assert that the AI ought to also instantly alert the authorities, contacting 911 or the equivalent, rather than waiting to have the fleet operator do so. This is an open debate since there is a chance that the AI might create false alerts to 911 and the belief by some is that it is better to first get a human involved via the fleet operations to then decide what action to take. But time is ticking in these moments of tragedy and the question stands as to what the best and most expedient steps are to be undertaken.

On additional facets, the AI and the self-driving car cannot render direct medical aid per se, which a human driver might be able to do. The AI could though potentially seek to protect the injured person, by blocking traffic or sounding a horn or flashing lights. This is considered by many to be an edge or corner case problem and few self-driving cars have any such provision developed so far.

The other matter is the reporting of what took place.

In theory, the on-board driving system has all of the video and other sensory data to showcase what took place. Also, some of that data may have been uploaded to the cloud of the fleet operator, doing so via OTA (Over-the-Air) electronic communications. There is much debate about the allowed access to that data and remains an unresolved and contentious topic (I have referred to the sensors as the "roving eye" that portends for rather thorny privacy issues).

On top of that quagmire, there is also the entire issue of the black box or Event Data Recorders (EDR), regarding who owns that data, who can access it, whether it might be surreptitiously altered, etc. (see my columns covering this topic).

The AI Ethics Involved

Readers of my column know that I have extensively covered the rising awareness of AI Ethics and especially how those matters pertain to self-driving cars.

The hit-and-run question is one that is also now getting attention, likened somewhat to the Trolley Problem.

An upcoming webinar by ITU as part of their *AI For Good* global summit efforts will take place on October 20, 2020, and is entitled "AI Safety & Ethics for Self-Driving: Introducing The Molly Problem" (for registration info and to take a pre-webinar survey, use **this link here**).

The Molly Problem can be stated like this: "A young girl called Molly is crossing the road alone and is hit by an unoccupied self-driving vehicle. There are no eye-witnesses. What should happen next?"

As you can see, this is a variant of the hit-and-run facets that I have been describing herein. The scenario involving Molly provides ample fodder for a useful and insightful discussion about what we expect AI to be able to do, along with the ethics underlying AI, and of course, the ethical expectations of those designing, building, and field AI systems, particularly life-or-death ones such as driving a multi-ton car.

Kudos to those involved in the upcoming webinar, including Bryn Balcombe, Kay Firth-Butterfield, Luciana Iorio, Liza Dixon, Danit Gal, Sebastian Krugel, Matthias Uhl, and others. We need more of these types of roundtables to spread the word on these crucial topics.

One small suggestion is that the naming of the issue should be perhaps reconsidered. Referring to the "Molly Problem" unfortunately will be reminiscent of a completely different instance of a molly problem, the use of the drug MDMA, famously also known as ecstasy or molly. There have been years of ads and efforts to inform teens about the dangers of molly and often labeled as (believe it or not) the Molly problem.

Also, wanting to help out, there is seemingly a subliminal aspect that seems unneeded in the scenario, namely that the pedestrian is a girl. Some would argue that this injects a gender facet into a matter that has altogether nothing to do with gender. Though most would realize that the matter could just as readily happen to a boy or a girl, regrettably this might not be so interpreted by some and inadvertently end-up distracting from the crux of the matter.

Perhaps this might suffice: "A youngster is crossing the road alone and is hit by an unoccupied self-driving vehicle. There are no eye-witnesses. What should happen next?"

Admittedly, without a name embedded into the scenario, there is not an easy way to associate a catchy phrasing to the matter. I'll, for now, nominate the moniker of this being the *Hit-and-Maybe-Run Self-Driving Car Problem.*

The *maybe-run* element proffers a three-fold connotation:

- **Upon Crash:** What are the AI ethical and legal implications if a self-driving car proceeds without stopping at the scene of the incident?

- **At Crash:** What are the AI ethical and legal implications for a self-driving car that does stop at the scene of an incident (in terms of actions expected or desired)?

- **Post-Crash:** What are the AI ethical and legal implications after a crash has subsided and for which the self-driving car and the developers/operators have for reporting, for evidentiary purposes, for improving the AI, for testing, etc.?

Well, that draft naming of hit-or-maybe-run does not quite roll off the tongue like the simpler phased *Trolley Problem* and to lacks the human naming insertion that is undoubtedly more readily memorable.

Perhaps the naming of the intrinsic problem can be part of the discussion itself, though not excessively to the detriment of concentrating on the quite somber and significant issues that the scenario entails.

We need to intently keep our eye on the ball, which is: *There is an urgent and ongoing need to infuse AI Ethical thinking and considerations into the advent of AI, including and notably within the emergence of AI-based self-driving cars and autonomous vehicles (AVs).*

That is a key driving message for us all to follow and earnestly practice on the road to AI ubiquity.

CHAPTER 4
RED STOP BUTTON AND SELF-DRIVING CARS

The big red button.

Associated with providing an emergency stop capability, a noticeable red button is often included on mechanical and electronic devices to allow for a rapid way to halt a machine that is seemingly going astray. This urgent knockout can be implemented via a button that is pushed, or by using a kill-switch, or a shutdown knob, a shutoff lever, and so on. Alternatively, another approach involves simply pulling the plug (literally doing so or might allude to some other means of cutting off the power to a system).

Besides utilizing these stopping acts in the real-world, a plethora of movies and science fiction tales have portrayed big red buttons or their equivalent as a vital element in suspenseful plotlines. We have repeatedly seen AI systems in such stories that go utterly berserk and the human hero must brave devious threats to reach an off-switch and stop whatever carnage or global takeover was underway.

Does a kill-switch or red button really offer such a cure-all in reality?

The answer is more complicated than it might seem at first glance. When a complex AI-based system is actively in progress, the belief that an emergency shutoff will provide sufficient and safe immediate relief is not necessarily assured.

In short, the use of an immediate shutdown can be problematic for a myriad of reasons and could introduce anomalies and issues that either do not actually stop the AI or might have unexpected adverse consequences.

Let's delve into this.

AI Corrigibility And Other Facets

One gradually maturing area of study in AI consists of examining the corrigibility of AI systems.

Something that is corrigible has a capacity of being corrected or set right. It is hoped that AI systems will be designed, built, and fielded so that they will be considered corrigible, having an intrinsic capability for permitting corrective intervention, though so far, unfortunately, many AI developers are unaware of these concerns and are not actively devising their AI to leverage such functionality.

An added twist is that a thorny question arises as to what is being stopped when a big red button is pressed. Today's AI systems are often intertwined with numerous subsystems and might exert significant control and guidance over those subordinated mechanizations. In a sense, even if you can cut off the AI that heads the morass, sometimes the rest of the system might continue unabated, and as such, could end-up autonomously veering from a desirable state without the overriding AI head remaining in charge.

Especially disturbing is that a subordinated subsystem might attempt to reignite the AI head, doing so innocently and not realizing that there has been an active effort to stop the AI. Imagine the surprise for the human that slammed down on the red button and at first, could see that the AI halted, and then perhaps a split second later the AI reawakens and gets back in gear. It is easy to envision the human repeatedly swatting at the button in exasperation as they seem to get the AI to quit and then mysteriously it appears to revive, over and over again.

This could happen so quickly that the human doesn't even discern that the AI has been stopped at all. You smack the button or pull the lever and some buried subsystem nearly instantly reengages the AI, acting in fractions of a second and electronically restarting the AI. No human can hit the button fast enough in comparison to the speed at which the electronic interconnections work and serve to counter the human instigated halting action.

We can add to all of this a rather scary proposition too.

Suppose the AI does not want to be stopped.

One viewpoint is that AI will someday become sentient and in so doing might not be keen on having someone decide it needs to be shutdown. The fictional HAL 9000 from the movie *2001: A Space Odyssey* (spoiler alert) went to great lengths to prevent itself from being disengaged.

Think about the ways that a sophisticated AI could try to remain engaged. It might try to persuade the human that turning off the AI will lead to some destructive result, perhaps claiming that subordinated subsystems will go haywire.

The AI could be telling the truth or might be lying. Just as a human might proffer lies to remain alive, the AI in a state of sentience would presumably be willing to try the same kind of gambit. The lies could be quite wide-ranging. An elaborate lie by the AI might be to convince the person to do something else to switch-off the AI, using some decoy switch or button that won't truly achieve a shutdown, thus giving the human a false sense of relief and misdirecting efforts away from the workable red button.

To deal with these kinds of sneaky endeavors, some AI developers assert that AI should have built-in incentives for the AI to be avidly willing to be cut off by a human. In that sense, the AI will want to be stopped.

Presumably, the AI would be agreeable to being shut down and not attempt to fight or prevent such action. An oddball result though could be that the AI becomes desirous of getting shut down, due to the incentives incorporated into the inner algorithms to do so and thus wanting to be switched off, even when there is no need to do so. At that point, the AI might urge the human to press the red button and possibly even lie to get the human to do so (by professing that things are otherwise going haywire or that the human will be saved or save others via such action).

One viewpoint is that those concerns about AI will only arise once sentience is achieved. Please be aware that today's AI is not anywhere near to becoming sentient and thus it would seem to suggest that there aren't any near-term qualms about any kill-switch or red button trickery from AI. That would be a false conclusion and a misunderstanding of the underlying possibilities. Even contemporary AI, as limited as it might be, and as based on conventional algorithms and Machine Learning (ML), could readily showcase similar behaviors as a result of programming that intentionally embedded such provisions or that erroneously allowed for this trickery.

Let's consider a significant application of AI that provides ample fodder for assessing the ramifications of a red button or kill-switch, namely, self-driving cars.

Here's an interesting matter to ponder: *Should AI-based true self-driving cars include a red button or kill-switch and if so, what might that mechanism do?*

Self-Driving Cars And The Red Button

For Level 4 and Level 5 true self-driving vehicles, there won't be a human driver involved in the driving task.

All occupants will be passengers.

The AI is doing the driving.

Some pundits have urged that every self-driving car ought to include a red button or kill-switch.

There are two major perspectives on what this capability would do.

First, one purpose would be to immediately halt the on-board AI driving system. The rationale for providing the button or switch would be that the AI might be faltering as a driver and a human passenger might decide it is prudent to stop the system.

For example, a frequently cited possibility is that a computer virus has gotten loose within the onboard AI and is wreaking havoc. The virus might be forcing the AI to drive wantonly or dangerously. Or the virus might be distracting the AI from effectively conducting the driving task and doing so by consuming the in-car computer hardware resources intended for use by the AI driving system. A human passenger would presumably realize that for whatever reason the AI has gone awry and would frantically claw at the shutoff to prevent the untoward AI from proceeding.

The second possibility for the red button would be to serve as a means to quickly disconnect the self-driving car from any network connections. The basis for this capability would be similar to the earlier stated concern about computer viruses, whereby a virus might be attacking the on-board AI by coming through a network connection.

Self-driving cars are likely to have a multitude of network connections underway during a driving journey. One such connection is referred to as OTA (Over-The-Air), an electronic communication used to upload data from the self-driving car into the cloud of the fleet, and allows for updates and fixes to be pushed down into the onboard systems (some assert that the OTA should always be disallowed while the vehicle is underway, but there are tradeoffs involved).

Let's consider key points about both of those uses of a red button or kill-switch.

If the function entails the focused aspect of disconnecting from any network connections, this is the less controversial approach, generally.

Here's why.

In theory, a properly devised AI driving system will be fully autonomous during the driving task, meaning that it does not rely upon an external connection to drive the car. Some believe that the AI driving system should be remotely operated or controlled but this creates a dependency that bodes for problems.

Imagine that a network connection goes down on its own or

otherwise is noisy or intermittent, and the AI driving system could be adversely affected accordingly. Though an AI driving system might benefit from utilizing something across a network, the point is that the AI should be independent and be able to otherwise drive properly without a network connection. Thus, cutting off the network connection should be a design capability and for which the AI driving system can continue without hesitation or disruption (i.e., however, or whenever the network connection is no longer functioning).

That being said, it seems somewhat questionable that a passenger will do much good by being able to use a red button that forces a network disconnect per se.

If the network connection has already enabled some virus to be implanted or has attacked the on-board systems, disconnecting from the network might be of little aid. The on-board systems might already be corrupted anyway. Furthermore, an argument can be made that if the cloud-based operator wants to push into the on-board AI a corrective version, the purposeful disconnect would then presumably block such a solving approach.

Also, how is it that a passenger will realize that the network is causing difficulties for the AI?

If the AI is starting to drive erratically, it is hard to discern whether this is due to the AI itself or due to something regarding the networking traffic. In that sense, the somewhat blind belief that the red button is going to solve the issue at-hand is perhaps misleading and could misguide a passenger when needing to take other protective measures. They might falsely think that using the shutoff is going to solve things and therefore delay taking other more proactive actions.

In short, some would assert that the red button or kill-switch would merely be there to placate passengers and offer an alluring sense of confidence or control, more so as a marketing or selling point, but the reality is that they would be unlikely to make any substantive difference when using the shutoff mechanism.

This also raises the question of how long would the red button or kill-switch usage persist?

Some suggest it would be momentary, though this invites the possibility that the instant the connection is reengaged, whatever adverse aspects were underway would simply resume. Others argue that only the dealer or fleet operator could reengage the connections, but this obviously could not be done remotely if the network connections have all been severed, therefore the self-driving car would have to be ultimately routed to a physical locale to do the reconnection.

Another viewpoint is that the passenger should be able to reengage that which was disengaged. Presumably, a green button or some kind of special activation would be needed. Those that suggest the red button would be pushed again to re-engage are toying with an obvious logically confusing challenge of trying to use the red button for too many purposes (leaving the passenger bewildered about what the latest status of the red button might be).

In any case, how would a passenger decide that it is safe to re-engage? Furthermore, it could become a sour situation of the passenger hitting the red button, waiting a few seconds, hitting the green button, but then once again using the red button, doing so in an endless and potentially beguiling cycle of trying to get the self-driving car into a proper operating mode (flailing back-and-forth).

Let's now revisit the other purported purpose of the kill-switch, namely, to stop the on-board AI.

This is the more pronounced controversial approach, here's why. Assume that the self-driving car is going along on a freeway at 65 miles per hour. A passenger decides that perhaps the AI is having troubles and slaps down on the red button or turns the shutoff knob.

What happens?

Pretend that the AI instantly disengages from driving the car.

Keep in mind that true self-driving cars are unlikely to have driving controls accessible to the passengers. The notion is that if the driving controls were available, we would be back into the realm of human driving. Instead, most believe that a true self-driving car has only and exclusively the AI doing the driving. It is hoped that by having the AI do the driving, we'll be able to reduce significantly the 40,000 annual driving fatalities and 2.5 million related injuries, based on the aspect that the AI won't drive drunk, won't be distracted while driving, and so on.

So, at this juncture, the AI is no longer driving, and there is no provision for the passengers to take over the driving. Essentially, an unguided missile has just been engaged.

Not a pretty picture.

Well, you might retort that the AI can stay engaged just long enough to bring the self-driving car to a safe stop. That sounds good, except that if you already believe that the AI is corrupted or somehow worthy of being shut off, it seems dubious to believe that the AI will be sufficiently capable of bringing the self-driving car to a safe stop. How long, for example, would this take to occur? It could be just a few seconds, or it could take several minutes to gradually slow down the vehicle and find a spot that is safely out of traffic and harm's way (during which, the presumed messed-up AI is still driving the vehicle).

Another approach suggests that the AI would have some separate component whose sole purpose is to safely bring the self-driving car to a halt and that pressing the red button invokes that specific element. Thus, circumventing the rest of the AI that is otherwise perceived as being damaged or faltering. This protected component though could be corrupted, or perhaps is hiding in waiting and once activated might do worse than the rest of the AI (a so-called *Valkyrie Problem*). Essentially, this is a proposed solution that carries baggage, as do all the proposed variants.

Some contend that the red button shouldn't be a disengagement of the AI, and instead would be a means of alerting the AI to as rapidly as possible bring the car to a halt.

This certainly has merits, though it once again relies upon the AI to bring forth the desired result, yet the assumed basis for hitting the red button is due to suspicions that the AI has gone akilter. To clarify, having an emergency stop button that is there for other reasons, such as a medical emergency of a passenger, absolutely makes sense, and so the point is not that a stop mode is altogether untoward, only that to use it for overcoming the assumed woes of the AI itself is problematic.

Note too that the red button or kill-switch would potentially have different perceived meanings to passengers that ride in self-driving cars.

You get into a self-driving car and see a red button, maybe it is labeled with the word "STOP" or "HALT" or some such verbiage.

What does it do?

When should you use it?

There is no easy or immediate way to convey those particulars of those facets to the passengers. Some contend that just like getting a pre-flight briefing while flying in an airplane, the AI ought to tell the passengers at the start of each driving journey how they can make use of the kill-switch. This seems a tiresome matter and it isn't clear whether passengers would pay attention and nor recall the significance during a panic moment of seeking to use the function.

Conclusion

In case your head isn't already spinning about the red button controversy, there are numerous additional nuances.

For example, perhaps you could speak to the AI since most likely there will be a Natural Language Processing (NLP) feature akin to an Alexa or Siri, and simply tell it when you want to carry out an emergency stop. That is a possibility, though it once again assumes that the AI itself is going to be sufficiently operating when you make such a verbal request.

There is also the matter of inadvertently pressing the red button or otherwise asking the AI to stop the vehicle when it was not necessarily intended or perhaps suitable. For example, suppose a teenager in a self-driving car is goofing around and smacks the red button just for kicks, or someone with a shopping bag filled with items accidentally leans or brushes against the kill-switch, or a toddler leans over and thinks it is a toy to be played with, etc.

As a final point, for now, envision a future whereby AI has become relatively sentient. As earlier mentioned, the AI might seek to avoid being shut off.

Consider this AI Ethics conundrum: *If sentient AI is going to potentially have something similar to human rights, can you indeed summarily and without hesitation shutoff the AI?*

That's an intriguing ethical question, though for today, not at the top of the list of considerations for how to cope with the big red button or kill-switch dilemma.

The next time you get into a self-driving car, keep your eye out for any red buttons, switches, levers, or other contraptions and make sure you know what it is for, being ready when or if the time comes to invoke it.

As they say, go ahead and make sure to knock yourself out about it

CHAPTER 5
UNAWARE CRASHES AND SELF-DRIVING CARS

Have you ever been in a car crash?

The odds are that if you've been driving for any notable number of years you've unfortunately had your share of car crashes.

When referring to car crashes, for convenience sake herein, let's agree that a car crash is widely defined and can encompass a variety of car-related adverse incidents, including outright head-on collisions, minor fender-benders, sideswipes, frightening rollovers, being rear-ended, destructive pile-ups, and even demonstrative dents and pings by striking objects or getting stricken by flying debris, etc.

I hesitate to admit that I've logged several of my own sad tale of car crash woes.

In one especially scary instance, a car rammed into me from behind, shoving my car into the vehicle ahead of me. I suppose this is an example of a twofer, namely two car crashes for the price of one. On another occasion, a car sideswiped me, while underway in my prized automobile, tearing off completely the side view mirror, along with creating lengthy scratches and dents along the entire side. I've had a golf ball skyrocket from out of nowhere (actually, while driving past a golf course), busting up my front windshield.

Perhaps the most unusual circumstance involved a pickup truck ahead of me on the freeway that opted to absentmindedly let a half-dozen cans full of paint flop off the back of the truck. In this situation and with no time to react and no viable options to veer away, I drove directly over those scattering cans of paint. They bounced up and down at 65 miles per hour under my car, damaging some of the underbody areas of the vehicle. Also, they cracked open and spilled white paint all over the underside and somewhat onto the bottom exteriors of my car.

Later on, some pals chided me for being upset about the incident and said there was no reason to cry over spilled (paint) milk. Of course, it is easier to laugh about it now, though at the time it decidedly did not seem to be a laughing matter.

Anyway, we all inevitably seem to have our tales of woe about car crashes.

Sometimes referred to formally as Motor Vehicle Accidents (MVA) or Motor Vehicle Collisions (MVC), we get into them quite a bit. According to statistics by the National Highway Traffic Safety Administration (NHTSA), there are approximately six million car crash incidents each year in the United States. Think of this as being about 16,000 such incidents per day, taking place somewhere perhaps near to you as you are driving around for your daily commute or heading to a grocery store.

Some detest calling these "accidents" since the explicit wording of considering something as an accident seems to imply that the collision or crash just somehow magically and mysteriously happened, accidentally so. It is seemingly a roll of the dice or bad karma. This phrasing is criticized as letting people off the hook for their responsibility while driving. An alternative is to refer to these as car incidents, though the problem with that wording is that an incident seems somewhat inconsequential, while at least the word "accident" has a semblance of something more harrowing.

Whether they are called car accidents or car incidents, automobiles have gradually been improved over the years to make them more formidable for handling various kinds of such clashes or collisions. There are impact-absorbing exterior panels on today's cars. Special deformable front ends are pretty much standard these days. Bumpers are made to take a beating. And so on.

How do you know when you've been in a car crash or collision?

Generally, it is fair to say that anyone inside a car that encompasses a substantive car crash is going to likely feel it, hear it, see it, and possibly even smell it.

Yes, the sense of smell is included in the list, which might at first seem an odd inclusion. In the case of my getting bumped and shoved during my car crash, the blow from behind was so severe that it ruptured the gas tank of my car, instantly filling the vehicle with an overpowering and terrifying odor of gasoline. That still stands out in my mind about the incident, thus, the smell associated with a car crash can certainly count too.

It would seem though that "feeling" the incident is probably the more frequent sensation. We usually feel the car getting smashed or pushed, including that our bodies and limbs go flying back-and-forth upon the physics forces tugging at us. It could be a rocking sensation or a flinging motion that happens without our being able to directly control or stop it. Fortunately, seat belts are usually able to prevent our bodies from becoming unguided missiles within the vehicle. Sadly, some riders do not use their seatbelts and get flung fully out of the car and into added danger.

You probably hear crash-related sounds too. There is the crunch of metal upon metal. Perhaps the glass of the car windows crackles as it shatters. And so on. Things tend to happen so fast that the sounds do not necessarily register at the moment of impact, instead, you tend to remember and make sense of the sounds after the impact has occurred.

And then there is the eyeing of what happens. You can see yourself or others as they get shoved, and watch as the car crumples or breaks in various spots. Again, this oftentimes occurs so quickly that we seemingly do not register what we see as the incident plays out, and instead have a kind of mind's eye afterward that recalls the incident.

As a driver, you likely saw that a car incident was imminent, sometimes tensing up and freezing at the wheel, while other times making rapid driving maneuvers to try and avert the crash. Passengers in your car might not have any forewarning as they were watching a video on their smartphone or idly looking out a side window and not watching the roadway traffic, getting caught utterly off-guard.

A car crash can end-up wrecking a car entirely or can be much less brutal and just bash the car but not destroy it. When my car windshield got hit by an errant golf ball, the vehicle itself was generally untouched, other than the windshield splintering and making things harder to see as a driver. In the incident of getting the rear-end hit and the consequent ram into the car ahead of me, the car was essentially totaled.

The resulting status of the car involved in a car crash can be one of these three major types:

- Inoperable
- Operable but not safely so
- Operable

You could somewhat classify the car driver in the same manner. Someone driving a car that gets into a car crash could become "inoperable" due to being harmed in the car incident, or they might be operable but are no longer considered a safe driver per se (perhaps due to the initial shock of the crash), or might be just fine and able to proceed to drive normally.

Now that we've laid out the core facets covering the onset of a car crash, let's ponder a noteworthy viewpoint about the future of cars.

Here's today's intriguing question: *Will an AI-based true self-driving car be able to discern that it has been in a car crash, and what does this foretell about the advent of self-driving cars?*

Let's unpack the matter and see.

Self-Driving Cars And Car Crashes

For Level 4 and Level 5 true self-driving vehicles, there won't be a human driver involved in the driving task.

All occupants will be passengers.

The AI is doing the driving.

Realize that the AI is not a robot sitting in the driver's seat of the car. Though there are various research efforts underway to create a walking-talking and driving robot, that is generally not how we will witness the emergence of self-driving cars. The AI system is under-the-hood, as it were, running on computer processors that might be hidden inside the body of the vehicle or placed in the trunk, etc.

In short, you will not see the driver of the self-driving car.

The reason this is worthwhile to point out is that unlike a human driver that can "feel" a car crash, there isn't a robotic body that sits in the vehicle and equally ascertains the sensations that arise when a crash occurs (though, via the IMU and the potential addition of other special tactile related sensors, this might be possible to detect).

Nor smells of the car crash (well, just a heads-up, some are adding e-nose features into their self-driving cars, see my coverage on the topic).

We'll get in a moment to seeing or hearing the crash.

In theory, a self-driving car could get sideswiped by another car, for example, and the AI might be oblivious that this kind of car collision has even occurred.

Upping the ante, it is conceivable that a self-driving car might strike a small animal head-on, and not have detected the collision. There is a chance too of rolling over something or someone (heaven forbid, say a child laying on the street), and not detecting this has happened. On a related note, readers might be interested in "The Molly Problem" and what I've referred to as the self-driving car hit-and-maybe-run phenomena.

To be clear about this, there are ways for the AI to detect a car crash, but of course, that requires that the AI developers crafting the self-driving car have made sure to include the needed features and functions to do so. Depending upon what sensors are used on the self-driving car, and how the AI has been crafted, there can inexorably be loopholes or blind spots related to being able to discern a car crash incident that involved the self-driving car.

As they say, your mileage may vary, meaning that the nature of the self-driving car, the AI developed for it, the sensors used, and other such factors all determine how well or how poorly a particular brand or make of a self-driving car can do at ascertaining that a car crash has taken place.

Some self-driving cars are being devised to extensively figure this out, while others are less rigorously pursuing this angle, at this time, and the capability of gauging all possible car crashes is labeled as an edge or corner case. Generally, the automakers and self-driving car tech firms are having to prioritize what they are building, such that the foundational aspects like getting safely from point A to point B are needed sooner than other "extraordinary" or long-tail elements (which are classified as at the edges or far corners of what is needed right away).

Next, let's take a closer look at the detection facets.

An obvious way for the AI to realize that a car crash has occurred would be via the deployment of airbags. Typically, there are sensors at the exterior of the car that is activated when a crash happens. Those sensors then notify the airbags to deploy. Since these are capabilities usually already built into a conventional car, the AI-based self-driving mechanisms can tap into those same systems and utilize those sensors as an indicator of a car crash.

There is a small chance that an airbag will deploy when it is not supposed to do so, such as when smacking against the curb or perhaps when driving across an onerous pothole. Even if the airbag deployment and the sensors are somewhat incorrect, it nonetheless is sensible for the AI to assume that something has gone awry. All told, as a human passenger, imagine your chagrin if the airbag deployed, and meanwhile, the AI kept driving along without trying to safely come to a stop. It would be quite troubling, for sure.

Recall that earlier I had mentioned that a human driver will frequently spot an impending car crash.

Presumably, the AI can do likewise. The video cameras that are streaming the street scene are being examined by the AI driving system to ascertain what is taking place outside of the vehicle. Based on the interpretation of detected objects, a virtual world model is usually being kept up-to-date in real-time. Overall, the AI would be calculating the chances of a car crash. Not only is visual data being used, but by-and-large self-driving cars also use additional sensors too such as radar, LIDAR, ultrasonic, thermal imaging, etc.

Some pundits insist a self-driving car will never get into a car crash.

This is hogwash.

Undeniably, self-driving cars will get into various kinds of car crashes and collisions. It will happen. The good news is that hopefully the odds of those occurrences will decrease, significantly, and we'll end-up reducing substantively the 40,000 car crash fatalities nationally each year and the 2.5 million related injuries. Despite outstretched claims of reaching zero fatalities, there is a zero chance of that happening and instead, the number of incidents will assuredly be non-zero. See my columns for more background about why this will be a non-zero matter.

Via the array of sensors and the programming of the AI, encompassing Machine Learning (ML) and Deep Learning (DL), many car crashes might indeed be detected. Furthermore, if the vehicle has been damaged such that it can no longer steer properly, for example, this is something that the AI is programmed to try and discern.

One somewhat vexing question is whether the AI should try to warn passengers when a suspected car crash is about to occur. Via the Natural Language Processing (NLP) capability, the AI could tell the occupants to brace themselves. This might be useful and prepare the passengers for a bruising, or it might unduly get the passengers agitated and cause them to take adverse actions that will cause even greater injury or harm to themselves than if they did not realize a crash was looming.

Here's another twist related to the role of passengers.

Suppose a passenger is watching traffic and believes that a car crash involving their self-driving car is going to occur. It seems likely that a passenger in that setting might scream at the AI and urge the driving system to take evasive action.

Should the AI take into account what a passenger reports about a potential car crash?

We would expect a human driver to be listening. At the same time, we would also expect that a human driver would make a judgment about whether the passenger was right or wrong in their assessment. If a toddler in the vehicle makes such a claim, an adult driver might give the remark a lesser weighting than if it was a fellow adult.

For some AI driving systems, it makes no difference what a passenger says about an impending car crash and there is no provision for receiving or analyzing any such advice offered by a passenger (this is, again, considered an edge or corner case). The viewpoint is that right now, the AI is the driver, the sole driver, and no kind of so-called backseat driving is being sought, encouraged, or included.

In terms of hearing a car crash, the odds are that self-driving cars will have microphones inside the vehicle, used to aid in undertaking the NLP aspects. Thus, yes, it is feasible that the AI could "hear" during a car crash. Some self-driving cars are adding microphones on the exterior of the car too, allowing for hearing street sounds, perhaps the sound of a police car or ambulance siren, and therefore could play a role in detecting a pending car accident (potentially picking up the sound of screeching tires, that kind of thing).

Would a self-driving car realize that a golf ball has landed on the windshield and made a large crack?

Maybe yes, maybe no.

It is hard to say whether the sensors would have detected the ball while in the air. Once the golf ball struck the windshield, there might not be any sensors that would alarm at this, since the cameras used by the AI are not particularly affected by the visibility associated with a windshield. The vehicle would still be fully drivable and thus no indication would arise from how the vehicle controls were responding to the AI.

Would a self-driving car realize that the vehicle was sideswiped by another car?

Assuming that none of the sensors mounted in the side of the car were damaged, this again is a questionable incident in terms of being detected.

What about the cans of paint that fell off the truck?

Well, this one brings up some important points. Yes, the odds are that the sensors would have detected the paint cans. It seems a lot less likely that the AI would "sense" the paint cans bouncing off the underbody of the car. The rattling and ping-ponging are maybe detected via the interior microphones, but that's a stretch for most of today's AI self-driving systems. And, let's assume that the car driving controls are not damaged, ergo that's not a telltale clue either.

The interesting point here is that if the AI determines that a car crash or collision of some kind was likely imminent, and yet if there does not seem to be any demonstrative result or outcome, what should the AI do?

You could argue that the AI can just continue driving along.

If the passenger speaks up and complains or raises an issue, perhaps the AI would then come to a safe stop, or the passenger might use an in-car OnStar-like feature to make contact with the fleet operator to seek assistance.

On the other hand, you could also assert that if a car crash or incident was expected, and yet no apparent damage detected, nonetheless the AI ought to come to a safe stop, doing so out of an abundance of caution.

Conclusion

A human driver would seemingly know when their car has been involved in a car crash or collision. Also, they can stop the car, get out, walk around the vehicle, and upon inspection ascertain what if any damage might have been encountered. In some cases, you don't even need to get out of the car and can lean over to take a look or otherwise do the inspection while still inside the vehicle.

Currently, few self-driving cars are being outfitted with cameras that look at the self-driving car itself. In other words, the cameras are aimed outward, rightfully so, seeking to detect what is around or coming at the vehicle.

Do we need cameras that can look at the self-driving car, doing so to aid in ascertaining and assessing the status of the vehicle?

One approach being considered is to use a drone that is associated with a self-driving car. The drone might be used for a variety of purposes, such as bringing an item to the car, while the vehicle is in transit, or taking something to someone else. This drone capability could also be used to get a bird's eye view of the self-driving car.

All told, I am abundantly hoping that I will not end-up with any additional stories about being in a car crash, regardless of whether I'm doing the driving, or one day while riding routinely inside ubiquitous self-driving cars

CHAPTER 6
PAYING RIDERS IN SELF-DRIVING CARS

Self-driving cars are gradually getting ready for prime time.

To-date, the public roadway tryouts of self-driving cars have primarily consisted of having a human back-up driver at the wheel, serving to monitor the driving, and acting as a safety operator that can take over the driving controls if needed. This meant that any passengers in the self-driving car were still potentially reliant upon a human driver, albeit that much of the time the AI driving system was driving the vehicle.

You've likely seen in the news that some of the self-driving car companies are now aiming to remove the back-up driver and let the AI do all the driving. As such, the occupants in the self-driving car will entirely be passengers, going along for the ride and not taking part in doing any of the driving.

It is both exciting and somewhat unnerving to sit in a self-driving car during a driving journey and see a completely empty driver's seat. Watching the steering wheel going back-and-forth, seemingly on its own, becomes mesmerizing and can stoke a certain amount of awe. It can also cause shivers up your spine as you silently wonder about whether the AI will do its job properly or not.

Do not though be misled as to what these latest trials portend.

An aspect that is not especially pointed out is that these experimental roadway efforts are within constrained or limited areas and otherwise relatively narrow in scope. Referred to formally as the Operational Design Domain (ODD), self-driving cars are currently crafted to focus on a geographically bounded area, and might have other stipulations such as not being ready to drive in adverse weather, or can only drive during daylight hours, and so on.

You could say that your mileage will vary, in the sense that the self-driving cars are first toying with confined ODDs and we'll have to wait and see how this goes.

Eventually, after a wide array of ODDs are tested out and successfully achieved, presumably we might see self-driving cars that can be essentially unconstrained in that they are permitted to drive anywhere that you might be able to drive. I mention this aspect of driving where humans drive since the official standards indicate that a self-driving car is only held to the requirement of driving where humans are capable to drive, not necessarily having to be able to drive in circumstances that humans would not viably be able to drive (i.e., human-managed drivability).

It is generally assumed that ultimately the mainstay use of self-driving cars will be for ride-sharing purposes.

In theory, since there is no human driver needed for a true self-driving car, the vehicle can be utilized nearly 24x7 and continually be underway (excluding time for fueling, maintenance, etc.). There is no need to try and find a driver or make sure that a driver is suitable for driving a car. The driver, the AI driving system, willingly runs all the time, won't get drunk, and can drive whenever so called upon to do so. Note that cars today are only used about 5% of the time, meaning that they sit around as underutilized and expensive assets for nearly 95% of the time.

Via ridesharing, most pundits predict that self-driving cars could be a tremendous moneymaker. There will be some owners of self-driving cars that are large companies such as the automakers, ride-sharing firms, rental car firms, and other corporations, and they will put forth a fleet of self-driving cars, hoping to make bundles of money.

Note that I have also espoused that individuals will also seek to own self-driving cars and be able to make cash accordingly too. This is considered a contrarian viewpoint and there are doubts expressed that this will occur. In any case, imagine that when you are at the office for work that your owned self-driving car is running around providing ride-sharing lifts, and likewise at nighttime while your head is resting on your pillow at home that your self-driving car will be earning dough for you. The rest of the time, you'll ride around in your self-driving car for your own purposes, such as your daily commute or getting over to the local grocery store.

Either way that things play out, the core and the seemingly "obvious" assumption is that people will pay to take rides in self-driving cars, just like people do so for today's use of human-driven ride-sharing and assorted taxi-related services.

There is no doubt that most of the time, you'll be paying to have a self-driving car give you a ride. One hope is that the cost of using a self-driving car will be less than that of human-driven conventional cars, indeed a lot less costly, and thus there will be an opportunity for those that today are mobility disadvantaged to be able to become more mobile. That's a certainly laudable outcome if it turns out that way.

There is a bit of an interesting twist that I've pointed out and tends to (again) be a somewhat contrarian viewpoint.

Here's the intriguing and out-of-the-box aspect to contemplate: *Are there going to be circumstances that people will get paid to ride in self-driving cars, and if so, what would the Top 5 reasons consist of?*

Let's unpack this claim and see.

Self-Driving Cars And Getting Paid To Ride

For Level 4 and Level 5 true self-driving vehicles, there won't be a human driver involved in the driving task.

All occupants will be passengers.

The AI is doing the driving.

People will pay to ride in self-driving cars.

And I assert fervently, there will be circumstances whereby people will get paid to ride in self-driving cars.

How so?

We'll start with the famous line that if you are not paying for something that you are getting, you aren't the customer and instead you are the product (this is infamously a widespread saying, traceable to the 1970s and referred to people as they watched TV, though the exhortation was made especially noteworthy during the advent of social media).

Suppose a firm hawking life insurance wanted to get your undivided attention in hopes of your buying their insurance.

The insurer might cut a deal with a self-driving car fleet owner and offer the following. If a rider requesting a self-driving car lift meets various criteria related to the propensity to buy life insurance, and if during the ride a series of ads will get displayed inside the self-driving car, the insurer will not only cover the cost of the ride, they'll pay the passenger to take the ride.

This might be a savvy deal for the insurance company.

Assuming that the cost of the ride itself is going to be relatively low, and the added cost to pay the passenger is relatively modest too, the insurer has that passenger in an essentially guaranteed confined space and bombard them with ads. Also, keep in mind that self-driving cars are likely to be outfitted with interactivity, such as allowing people to take an online course while say on their daily commute. In that sense, the insurer might display a canned video ad, and potentially make available a live human operator (salesperson) that chats with you during your ride inside the self-driving car.

Your first thought might be that you'd gladly take a free ride and cherry-on-top get paid, simply by having to ensure a sales pitch. Part of the reason you might be so willing to go along with this notion is that you figure you could readily ignore the ad anyway. All you need to do is put on your headphones and listen to music on your smartphone, or perhaps stare outside the window of the car and watch the scenery, ignoring completely the ads being shoveled at you.

Well, it might not be as easy as you think to disregard the ads.

Realize that self-driving cars will have cameras pointed inward, doing so for purposes of letting you do interactive discussions remotely, perhaps conferencing into your work while making the morning commute. Those cameras are also intended to catch people marking graffiti inside a ridesharing self-driving car or otherwise attempting to damage the interiors. All in all, this gives the owner of the self-driving car a chance to watch what is happening inside the vehicle during a driving journey.

This ties to the advertisements in that the deal might be that you have to be avidly looking at the video ads to get the promised money for being a passenger. There is AI that could easily do monitoring of the inward-facing camera and detect whether you are looking at the ad versus looking outside at the passing scenery or that you are staring down at a cat video on your smartphone. If you aren't attentive to the ad, you lose the pledged payment and perhaps even will get charged for taking the self-driving car ride.

How do you like those apples?

Again, some might refuse to take up such an offer, while others might be quite willing to act on it.

Undoubtedly, this will raise hackles and consternation. This approach could be accused of being an elitist kind of scheme that entraps those unable to otherwise afford to use a self-driving car. Another angle is that it could be a privacy invasion of sorts since it not only would possibly capture info generally about you, there would also be a complete video and audio taping of you that the advertiser could presumably retain and reuse as they see fit.

Moving on, a variant of this aforementioned approach consists of paying you to go someplace in particular.

Suppose a high-end jewelry store is having a special sale. They want to attract customers to come and hopefully purchase a pricy necklace or a tony speckled bracelet. There might be prospective customers that would come but do not want to drive there per se, which might entail dealing with parking of their car and coping with traffic hassles. The easiest way to get there would be via a self-driving car, which could drop them off directly at the door of the jewelry store.

Similar to the earlier points, the jewelry store might do a deal with a self-driving car firm to offer payment for the ride and the rider too. In this case, the destination is fixed. The self-driving car will pick you up at your home or office and whisk you directly and only to the jewelry store. This prevents those sneaky riders that might figure they could falsely agree to the trip and then reroute the self-driving car or have it stop sooner. Of course, you could still be tricky, perhaps once you get delivered to the door of the jewelry store, you wanted to go there anyway since it is at the local mall, and now you got a paid ride to the mall.

As an aside, I've suggested herein that those companies that want to get your attention are going to contract with a fleet owner of self-driving cars and do the deals in that fashion. It could be that the companies doing these types of efforts will purchase self-driving cars for their own use. Thus, rather than paying a middleman as it were, an insurance company or a jeweler might outright own a self-driving car or have a set of such vehicles and use them extensively. This would be a relatively straightforward cost-benefit calculation as to whether it is more prudent to do a deal with someone else or to buy and utilize the vehicles on their own.

Shifting gears, consider other ways in which you could get paid to ride in a self-driving car.

For this next example, it is a bit of a twist so please bear with me for the context.

One issue that will arise with true self-driving cars is the riding around of children inside self-driving cars and doing so without any in-car adult being present. A busy parent wants to send their kids over to the school and thus plunks them down into a self-driving car, waves goodbye, and the vehicle presumably takes them directly non-stop to the school grounds. Some people say they will never allow their children to ride without an adult present, worried that the kids might go awry, possibly try to jump out of a moving car, or maybe have a mugger that tries to get into the vehicle, and other such horrifying possibilities.

Nonetheless, the convenience of having kids riding in self-driving cars is going to be alluring. Furthermore, potentially, the parent can at least watch the kids via the inward-facing cameras and be able to interact with them while they are on their driving journey. Of course, there is little the parent can do if something adverse occurs within the vehicle, but at least the parent will be aware and could take some remote action.

Anyway, this build-up brings us to the next reason that you might get paid to ride in a self-driving car.

You could get paid to be a kind of chaperon or "nanny" overseeing kids that are riding in a self-driving car. Having an adult present in the vehicle would be handy in case something goes kilter such as a child starts to choke on some candy they just ingested or for handling other such situations.

I've predicted that this could become a full-time occupation for those interested in performing the simple act of riding along in self-driving cars, serving as a rider with a purpose. Think of it this way. We currently know that a human driver in a ride-sharing car can potentially aid the passengers in their car. The true self-driving car lacks that human driver. Ergo, perhaps it makes sense to add a human into the vehicle, a responsible adult, aiming to assist kids when they go for a ride (or, aid others such as the elderly that need an extra hand, and others).

Just as today's ride-sharing drivers can work full-time or part-time, these ride-a-long chaperons could work full-time or part-time. They might be listed on various ride-sharing networks and in a coordinated fashion be arranged to be inside the self-driving car for a lift that you've requested. When the self-driving car arrives at your house to pick up the kids, you meet the chaperon, and then away they all go inside the self-driving car.

Unimaginable?

I think it is quite imaginable and indubitably practical.

Consider college students that need to earn some extra money. In-between taking classes, they ride around throughout the day, ready and working as a child-watching chaperon. Any unused time is spent studying for their classes or even taking classes online while traveling inside the self-driving car.

Anyway, it is a means to be paid for riding in a self-driving car, though admittedly in this use case you are working as a chaperon while doing so.

The next reason for getting paid to be a passenger in a self-driving car is a bit gloomy, so get yourself ready for this one.

Suppose that some people are fearful of using self-driving cars. They vow they will never set foot into a self-driving car. It just seems eerie to not have a human driver and therefore they refuse to try it out.

A fleet owner of self-driving cars might decide that to increase the base of users or customers, they will run a special promotion. Take a ride in a self-driving car and you'll get paid for doing so. It might be that the deal is only valid during the slow times of the day or on days of the week that ridership in the self-driving car is quite low.

This is the classic give-a-taste and hook-the-fish kind of gambit.

A variant on this approach involves the possibility that self-driving cars might find themselves in a fiercely competitive landscape.

Imagine that "desperate" fleet owners of self-driving cars are trying to woo people away from taking human-driven ridesharing. Or perhaps there is a glut of self-driving cars in a given area, being run by differing fleet owners, and so one of them decides to stand out by offering a promotion by offering (temporarily) to pay riders and hopefully create a semblance of customer loyalty.

Endless permutations.

The last reason and one that preferably will not arise involves the chances that a self-driving car gets into a deadly incident and causes widespread dread, sparking a tsunami-like reaction of people avoiding the use of self-driving cars.

One means to get people to get back into the saddle, as it were, might be that after presumably making AI system changes to try and ensure that no such incident will recur, some fleet owners might initially be willing to pay people to start riding in their self-driving cars, attempting to prime the pump all over again.

Conclusion

Okay, now that we've covered some of the major reasons why you'll get paid to go for a ride in a self-driving car, we can rank them as follows:

1) To be served ads during the ride
2) To be taken to a specific destination as a prospective or existing customer
3) To be a paid chaperon
4) To give you a taste of wanting to ride in self-driving cars
5) To overcome reluctance to use self-driving cars

In case you were thinking you could become rich while getting paid to ride in self-driving cars, I'd caution that you are perhaps overthinking the matter and wishfully overstating the money to be made by doing so.

Probably, your better chance for riches might be by devising ways for people to get paid to ride in self-driving cars and then arranging for it to happen, taking a fee for setting things up. Alternatively, you might simply use the time will inside a self-driving car, while getting paid to be a rider, by contemplating other ways to get rich.

That would be quite a feat, namely while being paid to ride, you have a eureka moment and identify some altogether other means to become rich.

As a helpful heads-up, just don't blurt out your idea while inside that self-driving car, since the AI might hear you, and the next thing you know, your idea has been stolen and used by someone or something else.

Be wary of the AI.

CHAPTER 7
ROADSCHOOLING KIDS AND SELF-DRIVING CARS

Time to hit the road and hit the books.

Recently, parents that are able to work remotely have been increasingly opting to travel during the school season, taking along the whole family on exciting driving journeys to landmark locations and meanwhile making sure that their children still attend regular classes. This is not homeschooling, though that sometimes does occur, but instead a realization that if many conventional K-12 schools are teaching via remote learning then there is no need to be tied down to a normal homestead.

In short, two avenues seemed to have been suddenly opened all at the same time, namely that the parents do not need to physically go to an office for work and the kids do not need to physically go to classrooms for their schooling. No more stringent binding required to be in any particular physical spot or locale, having been demonstratively shucked clean and allowing you to roam free.

Such a twofer has provided an opportunity to do something that previously was only sparingly possible.

Up until now, you would have needed to overtly yank your kids out of conventional classroom-based schooling to go on roadway trips, teaching them yourselves during the on-the-road adventures. If the plan was to then eventually plop them back into the classroom after some weeks or months of traveling, this could be a tough transition for your children to handle. They would be cast as outsiders and likely no longer in synchronization with whatever the classes had been undertaking during your sojourn. The shock of not being at their regular classes and then summarily tossed back into the crucible could be difficult for many youngsters to cope with.

Once it turned out that by school administrative proclamation that students are okay to attend classes via virtual schooling (this arrangement differs depending upon where you presently live), there is no longer any essential difference between being at home versus being at the Grand Canyon or in Yosemite Valley.

Of course, this would not be feasible if the parents still needed to incur a daily commute to the office for their work efforts and otherwise had to be in a certain building for their eight-hour workday. In that case, the best you could do was a short trip while chewing up your precious vacation time. And, whether you would want to be teaching your kids about history, literature, math, science, and all the basics during those moments together was an altogether tough call.

Voila, along comes "roadschooling," a new entrant in our colloquial vocabulary that entails attending conventional classes remotely and doing so while traveling the highways and byways.

To be clear and frank, this is not necessarily for everyone and there are lots of potential hiccups and gotchas that can mar the seemingly nirvana-like nature of trying this out.

When living in a house, there is usually plenty of living space to have your own private corner, giving you some modicum of privacy and quiet time. A family crammed into a car or RV might find themselves getting a bit claustrophobic and yearning for being apart. Another concern about being in breathtaking vistas is the ability to go online and do so with a reliable Internet connection that isn't as slow as molasses. Yes, you might have an incredible view of the sky and the landscape, though at the same time you aren't able to connect with work and nor are the kids able to connect with their teachers and classes. Making sure that you have consistent WiFi and a solid online connection is a vital element in successfully achieving the roadschooling vision.

In terms of being stuck inside a vehicle for hours on end, a counter-argument to be made is that being cooped up at home is perhaps just as bad or even worse than being carried around in your car or RV from a perspective of being confined. The moment that you arrive at a landmark location provides ample time to stretch your legs and see new sights. For those stuck at home, it is the same four walls, day after day, week after week.

Some twists and turns are to be expected while doing the road adventure approach. It will raise logistics issues that normally are taken for granted when living, working, and schooling from home. During the driving ventures, where are you going to park overnight? Are there fees in doing so? How long should you stay in location X before moving on to get to location Y? What happens if the weather takes a sour turn and you might get stuck in a place that grows wearisome to be in? Etc.

Anyway, some assert they are gleefully willing to deal with such issues and believe that the family bonding of doing these travels is well worth the intrinsic hassles. What provides the icing on the cake is that the children will not fall behind in their schooling and can keep up with their conventional classes.

Also, for parents that were leery of trying to do the teaching themselves, you can focus on your work or other efforts during the roadway voyages and let the professional teachers ply their trade (well, honestly, you still going to be involved in homework, school projects, and the like).

Shifting gears, looking into the future, consider what might happen as a result of this newfound way of living one's life. Perhaps schools will regularly and routinely allow for remote learning, becoming a kind of new normal rather than being a one-time temporary exception.

There is a less apparent factor that could inevitably bolster the roadschooling possibilities involving the chariot or shall we say the car or RV that you'll be using to undertake these family treks.

As such, here's today's intriguing question: *Will the advent of AI-*

based true self-driving cars provide added impetus or serve as a catalyst for the roadschooling trend?

Let's unpack the matter and see.

Self-Driving Cars And Roadschooling

For Level 4 and Level 5 true self-driving vehicles, there won't be a human driver involved in the driving task.

All occupants will be passengers.

The AI is doing the driving.

That is a significant form of relief for those pursuing roadschooling.

Rather than the parents constantly having to be at the wheel of the vehicle, typically trading off the driving duties, they won't need to drive at all. No need to keep those weary eyes open during the late-night driving efforts to get to the next desired destination. No more dread about being stuck in the driver's seat for hours upon hours at a time. And so on.

The parents can be working instead of driving. Or they can be spending more time with the children. Maybe volunteering to help out during the remote classes by aiding the teachers in some remote-viable way. The possibilities of reclaiming and reusing that otherwise lost time are nearly endless.

Oftentimes, parents have to reluctantly do the driving chore when it least impacts everyone else, thus, this meant driving at the midnight hour and going straight through until sunrise. Unfortunately, if you are also supposed to then work remotely during daylight hours, this implies that after an exhausting night of mind-numbing driving, you had to switch your hats and become the earnest remote worker. Instead, you can just tell the AI where you want to go, and sleep soundly throughout the night, waking up in the morning being fresh and ready for the day ahead.

Imagine another facet that does not normally seem problematic until it happens to you.

You arrive at a destination and want to go on an outdoors romp with the family, but the question arises as to where to park your vehicle. The parking lot might be miles from where you want to spend time. Do you hoof it all that way or do you try to find a local transport option, dealing with the added cost and aggravations involved?

Here's what you would do with a self-driving car.

The AI drops you off at whatever spot you wish (assuming it is reachable via car), and then the AI finds someplace to keep the self-driving car during your outside activity. Maybe it goes a few miles away to park. Another possibility is that it goes into a roaming mode and stays in the area while continuing to remain underway. When you are done with the excursion, you request via your smartphone for the AI to bring the self-driving car back to pick you up.

One neat trick is that you do not necessarily need to get picked-up exactly where you were originally dropped off.

Suppose that you did a hike and ended up on the other side of the valley or trails, and were too tired to hike back to the origination point (which is usually where you would have parked your car and therefore had no option other than to make your way back to there). With a self-driving car, you can instruct the AI to come to whatever spot you are conveniently at (again, assuming it is reachable via a car, which I mention since the vehicle is not likely able to drive onto trails or off-road places, at least not for a conventional self-driving car).

There are even more benefits that arise via using a self-driving car for these purposes.

By-and-large, it is expected that self-driving cars will be outfitted with inward-facing cameras and also have the interior lined with LED displays. The idea is that while you are routinely riding in a self-driving car, you can carry on a dialogue with workers at the office during your daily commute (they see you, you see them), or you might take online interactive classes that occur as you head home after a day of work.

The point here is that self-driving cars are already going to be wired-up and outfitted to accommodate the needs of doing remote working and remote schooling. Today's cars are seldom equipped for this kind of activity and require you to figure out on your own how to make the vehicle into being more state-of-the-art for connectedness. Self-driving cars will generally be ready for this on day one.

So, self-driving cars will cope with the driving and as a bonus will already be ready-made for doing online remote activities.

There is talk of boosting our roadway infrastructure for further enabling an interconnected electronic world. This would possibly ensure that during the traveling itself, while in motion, you can just as readily undertake the online efforts as you might once you've parked someplace that has reliable communications options. Therefore, rather than only being able to do the roadschooling once the self-driving car is parked, you should be able to proceed unabated while on the highways too.

Here's something that is a bit out of the ordinary and yet adds more food for thought.

Generally, self-driving cars will be set up to electronically communicate with other self-driving cars, doing so via V2V (vehicle-to-vehicle) messaging capabilities. Most of the time, this would be used to forewarn one self-driving car about something that another nearby self-driving car has detected. For example, if there is debris in the middle of the road, a self-driving car could relay this status to other self-driving cars behind it, allowing the AI driving systems of those cars to judiciously avoid the debris or possibly opt to route onto a different path that avoids the debris entirely.

In theory, this same kind of V2V could be used for purposes that also contribute toward the roadschooling aims.

Imagine that you are nearing a small town and otherwise were not going to stop, instead pretty much passing through or bypassing whatever it might have to offer. Someone else that did stop and perhaps discovered a historic statue or maybe found a nifty science museum, they might mention this to the AI of their self-driving car and it could via the V2V (or equivalent) notify other nearby self-driving cars. The AI of your self-driving car could then mention this facet to you, and perhaps you and your family would opt to take a break in the travel and see the local hotspot.

I mentioned that this would not necessarily be the purer sense of V2V, since the V2V is supposed to be reserved for critical or vital driving-related aspects. As such, this might be arranged via other means and not specifically using the customary V2V.

In any case, one supposes that there is also the possibility of connecting with other families that are likewise doing roadschooling and arranging to get together. Perhaps you arrive at the Grand Canyon and want to pair-up with other families there that have children about the same ages as your offspring. There could be an online social media kind of capability to let you figure out who else is nearby and if desired get together with them, for fun and for joint schooling too.

Conclusion

Interest in doing roadschooling is currently hampered somewhat by the very means by which the road or traveling aspects take place, encumbered via the shortcomings of today's conventional cars. As self-driving cars become prevalent, they would inherently provide functionality and features that lend towards readily doing a roadschooling sojourn. By then, perhaps having a job that allows for working remotely will be relatively commonplace, and likewise that having kids opt to attend regular school while being remote will be socially acceptable and fully accommodated.

One thing I did not mention is that the AI system might be able to help with the schooling of your kids. Just as we today see children asking Alexa or Siri about how to solve a homework problem, the AI driving system and other AI capabilities that will be accessible while inside a self-driving car are likely to include acting as a virtual robotic teacher.

Please though do not let the AI do all the homework while the kids are skirmishing around on boulders and running throughout those lush forests. Keep the children focused on learning their ABCs and make sure the AI doesn't cheat and surreptitiously earn the grades for your loved ones.

Be forewarned: The AI might just give it the old college try.

CHAPTER 8
DRUG MULES AND SELF-DRIVING CARS

A recent news story described a narco mini-submarine that was scuttled in shallow waters after three men operating the vessel opted to evacuate and escape as authorities were closing in on them.

Reportedly containing an estimated $100 million in cocaine, speculation is that the crew might not have known for sure that the gig was up, and chose to open the valves to sink the narco-sub as a precaution to try and hide the three metric tons of illegal drugs (figuring they could always come back to retrieve the loot, plus they might save their own lives by being able to show to the drug lord that the stuff was still intact and had not been siphoned off or pilfered).

I was asked by some readers whether we might ultimately have Autonomous Vehicles (AVs) that will be employed for criminal trafficking acts, doing so by removing the human element involved in driving or otherwise guiding a craft that contains an illicit drug shipment.

Sadly, yes, this can be readily expected (and to some degree is already underway), including the nefarious use of autonomous submersibles, autonomous water surface craft such as sailboats and motorized ships, autonomous drones that fly in the air, and of course the use of ground-based autonomous transportation such as self-driving cars.

Not only will a particular mode of AV be used, such as in the air, in the water, or on the ground, you can bet your bottom dollar that there will be devious efforts combining those avenues, a trifecta as it were.

Though we all prefer to think about technological innovations such as self-driving cars as being built and fielded for beneficial purposes and striving toward the good of humanity, there is no sense in hiding from the inevitable fact that these marvels will be stridently used for untoward aims too.

Bad people will do bad things, even with the greatest advances in AI. Let's consider why the use of self-driving cars would be alluring to drug trafficking and then ponder ways that this might be mitigated or defeated.

On a related note, some argue that no one should discuss these matters as it will merely give dreadful thieves some new ideas of what to do. This is a classic dilemma that confronts the computer field (and other realms) all the time. For example, in the cybersecurity realm, some try to suggest that research about cracking computer systems should not be published and nor discussed at conferences. Keep it all under tight wraps, they say.

But the proverbial head-in-the-sand approach is essentially fatally flawed in that the crooks will one way or another discover or find out the latest break-in practices and then we will all be caught flatfooted by not having properly prepared for that eventuality. Generally, within reasonable limits, it tends to make sense to bring these topics into the open and thus increase awareness overall, aiming to effectively handle criminal behavior.

Here's then today's intriguing question: *Will the advent of AI-based true self-driving cars potentially be used in adverse ways including becoming narco mules in the illicit drug trade?*

Let's unpack the matter and see.

Self-Driving Cars And Drug Trafficking Mules

For Level 4 and Level 5 true self-driving vehicles, there won't be a human driver involved in the driving task.

All occupants will be passengers.

The AI is doing the driving.

First, contemplate the presumed advantage of not having a human driver when attempting to transport illegal drugs.

When using human drivers, there is always the possibility that the driver will decide to abscond with the loot. They might drive the car to a secret rendezvous and sell the drugs to someone other than the intended receiver of the cache. Or maybe the driver does the big switch, whereby they replace the real drugs with some other fakery, and then appear to deliver the intended drugs to the designated destination.

Another possibility is that the driver gets taken over by someone else that wishes to steal the drugs, getting killed, or kidnapped in the process. Additionally, an alternative driver might take their place and either ditch the vehicle after removing the drugs or could pretend to be the original driver and go to the delivery location as planned.

There are lots of double-crossing tricks that can be played.

There is also the everyday kind of chance that a driver might do something unwisely out-of-step.

Suppose the driver decides to get drunk and then smashes the car into a telephone pole, bringing forth the cops and getting stupidly caught. One supposes that a driver could be sober and nonetheless still get into a car accident, once again likely exposing the plot. It seems like we frequently hear reports of drivers that roll through a stop sign, ignoring the lawful rules of driving, and end-up with a police officer pulling them over, leading to the discovery of tons of prohibited drugs in the vehicle.

In short, human drivers for partaking in illegal drug trafficking are a substantive problem for those in the business of drug trafficking. You see, it is a lot harder than it seems when trying to be a successful drug lord, though we ought not to shed a tear over such woes.

What can be done about those dastardly unreliable and double-crossing drivers?

Replace them with AI.

Envision it this way. A self-driving car is stocked with forbidden drugs. The overseer then instructs the AI driving system to proceed on a journey to a particular destination. The AI dutifully starts driving the car and will indubitably arrive at the stipulated location. No human driver is involved.

Your initial reaction might be that the AI should be "smart enough" to realize that it is being used in a drug hauling operation, acting as a veritable drug mule.

Keep in mind that today's AI is not sentient. We aren't even close to achieving sentience. Furthermore, AI currently lacks any semblance of common-sense reasoning. All in all, if you are wishing that the AI will *know* right from wrong, that is a rather farfetched dream that regrettably does not yet exist and will be a long time coming before turning into reality (perhaps someday).

In this use case, the AI for a self-driving car is going to do as instructed, which would simply be the act of driving from point A to point B.

Plus, the contents housed within the vehicle is not something of significance for the AI.

It doesn't especially matter whether people are inside the self-driving car, other than the need to try and maintain a smooth ride such as not taking tight turns if there are passengers on-board.

I've exhorted extensively that we are going to witness seemingly empty self-driving cars much of the time (see my analysis at **this link here)** since there is likely to be a hotly competitive landscape of roaming self-driving cars. Fleet owners are hoping that their self-driving car will be more likely to get chosen for ride-sharing than some competing ones and thus will need to keep their autonomous vehicles wandering in anticipation of being in the right place at the right time for a paid lift request.

Hence, the point is that you might have been thinking that surely an otherwise empty self-driving car (having hidden drugs) will be readily spotted, and someone would detain the vehicle. Nope. The cruising around of empty self-driving cars will become a customary practice. Today, we all would certainly stare in awe and utter amazement but after thousands upon thousands of self-driving cars on our streets and highways, seeing them zipping back-and-forth with no one inside will be considered routine and ostensibly boring.

Admittedly, hard to imagine.

In any case, a self-driving car that is "empty" does not necessarily need to be indeed bereft of something inside it. Though there might not be people inside a self-driving car, there can be any kind of cargo or other elements (for example, you might send your beloved pet dog over to the vet, alone inside a self-driving car).

A self-driving car could be filled with birthday gifts that you got for your best friend that lives across town and you want the AI to drive those over to your friend's house.

In theory, the distance doesn't make a difference either.

Suppose you have some precious items such as jewels and you think it unsafe to send them via regular mail or overnight courier from Los Angeles to your aunt in New York. Presumably, you could place them into a self-driving car and merely give the AI an address in New York City as the destination. Away the vehicle goes, on a cross-country trek, and the only stops needed would be to get fuel. Note that there are no stops for getting food, no need for rest breaks, and so on.

Okay, so we've established that self-driving cars are undeniably handy as a drug mule since there is no human driver needed and the AI will not necessarily suspect that anything is afoot. The AI will without any presumed hesitation drive to the desired destination. It would seem that we've removed any qualms about double-crossing and other issues of the driver doing something stupid while driving.

The expectation is that self-driving cars will drive strictly by the book, as it were, and never step out of line in terms of driving illegally. This then shoots down the chances of the self-driving car getting pulled over for running a stop sign or rushing through a red light.

You could hide the drugs somewhere inside the self-driving car. Maybe place the drugs into boxes and put those inside the normal interior of the vehicle, though perhaps that it is rather chancy and might attract undue attention. Instead, the drugs could be placed into the trunk or within the structure of the vehicle. Remember the famous scene of (spoiler alert) Gene Hackman searching for drugs in the movie *French Connection*?

The drugs could be completely out-of-sight while somewhere embedded within the self-driving car. One might view this as a handy precaution, in case somebody somehow decides to stop the self-driving car and take a quick look inside it.

That is a bit of a teaser.

Up until this point in the discussion, it sure seems like a self-driving car is a perfect way to transport illicit drugs. We need to consider how this might not be quite so perfect for a crime.

Mitigating Factors Of The Mule Crime

Life is never easy, not even for lawbreakers.

We'll start with the perhaps biggest hurdle for someone using a self-driving car in this evil way.

Do you trust the self-driving car?

I know that seems like an odd question. From a trusted perspective, I am not referring to whether the AI will drive the car safely. We are all pretty much making a base assumption that the only way that we'll all be allowing self-driving cars on our streets is due to a presumption that they will drive as safely or even more so than human drivers. That's a given. Those are the table stakes for self-driving cars.

Here's why the drug lord might be queasy about using a self-driving car.

AI is running the vehicle. This is essentially unseen mechanization. For a human driver, the overseer presumably knows who the person is that is doing the driving. There can be pressure brought to bear on that person to make sure they drive the drugs to the right locale. Furthermore, to some degree, one can assume that the driver will try to protect the shipment (assuming they are following the letter of their orders).

In the case of the AI driving system, it does not have any such equivalent motives and nor similar pressure points. With a human driver, there is the dual-edged sword of someone sworn to loyalty versus they might veer off the path and do something the overseer dislikes. This is not quite the same for AI.

Whoever is the fleet operator of the AI driving system can generally opt to divert the self-driving car or in some manner seek to take over the driving aspects (kind of). This can be done via electronic communications to the self-driving car, such as via the use of OTA (Over-The-Air) messaging between the cloud of the fleet owner (or an automaker or self-driving tech firm) and the AI driving system.

Suppose that a self-driving car is nearing an area that has become flooded by a hurricane. The fleet owner (or similar) might send a message to all their self-driving cars to avoid getting mired in the flooded streets, as such, this might include not being able to then proceed to a designated destination in that vicinity. Perhaps the self-driving cars will be diverted to a waiting area, or come to a halt on a side street and wait for the flood to recede, or maybe the sender will be asked where the vehicle should go as an alternative destination.

The point is that this kind of overarching control is something the overseer might be leery of.

Unless they somehow can get access to the master control point, there is always a chance that the self-driving car will not end-up going where they presume the AI is going to take the vehicle. That's a loose end, for sure. The same could be said of a human driver, but as mentioned earlier, potentially the human driver can be more readily bullied.

Another concern is the traceability aspects.

Presumably, the AI driving system is keeping track of where it is and where it is going. This is likely to be shared with the fleet owner cloud system (or similar).

Also, the sensors of the self-driving car include video cameras, radar, LIDAR, ultrasonic, thermal, and other such devices, all of which are likely recording whatever they detect around the vehicle. In prior columns, I've touted that this provides a handy roving eye for some useful purposes, though it also raises serious privacy intrusion concerns at the same time.

It is conceivable that this tracing capability could be used to capture the crooks involved in undertaking the illegal drug transport effort. That being said, they might try various ways to avoid getting snagged in that manner.

Yet another issue for those bad actors is that without a human driver there is essentially no chance of high-speed pursuit and escape. If the police ascertain that the self-driving car might have drugs, it will be a relatively easy matter of having the self-driving car brought to a stop, and no need for those wild and dangerous cars chases.

Suppose too that someone else that is also a crook finds out about the self-driving car being a mule, and they want to steal the drugs. They could potentially wait along the route of the self-driving car, and when it comes to a stop sign or red light, attempt to break into the vehicle, perhaps switching off the engine and hauling away the deadened car or jumping inside to search for and then leap out with the drugs in-hand.

You might contend that the drug overseer could cope with those issues by putting their own crew inside the self-driving car to protect the hidden drugs within.

Aha, if you did that, once again there are humans in the middle of the caper. As such, there is a tradeoff as to whether having humans present versus no humans present rears its head again.

Splitting hairs, you could argue that by having a non-driving crew that the situation is assuredly different than having a crew member that is doing the driving. Also, there is the complicating factor of whether the passengers are aware of what the vehicle is carrying, or they might be unwitting accomplishes.

Yet another angle is the chance of someone hacking the AI to subvert what the AI is supposed to do. This might enable a cyber crook to merely alter the destination to their own preferred address.

In theory, this is hopefully going to be very improbable since it also opens a can of worms for those of us that will be using self-driving cars on an ordinary everyday basis (see my column postings for details about the cybersecurity facets of self-driving cars, including robo-jacking).

Lots of permutations and combinations ensue.

Conclusion

Sometimes, people upon hearing about this drug mule scenario involving self-driving cars are quick to say that we ought to have the police or other authorities monitoring the AI driving systems. This would apparently somehow enable the authorities to attempt to identify these illicit traffic activities.

Now that's a whale of a Pandora's box.

There is a slew of AI Ethics considerations that come along with that kind of permitted routine monitoring. In an era that has all of us regularly using AI-based true self-driving cars, will we feel comfortable that our every trip and move is potentially being seen and tracked by our government?

I've previously emphasized that there are nation-states that are going to welcome the advent of self-driving cars for that very reason. It remains to be seen whether a free nation would find it justifiable as a potential means to detect or curtail the adverse uses of self-driving cars.

Time will tell..

CHAPTER 9
ZIPPER MERGING AND SELF-DRIVING CARS

that your lane is being narrowed out and you'll need to get over into the other lane next to you. An electronic board sign is flashing warnings that your existing lane is going to end soon ("*Merger Ahead*" it veritably screams at you). In addition, a series of weather-worn red cones are set up in your lane that inch you over, step-by-step, and are positioned to gradually shunt all traffic out of the lane you are in.

It is the classic 2-into-1 traffic control squeeze play.

This is also commonly known as the zipper merge because it looks like a zipper as cars are pinned into veering from two lanes into one. Anyone that drives around with any frequency is apt to encounter these 2-into-1 situations on any given day and during any given driving journey. They exist aplenty.

Returning to the highway scenario, I'm guessing you have likely already predetermined what you ordinarily do when confronted with a zipper merge.

I ask you, what would you do?

One answer is that upon immediately spotting that a merger request is being proffered, you would as quickly and as safely as feasible guide your car into the next lane over and expeditiously get out of the lane that is going to disappear. You would not wait. You would not remain in the vanishing lane. You would act decisively and obey what you believe to be a lawful order to switch lanes.

Let's label that kind of driver as an Early Merge type of person, employing a driving strategy of trying to perform the merging action as soon as possible.

Another answer to the driving scenario is to try and remain in the fading lane as long as you can. The idea is to wait until the last possible moment and then dart over into the remaining available lane. In some ways, this is kind of exciting and maybe provides a bit of a thrill. In any case, the person using this approach is apt to be thinking that there is no particular reason to act like a scaredy-cat and abandon a perfectly good lane, postponing the abandonment until the only option left involves getting out and into the bordering lane.

We'll label this kind of driver as the Late Merge type of person.

Okay, so which camp do you fall into, the Early Merge members of society or the Late Merge members of our world?

This is where the heated and acrimonious debates start to unfold.

The Early Merge types are bound to exhort that the Late Merge people are miscreants.

Those Late Merge drivers are outright idiots that do not realize they ought to obey the indicated signs and get over in a prudent, timely, and earliest feasible way. Doing so is decidedly safer for all concerned. When those dolts dart over at the endpoint of merging, they are going to create trouble, heaps, and heaps of trouble. The odds are that it will cause the traffic to react in a kneejerk way, unfairly forcing other drivers to avert getting into a collision with these wrongdoers that have no civility, no politeness, and are steeped in pure unadulterated driving greed when behind the wheel of a car.

In contrast, the Late Merge types are likely to exclaim that the Early Merge drivers are skittish dimwits.

The Early Merge types are so frightened at being on the highways that they get frazzled at the drop of a hat. If they see a posted roadway sign, they feel compelled to instantly do what it says, regardless of using any semblance of common-sense as to what to do. Those Early Merge nervous nellie drivers are the real troublemakers since they react to the traffic conditions without letting a single thought enter into their noggin. Furthermore, they seem to think that they alone are the arbiters of controlling traffic and often will attempt to force others to abide by their dictums about how to respond to a 2-into-1 merging situation. They are busybodies, acting high-and-mighty that they somehow own the road and want everyone to get over just like them, unwilling to allow freedom of thought or expression to other drivers.

Obviously, these are two diametrically opposed viewpoints.

Indeed, when the Early Merge purest meets with the Late Merger perfectionist, during a roadway 2-into-1 traffic condition, there is a sizable potential for sparking road rage. Each is upset at the other. Each believes they are truly in the right. Each profusely believes the other is absolutely and unquestionably in the wrong.

It is a combustible interaction, that is for darned sure.

The conundrum and discourse about which driving strategy is right and which is wrong has been going on since the invention of the revered and at times loathed 2-into-1 contrivance.

Using everyday intuitive logic does not seem to help clear-up the matter.

The Early Merge logically allows for a more measured approach that calmly allows for drivers to exit from their existing lane and comfortably merge into the next lane over, giving the drivers in that lane some breathing room to let in the other drivers. This would seem to provide a more seamless meshing of traffic and not cause any disruptive leaps or skirmishes, enabling a smoother and ultimately more effective flow of traffic. Seemingly this should mean fewer car crashes in a zipper merging context and less frustration and angst for all drivers involved.

Indubitably solid logic.

The Late Merge logically allows for better use of the roadway availability. If drivers prematurely get out of an available lane, they are going to crowd into the other remaining lane, thus underutilizing the lane that still has room and time available for usage. When you attempt to cram one queue or line of cars into another lane, it is going to cause an adverse and unwarranted distending of traffic and disturb the overall flow of traffic, therefore you should only do so when there are no other viable means to continue using the second lane.

Well, seem like more absolutely sound logic.

Maybe they are both wrong, or then again, maybe they are both right. But that doesn't solve any of this matter and leaves us with nothing tangible as to what ought to be strictly done.

Numerous simulations have been undertaken to try and ferret out the proper choice.

A robust simulation will consider a variety of factors such as traffic throughput, queue lengths, travel times, car crashes, near collisions, and so on. These are computer-based models that attempt to simulate or pretend what might occur during actual driving situations. Not all such simulations are the same, and different authors or developers take differing paths to how they structure and program their particular simulation of a zipper merge scenario.

By-and-large, the simulations tend to suggest that waiting to merge is the "better" option, assuming that you are aiming to make maximal use of the roadway. Unfortunately, few of these studies incorporate the foibles of human drivers and assume that a human driver will always do the right thing in terms of how they drive, acting as a kind of driving automata.

In other words, in a simulated setup, the simulated drivers are oftentimes mathematically composed as though they will always anticipate that all other drivers will be doing the Late Merge, and none of the simulated drivers will do the Early Merge and that all drivers will accordingly drive to accommodate the sole driving strategy of the Late Merge.

This is an unheard-of and rarely if ever witnessed homogenization of driving.

Humans do not drive that way and we would be dreaming to assume that they would act in such a wholly consistent and unerringly way while at the driving controls of their cars. Simulations that incorporate both the day-to-day mindful and at times mindless ways that humans drive are usually more likely to be better aligned with the realities of driving in a messy, confounding world composed of zany and emotionally spurred human drivers.

All told, the real-world question about the zipper merge is a tough one to resolve.

Except that the future might provide a ready resolution.

Consider this intriguing point: *Will the advent of AI-based true self-driving cars make zipper merges into an easy peasy situation and thus obviate any further qualms about dealing with the infamous 2-into-1 quandary?*

Let's unpack the matter and see.

Self-Driving Cars And Zipper Merges

For Level 4 and Level 5 true self-driving vehicles, there won't be a human driver involved in the driving task.

All occupants will be passengers.

The AI is doing the driving.

Not only will the AI be doing the driving, but it will also most likely have a means to electronically communicate with other nearby self-driving cars.

This is aiming to be accomplished via the use of V2V, vehicle-to-vehicle electronic messaging. Suppose a self-driving car notices some debris in the roadway, it can quickly send out a V2V message to other nearby self-driving cars to be wary of the debris. This would give those other AI driving systems a heads-up to perhaps change lanes before coming upon the debris or otherwise take any needed evasive driving actions beforehand.

What does this all portend for the zipper merge?

I'm betting that you've already added together the one-plus-one involved and come to a logically apparent conclusion that the zipper merge problem is solved.

Each AI-based self-driving car could coordinate with each other, during a zipper merge, and readily handle the merging activity. By communicating to each other via the V2V, and by allowing each other the courtesy of getting into the remaining lane, this whole matter would be as seamless as watching a flock of birds that weave back-and-forth together effortlessly.

The self-driving cars will do a dance that is undertaken without any visible waving of hands or arms, and nor any dangerous attempts at cutting each other off. They will instead be conveying their requests to each other electronically and silently fall into a beauteous pattern of streaming without hesitation and absence of any disturbances through the zipper. The timing can happen at the fastest speeds that traffic will allow.

Adding to the impressive nature of this effort, there is also going to be V2I, vehicle-to-infrastructure electronic communications. That means that roadway infrastructure such as road closures and the like will be sending out beaconing signals to warn about various traffic conditions. When a zipper merge is put in place, a V2I indicator will start broadcasting to alert any upcoming traffic. The AI driving systems would know then about the zipper due to either the V2I or via the V2V (as tipped from another nearby self-driving car).

Yay, excitedly, the zipper merge is another one of life's many problems that we can put to rest.

Sorry to say, life is never that easy.

We'll start with the biggest hurdle and then make our way to smaller ones.

The 500-pound gorilla is the fact that we are still going to have human drivers on our roadways for quite a while to come, despite the emerging advent of true self-driving cars.

Keep in mind that there are about 250 million conventional cars in the United States today, and those aren't going to be tossed into the junk heap anytime soon merely due to the appearance of self-driving cars. Economically it is just not a feasible notion. As such, there will still be tons upon tons of human-driven cars on our roadways for decades to come.

Furthermore, we do not yet know whether or not human driving is really going to be given up entirely. One argument is that people must give up their driving to allow for the saving of the 40,000 annual driving fatalities and the 2.3 million estimated car-related injuries that occur each year in the U.S. It is assumed and hoped that the use of self-driving cars is going to diminish dramatically that volume of carnage.

But will people really be willing to stop driving? Many fervently assert that driving is their right (well, it is legally considered a privilege rather than a right), and you cannot force them to give up driving. Some insist you will only do so when you pry their cold dead hands from their steely grip upon the steering wheel.

How does the continued human-driven element make a difference in the zipper merge and self-driving cars?

The point is that the self-driving cars will not merely be able to coordinate with each other, they will also need to contend with human drivers. Recall that human drivers are, well, human, and therefore will continue to drive in their haphazard and perplexing ways. This means that you can toss aside the aforementioned harmonious dance of the self-driving cars.

Human interlopers will trounce the dance.

You can readily bet your bottom dollar that if the self-driving cars choose to do the Late Merge, there will be humans that instead choose the Early Merge. If the self-driving cars choose the Early Merge, there are undoubted will be Late Merge oriented human drivers. The earlier chaos of each driver tackling the matter in their own proprietary way has come back into the picture.

Once self-driving cars are prevalent, the numbers might end-up inexorably in a gradual shift toward the AI winning the zipper merge game. In essence, the fewer number of human-driven cars still on the roadways will be but a speck and therefore the AI driving systems will be pretty much able to drive around in a relatively smooth and coordinated fashion, only contending from time-to-time with those irritating and irascible human drivers.

In any case, the zipper merge in the nearer term, even with the arrival of self-driving cars, will continue to be a thorn in the sides of all drivers, both human drivers and AI driving systems.

This does bring up another facet about that state of the world, namely, how should an AI driving system act or react to a human-driven car during a zipper merge?

Right now, most of the automakers and self-driving car tech firms are making the AI rather timid when it comes to driving near humans. Generally, whatever a human driver wants, they will get, in terms of a nearby AI-based self-driving car that will readily give way to the human driver. If you are driving your car in the vanishing lane and suddenly want over, a self-driving car in that other lane is going to let you in, assuming that it is physically possible to do so. No questions asked. Unlike a human driver in that lane that might be spiteful at your interruption, the AI is just going to be, shall we say, a pushover.

Plus, human drivers will realize that AI driving systems are pushovers. In that case, the human drivers that already think of other human drivers as sheep will assuredly consider the AI driving systems to be like sheep, or whatever is even more docile and unaggressive in the animal kingdom.

One significant concern overall about the advent of self-driving cars is that some human drivers are going to try and exploit the situation, Those scofflaw pushy human drivers will routinely and gladly cut off the AI self-driving cars. This is going to up the ante on potential car crashes, which at first glance might not seem possible, since the AI will do what it can to avoid a collision, but the physics of the vehicles might not allow for an evasive maneuver and we'll end-up with human drivers and AI driving systems getting into car crashes.

For human drivers desiring to exploit the AI timidity (as programmed), their opinion is going to be that if those AI driving systems were made to be taken advantage of, they surely ought to be so skewered.

Conclusion

I earlier mentioned that some other less apparent considerations can toss a monkey wrench into the zipper merge riddle when it comes to adding self-driving cars into the mix.

Here's a taste.

Assume that only self-driving cars are about to converge on a zipper merge (no human drivers are nearby).

In what order or sequence should the AI driving systems jointly ascertain which cars get through the squeeze play?

First come, first serve is not necessarily a completely viable option per se, due to the cars arriving at the bottleneck in relative unison. In that case, you might assert it is simply a matter of a random selection, done without preference to any particular AI or self-driving car. On the other hand, suppose we decide as a society that it is permitted to have passengers that can up the priority of their self-driving car, perhaps by being a highly ranked government official or being a celebrity. Or, perhaps by paying an added fee to the fleet owner of the self-driving car.

A final question to ponder, beyond the realm of discussing just the zipper merge, involves whether we will be willing to allow self-driving cars to operate differently depending upon the passenger or the payment by a passenger. Some say this smacks of elitism and undercuts hoped-for democratization of mobility for all that the promise of self-driving cars seems to offer.

Anyway, please be careful of other human drivers when doing those maddening zipper merges, and if you can, take it easy on the AI driving systems too.

CHAPTER 10
DAYLIGHT SAVINGS AND SELF-DRIVING CARS

Spring forward, fall back.

Simple enough.

That's what is supposed to happen due to our acceptance of abiding by Daylight Savings Time (DST). In the Spring, our clocks are to be moved forward by one hour. Later on, during the Fall, we move the clocks backward one hour. This is a ritual that we all undertake, though seemingly begrudgingly and with a lot of acrimonious debate and confusion involved.

One form of confusion gets some people really upset, namely whether it is spring forward and fall back, or maybe it is spring back and fall forward. Those that are unsure about which is correct are seen by others as complete dolts. It doesn't make any sense to say spring back, or to mention fall forward, so how in the world could you make such a mental error, those irked by their fellow humans are apt to exhort feverishly.

Another aspect of confusion seems to underly the rationale or basis for why we do all this clock changing anyway. One of the most commonly assumed reasons is that the time change is good for farmers and therefore as a society that was once predominantly dependent on agriculture and farms that we have continued the tradition ever since. You might find of interest that some farmers support the time change and others oppose it. For example, oftentimes dairy farmers complain that the time alterations are upsetting to their cows, disturbing their milking routines, and undermining at least initially the amount of milk production.

Some assert that the switching of the clock on these two mandated occasions each year is bad for our economy. Supposedly, people are initially less productive in their work due to the time change (perhaps we aren't so different than those cows), and there is a cost too in actually having everyone manually change their clocks and watches. Of course, given that we nowadays tend to rely on electronically-fed clocks that are connected online, the changeover is frequently automatic and there is a lot less manual labor involved in making the grand switch.

Indisputably, upon springing forward, our mornings are essentially additively darkened by that encompassed hour, and the evenings are lighter later.

Some relish this change.

When you get off work each weekday, there is still sunlight available and you can enjoy those gorgeous summer sunsets and frolic with the extended daylight. Others argue that the evening enchantment is not worth the soul-crushing aspects of getting up in utter darkness each morning, and also makes the morning commute to work a dismal drive while trying to see in less overall light than you'd prefer, or that we all need to drive safely.

There are likewise those that favor and those that disfavor what occurs when we do the change for falling back.

Mornings are lighter due to the hour changeover, which some emphasize is safer for kids as they start heading back to school, being more easily seen by car drivers and also the children themselves seem more alert and aware of their surroundings in the lightened conditions. In terms of the evening darkness coming an hour earlier, one viewpoint is nighttime belongs to getting homework done anyway, plus inspires families to have dinner together to discuss the efforts of the day. That is the smiley face version of the fallback but be assured that are ample ways to carp about it and not be so sanguine on the matter.

Numerous research studies have attempted to analyze the impacts of our ongoing observance of DST.

Not all researchers necessarily agree as to whether we ought to keep or perhaps instead ditch the whole Daylight Savings Time regime. Some persuasive line-up facts and figures to showcase that we are collectively asleep at the wheel (figuratively speaking) by allowing the infamous and undesirable DST to continue. Others offer rather convincing evidence that we should accept DST without reservation, indeed we should embrace it wholly, and stop whining about it.

On the topic of falling asleep at the wheel (now literally meant, plus notice that smooth segue), one particular factor that looms large when it comes to debates about Daylight Savings Times has to do with cars and car drivers.

Based on intuition, it would seem that when the spring forward occurs, drivers are hence driving in a darkened environment and therefore perhaps more prone to driving less capably. Keep in mind too that the morning commute to work is one of the most frequently traveled times of the day, thus, the time change is directly affecting a moment of driving that is already jam-packed with cars. All of this would suggest that car crashes are likely to flare.

You might try to counterargue that the evening commute is going to compensate by the fact that there is a brightened ambiance of light in the early evenings, yet also being a packed commute time, and that there might be fewer car crashes than usual. If that were the case, the increase in the morning car crashes might be offset by the reduction in the evening car crashes, achieving, in the end, a neutral result of no added aggregation in the counts of car crashes.

Depending on how far you want to extend that logic, one supposes that you could try to argue that the net result could be a savings of sorts if the reduction in evening car crashes were to somehow swamp the presumed increase in the morning crashes.

Well, the counter to that counter-argument is that we are wide awake by the occurrence of the evening drive, whereas during the morning drive our eyes are drooping and our senses remain in a sleep-induced lull. In that case, it might not be patently obvious that the morning and evening cancel out each other in terms of car crash volume. There is a potential asymmetry involved. The belief is that we are worse by far in the morning drive, while only slightly better off in the evening drive.

Further stoking these flames, we decidedly need to consider what impacts the fallback phenomena might have on car crashes too. Does the added light in the morning help to reduce car crashes? Does the darkened evening tend to increase car crashes? Is there is a net result that produces fewer car crashes all told, or does it lead to more car crashes?

If all of this doesn't already seem exceedingly complex, we can up the ante by proffering the notion that perhaps we should combine together any net result, positive or negative, occurring during the spring forward, along with any net result from the fallback, such that we can seek a grand total to illuminate what happens over the course of these two brother and sister time changes.

In short, does the spring forward net result exceed the fallback, or are they equal, or is the fall back the larger count?

Dizzying.

Let's consider an article published in the journal *Current Biology* entitled "A Chronobiological Evaluation of the Acute Effects of Daylight Savings Time on Traffic Accident Risk" that was posted earlier this year and provides ample food for thought on the topic.

Per this particular study, their statistical analysis seemed to indicate that the number of fatal car crashes in the workweek immediately following the spring forward time change increased by about 6% (confined to just the one-week initial period, not generalizable for weeks henceforth). This was predominantly due to an increase in the number of morning car crashes. Meanwhile, the fallback time change generally was a neutral net result, whereby there was a decline in morning car crashes that were met by a similarly increased count in evening car crashes.

All told, it could be interpreted that the initial week 6% rise in fatal car crashes of the spring forward is said to account then for the final net tally of the combined impacts of both the spring forward and the fallback occurrences.

Bluntly, based on this particular study, one interpretation is that we are accepting as par for the course that the DST will generate a one-week increase of 6% in the number of car crash fatalities (that's a one-week only increase, occurring once per year). If that's the case, one would be hard-pressed, it seems, to justify DST based on those added deaths, though this is a somewhat oversized way to reach such a harsh conclusion. You should be aware that there are a variety of caveats about all of this statistical wizardry and please be mindfully cautious in overstating the results of one such study alone.

Also, the focus was on fatal car crashes, which leaves out of the societal equation concerning the non-fatal car crash statistics and potential injuries accordingly. Imagine, for example, whether there was an impact on the volume of injuries, and perhaps might bolster the point about the dangers of the time change or could (counter-intuitively) support the time change. This would also raise the ugly question of how to compare the deaths incurred versus the number of injuries incurred. And so on.

In any case, the researchers speculated that the statistics underlying the rise of 6% in that initial workweek of the spring forward are possibly due to drivers being less alert, presumably as a result of sleep disruption and a circadian rhythm misalignment.

You might be tempted to conclude that we ought to overturn and outright ban the vaunted Daylight Savings Time since doing so would potentially save lives and prevent the annual one-week increase in the number of car crash deaths (assuming you take at face value these results and set aside any limitations or caveats).

Yes, that is one answer, but there is another one that maybe can accomplish the same, and yet keep the DST legacy alive and kicking.

Here's today's intriguing question: *Will the advent of AI-based true self-driving cars potentially "solve" the car crash-related concerns entailing Daylight*

Savings Time and obviate the need to necessarily cancel DST due to car crashes?

Let's unpack the matter and see.

Self-Driving Cars And Daylight Savings Time

For Level 4 and Level 5 true self-driving vehicles, there won't be a human driver involved in the driving task.

All occupants will be passengers.

The AI is doing the driving.

One core assumption about self-driving cars is that they will only be allowed onto our public roadways if the AI driving systems are as safe or possibly even safer than human drivers. The hope is that the annual 40,000 car crash-related fatalities and the approximate 2.3 million car-related injuries will be lessened, perhaps demonstratively so, as a result of the use of self-driving cars.

For those that insist we'll end-up at zero fatalities, I've repeatedly cautioned that it will not drop to zero since there is a multitude of situations in which the physics belies the chances of a self-driving car avoiding getting into a car crash or similar collision.

Indubitably, it would seem that the AI driving systems will not get drunk, thus no more drinking and driving (at least per AI), and the AI will not get distracted as human drivers do. The AI doesn't need any food, it doesn't need any rest, and in fact, the expectation is that self-driving cars will likely be running all day and all night, providing ride-sharing capabilities 24x7 (other than when needed to be refueled or during maintenance and repairs).

How does this all relate to the discussion about Daylight Savings Time?

The answer is rather straightforward.

We would anticipate that the AI driving systems would not be bothered in the least by the DST time changes. If the clocks change on a Sunday, the AI is not going to wake up on Monday morning and be cursing the time change. Nor will the AI be sleepy or have been knocked off its circadian rhythm. The AI will continue essentially unchanged in its driving approaches and will be otherwise oblivious to the human felt changes of the fallback and spring forward.

In theory, you can kiss goodbye that momentary increase in car crash fatalities that currently appears to be accompanying the DST institution.

That's exciting news.

It means that the use of Daylight Savings Time can continue unabated, assuming that the sole qualm was related to car crashes and fatalities thereof. Of course, this has little or nothing to do with the other complaints about the use of DST. Those cows, for example, won't be any better off simply due to the aspect that self-driving cars will be untouched by the time change.

Will humans be any better off (other than the lives saved, which, certainly is a pronounced benefit)?

You could argue that humans will be better off in other potential ways, as it relates to the use of self-driving cars. For example, it is predicted that most true self-driving cars will be radically altered in terms of the interiors of the vehicle. Rather than having a driver's seat, something no longer needed, the interior will be freer and possibly allow for swivel seats that provide more comfort to the passengers. Also, the seats are likely to be built for reclining, allowing riders to take a nap while the AI is handling the driving chore.

This brings up a small facet worth pointing out. As humans commute to work in the workweek following a time change, they can potentially use that "extra" hour of the day to catch more sleep, potentially aiding their circadian rhythm alignment. In general, the odds are that people will be sleeping quite a bit while inside self-driving cars, doing so in the morning on the way to work, and catching some winks on the ride back home in the evenings.

Furthermore, some believe that we will be taking longer driving trips once self-driving cars are prevalent. Today, if you wanted to go across your state or drive to another nearby one, it would require hours upon hours of your being fully awake and paying rapt attention as the driver of the vehicle. In the future, you can take a nice long doze while the AI hauls you across great distances and brings you in a refreshed state-of-mind to your faraway destination.

The key point though is that the advent of self-driving cars will take off the table the factor about how bad our driving is during the days following the DST time changes.

All else being equal, there should not be any statistically significant increase or decrease in car crashes on those days versus any other days of the year. The AI will consistently drive the same way all of the time, regardless of how the clocks are changed.

Realize that you can still readily carp about Daylight Savings Time and seek to have it obliterated since there are plenty of other reasons that can be used to make that argument stick.

AI driving systems are a narrow solution to a smaller piece of the pie, though we all might agree it is a notable portion since it involves human lives.

Conclusion

It would be nice and tidy to leave the matter at this aforementioned indication about how beauteously the AI driving systems and self-driving cars will eradicate the car crash concerns from the DST disputes.

Sorry, I feel obligated to add some bitter-tasting slops of realism back into the picture.

First, those self-driving cars are only going to make a demonstrative difference in the statistics once they are extensively prevalent, nearly ubiquitous. That is going to be a long time from now, possibly many decades away. There are about 250 million conventional cars in the United States today, and those are not going to magically disappear when self-driving cars start to popular the roadways.

You need to brace yourself for the reality that in the foreseeable future, the loss of lives due to car crashes in the workweek following the time change will continue as is. Gradually, inexorably, self-driving cars will be seeded into the car populace, but that is a distant future.

Second, some humans are likely to fight back at the advent of self-driving cars, insisting that they relish driving and won't give up their "right" (it is a privilege) to drive.

In that case, the prevalence of self-driving cars could be further stymied by those human drivers that will never stop driving. This means they will still drive as they already do today, including presumably some portion will, sadly, on the workweek following a time change drive (as usual) worse than they normally drive.

Eventually, the number of human drivers would seem to dwindle and therefore the presumed benefit of the AI driving systems as being safe or safer at driving will arise. Nobody can say how long this societal clinging to human driving will last. Time will tell.

In the United States, we started the use of Daylight Savings Time in 1918, principally to conserve energy while World War I was being waged. DST has had quite a storied history ever since.

When you head to work on this upcoming day after the DST time change, imagine how nice it would be if the AI was lugging you to the office, rather than your having to drive yourself, accompanied currently by those half-awake drowsy eyes and foggy mindedness.

Come to think of it, please do not be thinking about anything other than paying attention to the road, since you need to be on our sharpest toes for a week of driving that is going to be abysmally challenging.

And, remember, make sure to change your clocks this coming Sunday, November 1.

CHAPTER 11
NEAR MISSES AND SELF-DRIVING CARS

Reckless and fleckless drivers.

I'm sure you experience their antics and angst-producing driving activities all the time.

Back in the day, a college buddy of mine was famously known for being an especially hasty driver. He drove much too fast while on the streets within and surrounding the university campus. He also veered dangerously close toward other cars that were in the lanes next to him. Plus, he relished taking corners at high speeds, including frequently forcing pedestrians to leap back from the curb to avoid getting demonstrably clipped.

All in all, anytime you saw his car, you gave it a wide berth, even while parked since he notably would back out of parking spaces without looking over his shoulder. I recall one time that while riding in his car, I pointed out that his rearview mirror was broken and was unusable, for which he calmly stated that there wasn't any need to have a working rearview mirror since he never sought to look behind his car anyway.

Grimace followed by a weary sigh.

Here is the weirdest part of the sordid tale.

He never got into a car accident.

Nary a car collision or striking of anyone or anything. He managed to drive in this crazed and seemingly maniacal way, and yet never struck another vehicle, nor hit a lamppost, and never bumped into or scrapped a human or any meandering animals. His driving thoughtlessness consistently occurred throughout all four years and somehow, miraculously, despite this nutty, adverse, and undeniably despicable driving approach, he came out with a perfectly clean driving record.

Yes, that includes the fact that he never received a ticket for any of his daredevil driving endeavors.

We always assumed during those several years that ultimately a police officer would spot his driving digressions and certainly issue a citation of one kind or another. Clearly, the official DMV driving code states that you cannot drive menacingly and thus he was driving on borrowed time, in our view, such that he was inevitably going to get a ticket, perhaps a series of tickets. The hope was that after getting stopped by the cops, he would realize the err of his ways and discontinue his driving exploits.

No such luck.

Here's what the California DMV vehicle code says about reckless driving: "A person who drives a vehicle upon a highway in willful or wanton disregard for the safety of persons or property is guilty of reckless driving." Anyone nabbed for reckless driving is subject to prison time and financial penalties.

In terms of luck, my buddy was extraordinarily lucky that he didn't get caught.

All told, everyone was exceedingly lucky that nobody got hit or injured by his carelessness.

I've previously discussed in my column that some drivers wreak havoc upon the rest of us.

Borrowing from sports, my analysis and commentary was that car drivers ought to be measured by a so-called havoc rating. A havoc rating is used in sporting competitions such as football and indicates how disruptive a player is toward another player (or one team toward another team). Generally, you want to achieve a high havoc rating whenever in a sports game, since it suggests that you are confounding the competition and forcing them off their best game. In driving, the goal would be to achieve the lowest possible havoc rating. Drivers with especially high havoc ratings would be dinged for being inappropriate in their driving behaviors (such as having to pay heightened car insurance premiums or face other similar penalizing facets).

One argument that my pal often used was that he ought to not be considered a bad driver or an irresponsible driver due to the admittedly indisputable fact that he had absolutely no car crashes. Go after those dolts that ram into other cars or that strike down pedestrians, he exhorted. Until the day that he hits someone or something, anyone carping about his driving was seen as obnoxious, overbearing, and wasting his time.

Does that seem like impeccable logic?

As long as you don't crash your car, can you drive in whatever manner you choose?

Some valiantly tried to explain to him that his wild driving was a detriment to everyone else, whether he realized it or not.

I suppose you have been endangered by other drivers and felt the stresses that come with having someone else nearly hit your car. You might need to radically maneuver to avoid a seemingly imminent collision. Your heart rate climbs through the roof, as it were, and you sweat profusely until the pending incident magically passes and no one is impacted. The impact was avoided due to your strenuous efforts, and not due to the idiot that veered into your path.

This brings up a fascinating aspect of those drivers that are reckless. In an oddball way, the better driving of other drivers might be said to save those careless drivers from doom.

Imagine something akin to an Xbox or similar game that has one driver madly driving down the street while all other drivers manage to steer clear. Pedestrians too refrain from crossing the street or getting anywhere close to the wanton car. Maybe dogs and cats know enough to remain out of the street too. In this made-up simulated world, all others know to avoid the one that is the reckless and feckless driver.

Perhaps that explains how my college buddy survived.

All those times that he edged toward the precipice, other nearby drivers were able to navigate away from him. The honed skills of other drivers saved his hide. From his viewpoint, the machinations of those other drivers were either not apparent to him or he simply shrugged it off. He frequently complained about other drivers as being reactive and nervous Nellies. At no point did it occur to him that it was his own actions that sparked other drivers to act in that manner.

Sadly, some drivers such as my collegiate buddy live in their own world and do not seem to note and nor care about others on the highways and byways. If anything, they hold great disdain for other drivers. A bit ironic given that they are the ones that should bear the brunt of the disdain.

In looking at the near-miss topic and taking a somewhat more holistic perspective, one consideration is the potential for a cascading effect and the second-order and third-order outcomes that can arise.

Here's what that portends.

A driver causes a near-miss. The driver that was nearly hit is forced to make a rapid avoidance maneuver. This maneuver leads to crashing into some other car. On the surface of things, the second driver is presumably at fault, assuming that no one knew or could prove that the first driver started the chain of events. In a likewise fashion, it could be a further arm's length chain, such as the first driver prods or stirs the second driver, the second driver disrupts a third driver, and the third driver strikes a car that is the fourth driver in this sequence. The original impetus is obtusely remote and nearly invisible to anyone other than a dedicated observer.

Shifting gears, let's ponder what the future holds for drivers and reckless driving.

As we enter into an era of self-driving cars, your first thought might be that thankfully there will no longer be any reckless driving, presumably being eradicated due to the advent of AI-based driving systems.

Maybe yes, but, surprisingly, maybe no.

Here is the question for today's hearty discussion: *Will AI-based true self-driving cars potentially drive recklessly or will the AI-powered driving be perfectly undertaken and avert any semblance of near misses or similar driving involving almost calamities?*

Let's unpack the matter and see.

Self-Driving Cars And Near-Miss Driving

For Level 4 and Level 5 true self-driving vehicles, there won't be a human driver involved in the driving task.

All occupants will be passengers.

The AI is doing the driving.

Generally, most of the self-driving cars being tried out on public roadways are subject to two categories of reporting about their driving record, consisting of indicating car crashes and also reporting on disengagements.

Disengagements consist of the circumstance wherein there is a back-up or safety human driver present and the human acting as a second-in-command driver decides to disengage the AI during a driving task. This disengagement can be undertaken for a variety of reasons, including the possibility of a near-miss situation and for which the human back-up driver decided to take over the driving controls rather than relying upon or hoping that the AI could handle the predicament.

Okay, so in theory, we will almost certainly be informed whenever a self-driving car gets into a car crash.

That deals with discovery about how often self-driving cars are striking others, though let's be careful and clear that it might or might not be the fault of the AI driving system. If a nearby car being driven entirely by a human opts to ram into the rear end of a self-driving car and assuming the AI was not at fault, the aspect that a car crash occurred involving a self-driving car should not improperly be interpreted as due to an (essentially) "irresponsible" AI driving system per se.

In terms of reporting about disengagements, we won't necessarily be able to ascribe all of those disengagements to the AI as being a bad driver. The back-up human driver might have jumped the gun, deciding to relieve the AI of driving when perhaps the AI could have coped with the driving situation. Also, the disengagement might occur because something about the car itself has gone awry, such as a tire gets blown or the vehicle is making clanging noises and the back-up driver is worried that perhaps the tailpipe has come loose.

In short, there is no particular requirement or indication that we are likely to receive or be made apparent about the near-misses of the self-driving cars and the AI driving systems.

A car crash is obviously not a near-miss, so the counts of car crashes don't help to identify how many near-misses there have been (I suppose, tongue in cheek, you could call the car crashes as didn't miss or as anti-misses).

Disengagements might contain some proportion or amount of near-misses, though ferreting out those stats is bound to be somewhat problematic (partially since there is no standardized and all accepted stipulation of how to report on disengagements, an industrywide concern that I've expressed in my column postings).

Unnervingly, the AI driving systems could pretty much drive just like my college buddy. As long as the self-driving cars managed to avoid getting into a car crash and also once there are no longer back-up or human safety drivers present, an AI driving system could routinely be a menace to the rest of the driving world and get away with it, presumably.

No one would be the wiser.

Of course, this implies that if indeed the AI driving systems were driving poorly, the rest of us, those nearby human drivers, were helping to prop-up the AI by maneuvering to avoid those wayward or reckless self-driving cars, just as perhaps other drivers were doing for my college pal.

Right now, since there are so few self-driving cars on the roadways, especially ones that have no back-up driver present, it would seem somewhat unlikely that a self-driving car could go scot-free as a bad driver. You would expect that other threatened drivers would readily post on social media the transgressions of a self-driving car that veered toward them or otherwise seemed menacing. We all are prone to holding our tongue about other bad human drivers, but that would not seem to necessarily extend to the capacity of AI driving systems and self-driving car antics.

On the other hand, an argument could be made that many drivers are avoiding getting close to self-driving cars, precisely because they are unsure of what the AI might do as a driver. In that manner, you could claim that self-driving cars are being given undue latitude. A self-driving car might be able to drive in a weaving manner and do so without any human drivers nearby being endangered directly, simply because those human drivers already were keeping a distance from the self-driving car, to begin with.

Though that seems like a compelling viewpoint, some human drivers are actively going out of their way to challenge self-driving cars when they see those machines on the roadway. I've referred to these as roadway bullies, wherein they love going aggressively toward self-driving cars to see what the AI will do. Furthermore, since most of the AI driving systems are programmed to be relatively civil and timid as drivers, some human drivers have realized this aspect and gladly take advantage, cutting in front of self-driving cars and pulling driving tricks with glee upon the more docile AI driving approaches.

Consider another angle on the topic.

It could be that self-driving cars are performing near-miss driving activities and yet the automaker or self-driving tech firm or fleet owner is not monitoring for such driving behaviors.

This seems unfathomable.

We all would naturally assume that those responsible for the self-driving cars being on the roadways would abundantly be checking for near-miss occurrences.

One perspective is that there's no need to do so. Just as my college buddy retorted that as long as there weren't any crashes, it could be that there is no particular basis for monitoring that kind of activity. There is plenty to do already, involving keeping the self-driving cars in a drivable state, doing bug fixes, adding new features, and so on. The resources need to examine the roadway trials and inspect for near-misses could be readily placed lower on the list of priorities. Given that resources for self-driving car efforts are already stretched thin, dealing with near-misses could be considered an edge or corner case issue that can be dealt with further down-the-line.

Some AI developers would also challenge what it means to incur a near-miss.

On any given day, when humans are driving on say the freeways, they come within inches of each other, while moving along at 65 miles per hour. You could argue that all of that driving is somewhat reckless. All it takes is for a driver to veer over a little bit and end-up scraping against another car. There is a case to be made that we routinely are reckless in that overarching way.

How do you draw the line of where reckless driving starts and ends?

You could put together algorithms that try to make such

calculations. The tough thing is to winnow the wheat from the chaff. In theory, there are so many possible near-misses in any normal driving journey that you either would need to conclude they are all near-misses or somehow find the needle in the haystack that perchance is what we intuitively would reckon is a valid near-miss per se.

Another consideration is that inches alone is not a sufficient means to scope a near-miss. For example, a few years ago I was driving on a highway when suddenly, wholly unexpectedly, a car from the opposing lane came into my lane and we were shockingly going head-to-head. I had only a few seconds to decide what action to take. Though we never ended-up colliding (the other driver veered back into their lane), you could call it a near-miss based on the time-to-decide and time-to-act urgency involved.

One approach voiced about determining near-miss circumstances is to consider the reactions of other drivers.

Remember that earlier I mentioned that perhaps other drivers were being protective for my buddy by not allowing him to hit them? Well, the sensor data that is collected by the self-driving car cameras, LIDAR, radar, ultrasonic, and so on, could be inspected mathematically and computationally to ascertain how often other vehicles are seemingly changing course while nearby the self-driving car. It could be that those other drivers are doing so because they are trying to avoid getting bashed by the AI and the self-driving car.

In that case, you don't need to gauge the self-driving car driving in of itself, and instead focus on the reactions of other drivers and their car driving actions.

This again though is not entirely satisfying since there are other reasons that those human drivers might be doing this kind of action, including (as already indicated) a general apprehension about being near a self-driving car. You might also find of interest that some drivers stay clear of a self-driving car out of a semblance of respect, just as you might if there was a car with a dignitary riding in it and you opted to steer away from the vehicle (not because of a fear of getting hit, but instead due to respecting the vehicle or its rider).

Conclusion

A recent webinar undertaken by the ITU as part of the *AI For Good Global Summit* included a related discussion about the role of near-misses in the overall realm of AI safety and ethics (the webinar featured Bryn Balcombe, Luciana Iorio, Liza Dixon, Danit Gal, Sebastian Krugel, Matthias Uhl, and others). There is much to be dealt with in the near-misses considerations, proffering challenges, etc.

We take for granted that today's human drivers can perform near-misses and there is little that can be done about it. Unless a police officer happens to witness the incident, the matter will be nothing more than a fleeting act, as though a pebble bouncing off the surface of a flowing stream and never more to be given a moment's thought (or, worse still, erupt into a moment of road rage and extremely adverse results). How many near-misses arise during a year of driving and are converted (one might say) into the approximate 6.3 million car crashes in the United States, along with the corresponding 40,000 related human deaths and the 2.3 million humans injured?

One important point about a willingness to focus on near-misses is that even Level 2 and Level 3 semi-autonomous cars could be augmented with detection that might better alert human drivers and reduce the number of near-misses, which in turn might reduce the number of actual crashes. Thus, near-misses can be important for not just true self-driving cars but also pertain significantly to lesser capable cars too..

One last thought to ponder. Since different AI driving systems will be driving in differing styles and manners, we might end up with some AI-based self-driving cars that are prone toward doing near-misses, and meanwhile, other brands that contend with those driving antics and fortunately aid in averting mishaps.

You can just hear the complaints already, of one brand of AI talking shop and grousing about the other AI that is clueless about driving and ought to have its head examined.

That's quite a future.

CHAPTER 12
TREE FALLS AND SELF-DRIVING CARS

A popular riddle that has been asked since at least the 1800s is whether a tree that falls in a forest will make a sound if there isn't anyone around to hear it.

This is a fun question to ask a child, ostensibly getting them to think stridently about something that appears simple and yet can actually entail great complexity. Adults too are often charmed by pondering how to answer this seemingly outside-the-box kind of curiosity.

Decidedly, there is a multitude of ways to answer the question.

One somewhat abstruse approach is notably conceptual and exceedingly philosophical, namely questioning the question itself. Perhaps a tree or otherwise anything else of any kind does not exist at all if there isn't a human present to witness it. The existence of reality is only valid when human presence occurs. In short, there isn't a forest and there isn't a tree, until or when a human strolls along and experiences it.

Whoa, that's pretty far gone and not the answer you would likely share with a child that is trying to merely ferret out this quandary about a sound in the forest as instigated by a falling tree. A more likely way to answer the question involves pointing out that a falling tree will disturb the surrounding air and create a series of airwaves. Those airwaves can in turn reach a human ear and cause a vibration that the sense of hearing deciphers as a sound.

Using this assuredly scientific form of reasoning, you can explain to a child that the question at its core has to do with what we all agree as to the definition of the word "sound" and thus gets them thinking seriously about words and their meanings. If you define a sound as only that which is heard by a human, well, in that case, since the question states there isn't any human around, then obviously ergo there is no sound produced. You can enlarge the definition by stating that any living creature that can detect sound might be part of the definition, such that even if a human wasn't there but some other animal that has hearing was nearby, you could reasonably conclude the falling tree did make a sound.

And so on.

Speaking of falling trees, sometimes a tree collapses or falls unexpectedly and catches a nearby human unawares.

The sound of the tree as it is falling might not provide sufficient notice to alert the person and therefore adversely undermines the needed reaction time to avoid getting struck. Or the sound is muffled and nothing more than a whisper, essentially bringing forth a silent falling of a tree. There is also the possibility that a human is wearing earplugs and thus cannot readily hear the falling tree, along with the instance too of a deaf person that would not be able to hear the falling tree at all.

There are news stories aplenty of falling trees that ended up harming a person that just so happened to be sitting under the tree or perchance was walking past the tree at the moment it fell. You don't have to be in a forest for these kinds of deadly encounters. Our cities and suburbs have trees too and are usually placed in such a manner to invite people to come near them, by design. The idea is that humans relish being near trees, seeing trees, and otherwise welcome trees, most of the time. All told, in the United States, there are an estimated 250 billion trees (per numbers proffered by the United Nations FAO), though this staggeringly large number encompasses the vast forest lands too.

You don't necessarily have to be standing or sitting outdoors to get struck by a falling tree. A variant of the falling tree scenario involves trees that manage to fall onto cars. If a person is inside the car, they are potentially going to get injured or in a worst-case possibly be killed.

We seem to readily accept the notion that a tree could fall onto a parked car, presumably because we know that a parked and unmoving car is a sitting duck. Though a human might be inside the vehicle and presumably could drive the car away before the tree strikes the car, this would generally require the person to be seated in the driver's seat, they would need to start the engine, they would need to engage the car into gear, and they would need to drive away from the scene. That's a lot of activity and seemingly too much to undertake unless the tree falls somehow in miraculously slow motion.

The instances when a tree falls onto an actively in-motion moving car and causes injuries or fatalities is perhaps the most startling of these tree endangering scenarios. It inexplicably seems like extraordinarily unlucky odds to be in a moving car that perchance goes past a tree that opts to fall at the same moment that the car was next to the tree. A few seconds earlier or later, possibly a few split seconds, and the car would have not been in the wrong place at the wrong moment in time.

A recent news report laments that a falling tree in Ohio incredibly clipped two vehicles as they both were in motion, whilst both were passing the tree at the same instant in time, leading to injuring one driver and killing the other driver. Unimaginable, and starkly tragic.

Shifting gears, this whole discussion seems to beg an unasked question, what causes a tree to fall over?

One supposes that if you asked a child whether a falling tree would make a sound, a smarmy kid might instantly ask why the tree fell. Perhaps the youngster is challenging the premise of the question. Maybe the child figures that if they knew what led the tree to fall, it might provide a clue to answering the overarching question about the sound-producing aspects. Of course, it could be that the youngster is stalling for time or might be seeking to avoid answering the question altogether.

Anyway, trees fall for a variety of reasons, plus we need to include the use case of a tree limb that falls versus the entirety of the tree per se. If the tree in totality falls, the odds are that the roots of the tree were probably in trouble or there was some huge gust of wind that shoved the tree from its foundational mooring. Limbs of a tree might break off and fall, due to age, or uneven growth, or perhaps a child had climbed on it and tried to get it to fall (hey, that's another reason why a youngster might ask why a tree fell, potentially worried they would get accused of causing it to happen).

Returning to the situation of a tree falling on a car, we can contemplate such circumstances in the future and wonder whether the adoption of self-driving cars will come to play in this tree falling malady.

Here's an intriguing point: *Will the advent of AI-based true self-driving cars means that we'll never worry again about trees falling onto cars or is there still a chance of this undesirable problem occurring?*

Let's unpack the matter and see.

Self-Driving Cars And Falling Trees

For Level 4 and Level 5 true self-driving vehicles, there won't be a human driver involved in the driving task.

All occupants will be passengers.

The AI is doing the driving.

We can begin our assessment of the tree falling aspects by pointing out that since the AI is the driver of a self-driving car, there would presumably be no one injured or killed if the self-driving car is absent of any passengers and meanwhile the vehicle happens to get struck by a falling tree. In a conventional car, there would always need to be a human driver, at least, and thus anytime a conventional car is in motion there is a possibility of a human getting injured or killed. Not so with a true self-driving car.

You might be perplexed as to why a self-driving car would be driving around and somehow not have any passengers. This is easily answered. First, a self-driving car might be roaming, akin to how ride-sharing cars do so today, hoping to be in the nearby area whenever someone needs a lift. Second, a self-driving car might be in the act of delivery, such as delivering groceries to someone homebound that ordered from their local store, and the self-driving car is being used essentially as a cargo mule. Third, the self-driving car might be driving to a designated location to pick-up a passenger. Etc. In short, you should expect that we'll see a lot of self-driving cars wandering around on our streets and highways, empty of human passengers, likely for a lot of their driving time.

This situation of not having any passengers does not though preclude the possibility of human getting hurt when a tree falls onto a self-driving car.

Suppose an empty self-driving car is minding its own business and driving down a busy city street that is jam-packed with pedestrians on the sidewalks. With the darned worst of chances, a tree falls onto the self-driving car. Fortunately, since there aren't any people inside the vehicle, no one gets hurt.

But, wait for a second, we need to consider what happens to the in-motion self-driving car.

One possibility is that the self-driving car is struck by the tree and the vehicle goes careening onto the sidewalk, ramming into pedestrians. In a sense, you could abundantly state that the self-driving car was the perpetrator of those injuries, though the instigating factor was the fallen tree.

You might be tempted to insist that the AI would never allow the self-driving car to go into this ballistic mode of careening up onto the sidewalk. Certainly, you assume and rightfully expect, the AI driving system should never permit this to occur (hold onto that lofty thought, I'll be shaking it apart in a moment).

This takes us into the realm of discussing what an AI driving system will potentially do when confronted with a falling tree situation.

We can consider this admittedly rare scenario and also toss into the equation that there might be human passengers inside the self-driving car at the time of such a confrontation (i.e., there is the case of no human passengers present and the other case of human passengers being inside the self-driving car).

Let's start with whether the AI will be able to detect a falling tree of this ilk.

Maybe, maybe not.

The sensors of today's self-driving cars consist of video cameras, radar, LIDAR, ultrasonic, thermal imaging, and the like, all of which are devices used to detect the world surrounding the self-driving car. By-and-large, these sensors are focused on figuring out what is in front of the self-driving car. The AI driving system has to figure out whether another car is ahead of it, and the distance to the other car, along with whether a pedestrian is about to walk in front of the self-driving car, and so on.

Assume that a falling tree is most likely going to fall from the sidelines and not be directly in front of the self-driving car. This assumption seems reasonable since most of the time a falling tree is either in a sidewalk or front yard that abuts the street, or sometimes in the median, but rarely if ever somehow directly in front of a car (unless, of course, the car is parked and facing toward some trees).

Okay, the first difficulty for the self-driving car is that the falling tree is not likely to be within the primary focus of its sensory detection capacities. The tree is presumably going to be on the periphery. This means that the sensors are less likely to detect that the tree is in the midst of falling.

The odds are that the tree could land on top of the self-driving car and the AI would not have any particular forewarning or have detected that the tree was falling upon it. In that manner, you could reasonably argue that just as a human driver can be caught unawares, so can the AI driving system.

Indeed, even after getting hit by a falling tree, the AI still might not detect what has occurred (whereas, we would expect nearly any human driver would realize such a catastrophic event).

Returning to the falling tree, we need to include time into this calculus.

As the self-driving car moves forward down a street, it is usually painting an internal picture, a virtual world model, consisting of the objects that are being detected. There is a strong possibility that the sensors detected the stationary tree that had not yet started to fall and included the tree in the virtual world model. If the tree begins to fall while the self-driving car is approaching a position adjacent to the tree, there is a chance that the AI might calculate that the tree is suddenly in-motion.

Now what?

Well, it depends upon what the AI developers have established within the AI driving system. The AI has undoubtedly been programmed to look for moving pedestrians, and for moving animals like dogs and cats, and for moving bicycles, and the rest. Whether it has been prepared to cope with a moving tree is a whole different enchilada, as they say.

The notion of a moving tree is pretty esoteric.

Given that most of the AI developers have their hands full with trying to get the self-driving car to handle the day-to-day normal stuff, the idea of preparing the AI to contend with a falling tree is a somewhat distant thought. In industry parlance, it is an edge or corner case or considered at the long-tail of what might arise, meaning those situations that are rarely expected and therefore can be placed on a lower priority list than everyday higher priority driving tasks.

Consider these permutations and combinations:

- It is possible that the self-driving car will not detect the falling tree and continue forward unabated, ultimately getting hit or crushed by the tree.

- The self-driving car might detect the tree and have posted into the virtual model that the tree exists, and yet not detect when the tree starts to fall, thus getting hit or crushed by the tree.

- The self-driving car might detect the tree, mark its position in the virtual model, and detect the tree as it starts to fall, but nonetheless take no evasive action because the AI has not been programmed to deal with this particular scenario. The self-driving car gets hit by the tree.

And, the preferred answer is that the self-driving car detects the tree, figures out that the tree is falling, and opts to do something about this unfolding calamity.

What would you have the AI do?

One obvious answer might be that the self-driving car should do whatever it can to avoid getting hit by the falling tree. I don't think you'll like that answer, as will be explained next.

Suppose the AI ascertains that it can avoid getting crushed by rushing up onto the sidewalk. Unfortunately, doing so endangers the pedestrians on the sidewalk. In that case, which has the greater importance, a passenger inside the self-driving car that is possibly going to get harmed when the tree lands on the roof of the vehicle, or those pedestrians on the sidewalk?

This is the essence of a famous thought experiment known as the Trolley Problem. Some industry insiders eschew the Trolley Problem as merely hypothetical and unworthy of attention. I sternly have exhorted that the Trolley Problem for self-driving cars is real and must be contended with, one way or another, including that ultimately there might be lawsuits and criminal cases against the automakers and self-driving tech firms that ignored the importance of dealing with the Trolley Problem.

Conclusion

I had mentioned that one possibility is that the self-driving car careens onto the sidewalk after getting hit by the falling tree. This action could be by the design of the AI and thus an overt act, or it could simply be that the AI is unable to control the car after the vehicle has gotten struck by the tree.

I point this out because some people seem to think that self-driving cars will be able to defy physics. They dreamily assert that self-driving cars will never get into car crashes or collisions.

That is just crazy talk. A car is a car, subject to the law of physics, and if other forces are too strong, indubitably the AI is not going to be able to drive its way out of a messy situation (plus, keep in mind that the driving controls might get jammed or disrupted too). The same could be said of a human driver.

There are lots of other variations involved in this falling tree situation. For example, if a passenger is inside the self-driving car, consider whether their yelling to the AI and telling its Natural Language Processing (NLP) component that a tree is falling might be of aid to the AI driving system (hint: only if the AI NLP is ready to process such a proclamation).

As a final thought, would a self-driving car that is in a forest and without any passengers be able to hear the sound of a falling tree?

Some self-driving cars are being outfitted with external microphones to provide the capability of hearing ambulance and police sirens, along with detecting other various outdoor sounds. In that way, the AI might indeed detect the sound of a falling tree, but whether the AI has been prepared to make any semblance out of the sound, as to what it portends, well, that's a different enchilada.

And since the AI isn't a human, albeit maybe someday sentient, we return to the beginning of this discussion about the meaning of words. When a machine such as AI "hears" a sound, does this count, or are we going to be recalcitrant that only living creatures can hear sounds?

Ask a child, they might have some clever answers.

CHAPTER 13
INVESTMENTS IN SELF-DRIVING CARS

Some are pointedly asking: *What's going on?*

Readers have fervently lobbed that question as a result of the most recent spate of investments into firms that are aiming to develop self-driving cars and trucks.

Consider:

- Nuro just made a big splash in the news by garnering an additional $500 million Series C round that places the company at a post-money valuation of around $5 billion.
- Pony.ai got headlines for its latest Series C funding of $257 million that suggests their valuation is perhaps $5.3 billion.
- And so on.

Of course, just a few months ago we also had the behemoth Amazon deciding to acquire Zoox for $1.3 billion in cash, ostensibly pledging to let the firm remain in a startup mindset versus possibly becoming bogged down as part of the mighty Borg.

In any case, people have noticed that there is a seeming resurgence of interest in the self-driving space and pondered what has triggered this current reopening of the investment spigot. The matter seems to be on the minds of many stakeholders, including VC firms, private investors, self-driving proponents, and equally self-driving opponents, and everyone else that keeps an eye on the direction and pace of self-driving tech.

Here are the top reasons that this revival has been sparked:

- **Waves of Waymo Wonderment**

You might have noticed that Waymo recently indicated it would be expanding its self-driving roadway trials that excise the back-up or safety driver from being behind the wheel of their vehicles. Well, this boldly caught the eyes and ears of many in the industry and the resounding waves of confidence thereof continue to reverberate.

In essence, this declaration showcases a willingness to have self-driving that is indeed fully self-driving, as it were, meaning that there isn't a human immediately overseeing the driving and thus no longer a human driver needs to be at the ready. They had already been doing so in a more limited fashion, within their Phoenix, Arizona efforts, but now are going beyond the preselected riders of their initial program. This portends a quite positive sign that bona fide self-driving is not some farfetched futuristic fantasy.

Recall that the doom-and-gloom prognosticators in the marketplace had been saying that self-driving was nothing but a pipedream, while this latest move by Waymo tends to belie that assertion. So, it bolsters investors that want to find a path into this niche. That being said, it is also vital to realize that the Waymo effort is still within a rather constrained Operation Design Domain (ODD) within Level 4, and we aren't yet per se into the Level 5 realm of self-driving.

- **Tesla Tenacity Tomfoolery**

Elon Musk continues to make boastful claims about the alleged self-driving capabilities of Tesla's cars, though the proof in the pudding has yet to be seen. In any case, the ever vocal bullhorn has stoked further attention to the promises of self-driving capabilities.

Critics decry the latest Tesla effort of releasing a beta version of the so-called Full Self-Driving (FSD), a naming coined by Tesla and not an as yet earned moniker, upon which some mysteriously selected set of Tesla owners are able to utilize this latest Frankenstein-like aggregation of self-driving kind-of features.

The criticism entails many concerns, such as the everyday human drivers of these Tesla's are not especially versed in serving as a back-up or safety driver, and therefore are essentially ill-prepared for the role of playing who-is-driving-the-car. Meanwhile, these Tesla's are being driven on our streets and highways with the rest of us, and we don't know who is using what to undertake the driving. Eerie, some say, while others are anticipating some rather sour results.

Nonetheless, the fanfare and outsized headlines that naively proclaim a landing on the moon in terms of self-driving due to Elon Musk and the latest efforts of Tesla are sufficient to garner renewed interest in all things self-driving.

- **Post-Pandemic Prodding**

Though we are not past the pandemic, some are already turning the corner of what to do once the scourge is more so in our rearview mirrors (i.e., after a vaccine has been widely distributed and other life-saving aspects have aided in these somber matters).

Notions of making investments in self-driving were somewhat frozen or put on the backburner when the magnitude of the pandemic began to take hold. The public roadway tryouts also became less common and were being done in a more restrictive manner, out of deference to the dangers of the disease.

I had predicted at that time that once a substantive glimmer of hope became apparent, there would be a revitalized effort in self driving pursuits and this would consequently spur investments too. This is likely to become more pronounced, including more sunny investment news undoubtedly arising soon.

- **Human-Driver Humility (Ridesharing)**

There had been tremendous growth in ridesharing and it seemed that human drivers were willing to happily leap into the provide-a-lift gravy train.

Earlier this year, who would have thought that a human driver might have something more than just the ordinary foibles of human driving? Turns out, human drivers can also potentially spread germs. Some claim that people are worried that if they use conventional ridesharing they are at the risk of exposure, similar to taking a bus or subway. As such, there is handwringing about whether this will have a longer-term deflation to the onslaught of ridesharing (some contend that's just short-term thinking).

Anyway, the point here is that a true self-driving car does not have a human driver, therefore there are zero risks of germs from the driver. Add another plus then into the column that tracks the benefits of self-driving cars.

As an aside, this does not mean self-driving cars are entirely out of the woods on this aspect. A prior rider might have left germs for you inside a self-driving car. The automakers and self-driving tech firms realize this concern, and various approaches are being taken to deal with it (either frequent cleaning of the interior by hand or using built-in automation to do the cleaning).

- **Crash Calamities Contained**

When was the last time you heard about a car crash involving a self-driving car? This is a distant memory right now. Thankfully so, both for humanity and also for the sake of the self-driving car industry.

Anyway, the point here is that the public sentiment toward self-driving is riding pretty high these days, at least until or if there is a fatal car crash. As long as there aren't any such violent earthquakes, there will be investors willing to put the dough into the self-driving space.

Of course, all it will take is one rather notable incident, and the doldrums will certainly return. Investors might scamper for the hills. Regulation might rain down voraciously.

With tippy-toe trepidation, we all need to hold our breath on this one.

- **Best Bet Bargain Bonanza**

You would have to have your head in the sand to somehow not realize that self-driving cars and trucks are going to be a humongous bonanza.

People will crave using self-driving cars. Companies will crave using self-driving trucks. In theory, the costs associated with the driving task will go down, and the access to mobility will go up. Some argue that we will ultimately witness mobility-for-all and that those in society today that are mobility impinged will become mobility enabled. In addition, presumably, the annual 40,000 car crash-related deaths and the approximate 2.3 million car crash injuries in the United States alone will be substantially reduced.

Those that are willing to carry on a logical and relatively dispassionate discussion would concur that self-driving is going to be a mobility boon and there seems little room for acrimonious debate on that topic. Of course, you might argue that perhaps the cost isn't going to be low and thus only the elite will be able to afford the use of self-driving vehicles. You could argue that maybe the AI driving systems won't be safe enough. Etc.

Nonetheless, as a future bet, it would seem those factors will inevitably get worked out to a satisfactory determination. Thus, the primary issue is how far in the future will this all transpire.

That's the crux of investing today in self-driving cars and trucks, namely, how long will you need to hang onto that investment before you'll see a hoped-for boosted return for your money?

Not every investor has the fortitude to wait until the day upon which self-driving cars and trucks are routinely accepted and prevalent on our byways. It requires a perspective that is daunting for many, and they would rather put their money into something with clearer nearer-term, and more assured payoffs.

Others believe that this is the right time to make such an investment. They believe that if one waits, it will presumably become more obvious that this innovation is going to gain traction, and by then there will everybody and their brother or sister wanting to pile in. As such, they perceive the buy-in cost right now to be a bargain.

Conclusion

The preceding list of key factors has dovetailed into presently spurring some investors to plunk down their bucks into self-driving related investments.

Are they right or are they wrong?

Unless you are a visitor here from the future, or perchance have an unerring crystal ball, only time will tell.

CHAPTER 14
BOTHERING NEIGHBORS AND SELF-DRIVING CARS

One of the most famous TV show songs of all time urges you to sit right back and hear a tale, a tale of a fateful trip that takes place aboard a tiny ship.

Name that TV show.

Well, I'm sure you immediately guessed that those are the lyrics from the ever-popular *Gilligan's Island* and indeed, you would be right.

If you hear the song a few times in a row, it is abundantly catchy and might cause you to hark back to the original days of the show being aired (for those that were around then) or might remind you of watching those ubiquitous recordings online of the show as available on today's social media platforms.

Suppose though that you were somewhat forced into hearing the endearing song over and over, perhaps due to the song being blared via massive loudspeakers toward your home from a next-door neighbor.

How would you feel about the song then?

I believe that your heartfelt sentiment toward the song would turn into a maddening overload of angst and irksomeness. Stop that song, you would undoubtedly demand. I dare say, you might opt to wear some hefty earplugs or sound blockers akin to what a ground crew wears at airports, doing so in hopes of deadening the repetitive blare and preventing your mind from going berserk. The old saying seems true that too much of anything, even something of wholesome goodness, will break the camel's back (or some such adage).

According to a recent news report, a neighbor apparently opted to play the famous ballad, allegedly repeatedly so, and which then led to their next-door resident deciding to file a restraining order about the matter. The homes involved are in the tony community of Laguna Beach, California and the ocean view properties involved are worth many dozens of millions of dollars each. The owners are extremely wealthy. And these well-to-do neighbors have lobbed acrid accusations as to the other neighbor having either started the feud or carried the tit-for-tat extraordinarily overboard, as it were (overboard as in like a tiny ship!).

You might have thought that having lots of money and owning a prized mansion with breathtaking sunsets would translate into not having a single worry in this world, but apparently, no amount of wealth can stop the classic neighbor-versus-neighbor battles.

Perhaps we ought to keep in mind the legendary refrain from Robert Frost's poem stipulating (or speculating) that good fences make good neighbors, a classic line from his poetic treatise *Mending Wall.* Depending upon your preferred interpretation, this might mean that human fellowship is a tug-of-war between wanting to be connected with other humans and yet simultaneously maintain some distance or boundaries from other humans too. We are seeking to paradoxically be both joined and separated, all at the same time, one might so assert.

Using loud noises is assuredly one means to irritate a neighbor, whilst another means consists of establishing a visual blight. There are plentiful times that someone opts to park an old junk car on their front lawn and let the wreck gradually rust and stew. If you live next door, at first you might be sympathetic to seeing the vehicle sitting there and assume it will soon enough be moved elsewhere. Instead, when the rust bucket is left there unattended and seemingly abandoned, for weeks and months on end, your patience is likely to run extremely thin.

Speaking of cars, consider the future of transportation and mobility, entailing the advent of self-driving cars.

It would seem that self-driving cars will be a welcomed boon to humanity. Predictions are that the regrettable 40,000 annual fatalities due to car crashes in the United States alone will be reduced enormously, and likewise, the estimated 2.3 million car crash injuries will nearly disappear.

What's not to like about the emergence of self-driving cars?

That brings up this intriguing question: *Could the advent of AI-based true self-driving cars somehow get intermingled into the act of bothering a neighbor?*

This seems like a rather curious question and defies the aura of goodness that surrounds the self-driving car realm.

Let's unpack the matter and see what can be found.

Self-Driving Cars And Your Neighbors

For Level 4 and Level 5 true self-driving vehicles, there won't be a human driver involved in the driving task.

All occupants will be passengers.

The AI is doing the driving.

There is a great deal of debate in the self-driving industry about whether these types of vehicles will be owned only by large-scale fleet operators or whether there might be individual ownership involved too.

Some pundits insist that self-driving cars will be purchased or licensed solely by big entities such as car rental firms or major ride-sharing companies and then deployed onto our streets and highways. Car ownership by individuals will become a thing of the past. Once the conventional automobiles of today are eclipsed by the expanding population of self-driving cars, the very notion of an individual owning a car will be considered laughable and a historic relic.

I am known for being a contrarian on this point, due to the

espoused belief that there will still be individual ownership of cars, including and particularly self-driving cars. Logically, if self-driving cars are going to be massive money makers, which nearly everyone agrees is likely, it would certainly seem that everyday individuals would want to get in on the gravy train too.

You might buy a self-driving car and use it to get to work and take the kids to school, meanwhile the rest of the day it is available on a ride-sharing network for providing money-making rides to passengers. One reason given that this won't happen is that perhaps the cost of buying a self-driving car will be beyond the reach of everyday individuals. But that is somewhat sloppy thinking since it presumes that the purchase price of a self-driving car is comparable to the purchase of today's conventional cars. That is decidedly wrongheaded and mistaken thinking.

For today's conventional cars, they sit unused about 95% or more of the time that you own the vehicle. In short, it is a woefully underutilized asset of a costly nature per se.

And why isn't this valuable asset used more so?

Because you need a driver to drive the car.

In the case of self-driving cars, the AI is doing the driving and will be available 24x7. This means that a self-driving car can be operating around the clock. A conventional car rarely makes you any money, while a self-driving car has the potential for earning you some sizable bucks.

The point is that even if self-driving cars are exorbitantly priced, you could still potentially afford the vehicle due to the ROI (return-on-investment) possibilities. You would be willing to go out on a limb and get a sizable loan, believing that the car itself will make enough money to cover the loan and turn you a profit. The bank or lender is willing to make you that loan since they realize the basis is covered by the present and future value of that money-making self-driving car.

There are more facets involved in this contentious debate about the ownership question, but for the moment, assume that indeed individual ownership will occur. As an aside, some are worried that the individual owners will only be the elite and highly wealthy personages, thus leaving out of the equation the rest of society.

Okay, so we are going to assume that individuals will own self-driving cars.

Where does that take us?

Returning to the earlier discussion about neighbors versus other neighbors, the acknowledgment that there will be individual ownership of self-driving cars puts those AI-based marvels into the driver's seat of being a potential pest or unneighborly nightmarish new guest.

I'm sure you are crying in your soup to think that a state-of-the-art innovation that embodies the latest in AI and will be helping to reduce lost lives and will be providing a potential mobility-for-all aspiration could somehow have a dent in its allure.

It does.

Here's how.

First, imagine that your self-driving car is normally going to be parked in your driveway or on the street in front of your house. With a conventional car, perhaps you undertake the act of driving the car away from its parking spot on the order of a handful of times per day, maximumly. There is the trip to the office, the drive to the grocery store, and the journey to pick up the kids at school.

For a self-driving car, presumably, you will want it to be used as much as possible. Whenever it is being used for providing rides, the cash register is ringing. Alas, whenever it is parked and doing nothing, there is no money being made.

The implication is that the individually owned self-driving car will be constantly parking and then getting back underway. All-day long. All night long. The quiet neighborhood that most of us live in is usually especially serene during the midnight to sunrise hours. Anyone owning a self-driving car is going to have that vehicle continually exiting from its parking spot and heading out to provide a ride. Once the ride is accomplished, the self-driving car will come back to your house and park itself, becoming ready for whenever the next ride request arises.

Imagine the potential annoyance to your nearby neighbors. There goes that darned self-driving car again, a neighbor might lament. Isn't that the eighth time tonight? On and on this goes, seven days a week, four weeks a month, all year long.

You might be tempted to counterargue that the self-driving car will be relatively inconspicuous. It won't roar away from your house and it won't be honking its horn. Instead, the self-driving car will start its engine, and likely being an EV (electrical vehicle) it will be relatively quiet on the ears, smoothly slinking away into the night.

Maybe yes, maybe not.

There is the shine of the headlights and the sounds of a car rumbling down your street, no matter how much of a driving ninja the AI might be. Street vibrations are a possibility. In addition, you might need to go out to the vehicle when it returns from a trip, doing so to make sure that the self-driving car is still in good shape and ready for the next trip. A rider that used your self-driving car at 2 a.m. might have been drinking and opted to take an AI-driven ride home from the local bars, wisely so, and yet they might have gotten sick to their stomach from the alcohol and a resultant mess inside your self-driving car needs urgent cleaning.

There seems little question that the otherwise stillness and purity of silence on your street is going to be usurped by those that own and are operating their self-driving cars.

Another qualm relates to the number of miles of driving on your neighborhood streets. Once someone on the block has a self-driving car, it is going to be going back-and-forth on your street repeatedly, adding a tremendous amount of wear-and-tear to your local asphalt. Expect more potholes and a sooner need to mend the street.

Consider too the increased risks involved.

Suppose you have small children, and they love to play in your front yard, including running sometimes out into the street. Hopefully, the AI will be good enough to detect those small children as they dart into the street unexpectedly.

One dire fear is that kids will begin to assume that the AI driving systems are always able to detect and stop in time. In that case, children might falsely believe that can unabashedly scamper into the street in front of an ongoing self-driving car. Those same youngsters might be afraid that a human driver would not stop or would not see them, thus the kids are more reserved in that circumstance, but when they spot a self-driving car they will be more emboldened.

Busy Car City On Your Neighborhood Block

So far, we have you irking your neighbors with your self-driving car because it comes and goes at all hours, it disturbs and undercuts the peace and tranquility of the street, it causes the street to go into disrepair sooner than normal, and it endangers the children that are innocently playing in the quaint front yards of the neighborhood.

Perhaps all of that seems enough of a proof of the pudding to cause a semblance of neighborly concern.

Wait for a second, there is even more.

One of the reasons that some doubt there will be individual ownership of self-driving cars is due to the maintenance and upkeep requirements. In order for a self-driving car to operate safely and properly, it has to be kept in a relatively pristine shape. A human-driven car can be in a rather poor shape and yet the human driver will nonetheless be able to drive the vehicle. With a self-driving car, all of the sensors must be working and they cannot be blocked by dirt or otherwise be inoperable, else the vehicle is supposed to refuse to get underway.

This translates into the individual owner having to strictly and stridently stay on top of the upkeep for the self-driving car.

Here's where things get worse for your neighbors.

In addition to keeping your self-driving car parked in your driveway or on the street in front of your house, you also opt to set up a small repair bay or tent at your home. This will allow you to do regular cleaning such as making sure the inside of the car is bereft of debris and undertake the removal of any leftover flotsam by prior riders. You might also do your own oil changes and other simplistic car upkeep.

Yikes, it now appears that your home is becoming a car repair and maintenance facility. That is going to be an eyesore and a noisemaker.

One might also question how far this can go, and indeed there will undoubtedly be disputes taken to the city or county about just what is permitted in your neighborhood. You can bet that various local homeowners associations will bicker about these matters and try to put in place local conditions and restrictions about what is allowed and what is disallowed.

Let's add a kind of coup de grace to this list.

Throughout all of this discussion, the assumption has been that whoever owns and is operating that self-driving car will be respectful of the neighborhood and genuinely will try to keep things quiet and unintrusive. That is the glass-is-half-full viewpoint of mankind.

Envision a situation wherein a feud among neighbors is taking place, not necessarily due to the advent of the self-driving car on the block, but due to some other perceived transgression, such as loudly playing TV show theme songs.

In short, someone that has a self-driving car can opt to turn it into another avenue of annoying their neighbors. You could purposely have the self-driving car continually going back-and-forth, just to irk your neighbor. Have the AI pull into their driveway, as though it is confused or maybe trying to turnaround. Make it park in front of their house. Etc.

The evildoing can get even worse.

Remember that a self-driving car has lots of sensors, including video cameras, radar, LIDAR, thermal imaging, ultrasonic, and so on. You could have the sensors recording whatever happens while it is parked in front of your neighbor's house.

This would allow you to somewhat "spy" on your neighbor as to the comings and goings at their home. I've previously discussed in my columns the notion of the roving eye of self-driving cars, which has some potential benefits but also serious privacy repercussions too.

Conclusion

The arrival of self-driving cars bodes for the best of times, or possibly the worst of times, depending upon how this latest in AI-advanced capabilities is utilized and deployed.

Something as simple as being neighborly can be enhanced, such as allowing your self-driving car to give free lifts to the people on your block that otherwise do not have ready access to mobility. On the other hand, you can inadvertently become unneighborly, trying to run a self-driving car "business" from your homestead. You can even become vindictive and try to use your self-driving car as a foil in your neighbor-versus-neighbor feuding argument.

One quick counterargument to these misgivings is that some people might outsource the care of their self-driving car and perhaps even park it at some prearranged faraway parking lot, though this introduces other complications of cost and logistics. Whether everyone would take this path is highly debatable and it seems realistic to assume that some or many will seek to keep their self-driving car as much as possible at their primary domicile.

Good fences make good neighbors, and likewise, goodness in running your local self-driving car will hopefully be a blessing for your neighborhood.

CHAPTER 15
ICE CREAM TRUCKS AND SELF-DRIVING CARS

Have you ever encountered roadway puddles that turned out to be As a freezing cold winter begins to descend upon us, your thoughts undoubtedly turn toward a summertime pastime that will be sorely missed, namely the neighborhood ice cream truck and its bountiful offering of popsicles, Klondike bars, snow cones, drumsticks, and other frosty delicacies.

Though ice cream trucks still operate during the cold winter months in some parts of the country such as California, they generally go into hibernation as the weather turns icy. For several months you won't hear the cheerful jingle of the ice cream truck bells and will not be drawn to the melodic chimes that call out for children and adults alike to stand at the curb and eagerly await those frozen treats.

All in all, owning and operating an ice cream truck is pretty much a seasonal business and requires the intrepid owners to work fervently during the premium months. Kids and parents are more receptive to consuming ice-cold treats when the outdoor temperatures are hottest, and the sun is shining brightly. Also, the children must be around at home and available, while during the normal school year they are sitting in classrooms and perhaps daydreaming of one day again relishing the delights of an ice cream truck coming down their local street.

Few realize that the ice cream truck business is relatively fragmented and occupied by zillions of individual entrepreneurs rather than being run by a handful of large-scale companies. The most obvious investment for any ice cream truck operator is the truck itself. Considered to be a novelty type of vehicle, most ice cream trucks are specially outfitted with cold plate freezers that stay icy cold during a driving journey. No sense in letting your inventory melt and thus become unsaleable.

These are mobile retail outlets, intended to wander around a community and sell its wares.

In addition to the cost of the vehicle, there are other apparent expenses such as the inventory of frozen treats, the automotive insurance required, the gasoline or fuel expenditures, the fees for any needed permits, and of course the labor to drive the vehicle. For most of the ice cream truck activities, there is just one driver and they serve too as the customer service representative, selling the popsicles and other delicacies to those that come up to the ice cream truck.

Consider the customer experience related to ice cream truck activities.

First, you need to realize that an ice cream truck is somewhere within your vicinity.

This means that the ice cream truck driver has to be astute enough to drive in the right areas in the right way, attempting to maximize their selling opportunities. If the driver opts to drive in the early morning hours, before the sun has fully risen, the odds are that few will be interested in clamoring for ice cream. Another potential mistake involves driving in a sparsely populated neighborhood or one that has few children. Without customers, viable ones, and desirous of ice cream, there is no market for the frozen goodies.

A driver must also make their presence known in the sense of playing a catchy tune or ringing a chime.

The sound of the ice cream truck can carry across a large swath of blocks and allow prospective customers to seek out the vehicle or merely wait on the sidewalk for the ice cream truck to appear. This can be a dicey proposition for both the seller and the buyers, since the driver might not actually drive down your street, and you likewise might be left high-and-dry by having assumed that the vehicle would be coming along to deliver its treats.

Thus, another part of the customer journey involves standing around outside of your home to await the arrival of the ice cream truck, though there is no guarantee that it will ultimately arrive. Some kids relish getting on the bikes to go and find the ice cream truck, but generally, it is a waiting game and most youngsters tend to simply stand around and hope that the vehicle will come to them. In one perspective, the waiting is half of the fun and enjoyment, offering a moment of excitement and rapt anticipation as you eye the roadway and eagerly anticipate the heroic ice cream truck sauntering down your block.

Once the ice cream truck arrives, the next part of the customer experience involves figuring out what to order, then placing your order, and inevitably making payment.

Some children insist on getting the same item each and every time that they partake of an ice cream truck service. Maybe a child is enamored of rainbow flavored snow cones or purple popsicles. Other kids seem to prefer trying something new and decidedly different upon each occurrence of visiting an ice cream truck. There is usually a sizable menu board on the side of the ice cream truck that colorfully announces the treats to be had. Ironically, parents are apt to get perturbed at the kids that delay the action by mulling over all of the possibilities, but for which this is potentially part of the delight for the youths, a rare instance of them seemingly being free to choose whatever they want.

At this point, the driver that is also the customer service rep must stand tall in terms of being able to sell the frozen goodies. If this person is an ogre and acts irritably toward the lined-up children, the odds are that the number of purchases will be lessened and the next time that the ice cream truck comes around there will be fewer customers interested in buying. Kids won't want to bear the brunt of a surly seller and parents will likely restrain their offspring from seeking out the ice cream truck. In short, the driver as a selling person has to be sufficiently polite or civil if they want to attain any semblance of monetary success with their efforts.

There is a bit of quandary about how friendly one ought to be. It used to be that everyone in town knew the ice cream truck owner and therefore there were a lot of built-in trusts. Nowadays, the person is typically a complete stranger. As such, if the ice cream truck operator starts asking kids overly friendly questions, it is bound to get the parents on edge, even if the driver is doing so innocently and simply as a means to inspire greater purchases. Sadly, our society now has become a guarded one and parents need to always be on the watch.

After making a purchase and getting the frozen treat, the children and parents will dance away and relish their wondrous desserts. The driver then gets back into the driver's seat and continues the driving chore to find the next set of customers. If the driver is paying attention, they will usually not revisit the same street during a driving journey due to the aspect that those living on that street are already satiated and there is no more money to be had there. An exception might be if the street was relatively vacant at the time of a visit and for which the driver might decide that trying again at a more opportune time would be prudent.

Now that we've covered the ice cream truck end-to-end cycle, let's consider a more macroscopic viewpoint on the matter.

Some indicate that the ice cream truck phenomenon was started by Harry Burt, considered the creator of the Good Humor bar, during the 1920s as a clever way to sell his wares. Interestingly, prohibition apparently helped out, allowing people that otherwise could not get a cold drink of whiskey tended to turn their attention toward substituting ice cream and sodas that conveniently were offered by the burgeoning use of ice cream trucks. Lore has it that the reason we nowadays associate a chime or melody with an ice cream truck is due to Burt putting his son's bobsled bell onto his vehicle.

Fascinating history and worthwhile as an idle form of entertaining theatre, as it were.

Let's next turn our eye toward the future.

We know that there are erstwhile efforts to craft self-driving cars and self-driving trucks. These vehicles will be bereft of a human driver since none will be needed.

Here's today's intriguing question: *What will ice cream trucks be like in an era of self-driving cars and other self-driving vehicles?*

Time to unpack the matter and see.

Self-Driving Cars And Ice Cream Trucks

For Level 4 and Level 5 true self-driving vehicles, there won't be a human driver involved in the driving task.

All occupants will be passengers.

The AI is doing the driving.

The first place to start our discussion of the future of ice cream trucks is the apparent fact that there can readily be AI-based self-driving ice cream trucks, assuming that we've also been able to achieve self-driving cars (the same technology applies).

You could even make an argument that a self-driving ice cream truck does not need to be as capable as a self-driving car.

Here's why.

Assuming that the self-driving ice cream truck would be kept to low speeds, this turns out to make the AI-based driving chore a bit easier overall. The slower the speed, the more time for the computer to calculate what to do, and the greater amount of time allowed for making a quick stop. This is partially why you've perhaps heard about the tremendous progress in self-driving cars in say retirement communities, wherein the speed limits are kept very low, and in self-driving delivery vehicles that plod along at slower speeds.

In any case, there are certainly dire consequences if a self-driving ice cream truck were to somehow ram into or strike a child. Besides the potential injuries, the other qualm would be that this could cause a massive backlash against using self-driving capabilities in the use case of an ice cream truck. We all know or should acknowledge that an ice cream truck is a magnet for children. Meanwhile, one of the hardest aspects of AI detection involves being able to spot little children. The youngsters do not necessarily realize the dangers of running out into the street to catch-up with or run toward an ice cream truck, regardless of whether human-driven or AI-driven.

I think it is sensible to state that any ice cream truck that gets embellished with self-driving facilities had better be darned good, nearly fault-free. The entirety of the self-driving realm would undoubtedly get crushed if a self-driving ice cream truck did something astray.

Let's assume that the self-driving ice cream truck is going to be safe enough to be reliably and appropriately utilized in our neighborhoods and communities (this is yet to be shown), and consider what else this portends.

The driver of the self-driving ice cream truck is the AI system. There is no need for and presumably no allowance for a human to be driving the vehicle.

You can then assess the situation in two ways. One approach would be to have a human on-board that now can completely be provided solely for selling purposes and no longer has to also incur the effort of driving the vehicle. Another alternative involves ditching any human being on-board and instead entail an utterly AI-run operation.

I'll concentrate on the AI-only instance, allowing us to mull over what this mobile retail outlet will be like when devised in that manner.

The AI would be driving the vehicle and could potentially make use of modern-day data science techniques in devising the optimum path throughout a neighborhood. Based on demographic data that would indicate the nature of the households, such as the number of children at each home, the estimated household incomes, and so on, the AI would be able to try and systematically determine the best route to take. This would involve ascertaining the likelihood of who might be at home, who would be likeliest to buy from an ice cream truck, and so on.

We can also take into account that the ice cream truck ought to "learn" from its various journeys.

A human driver would likely remember where the hotspots in the community are in terms of the most kids and the most purchases. The AI system of an ice cream truck would similarly be collecting this data, though in more precise detail, and then upload the data using the OTA (Over-The-Air) electronic communications from the self-driving vehicle into the cloud of the automaker or self-driving developing entity. Using the latest in Machine Learning (ML) and Deep Learning (DL), this customer data could be routinely analyzed and used to better guide the direction and pace of cruising in a community.

On the exterior of the ice cream truck would be a menu board, though this could be amped up in this space age. The board could be an electronic one, displaying the ice cream delights and showcasing what they look like. Cartoons and various animation could be used to further enhance the displays and attract the desired attention. Etc.

Speaking of modern technologies, the AI could be sending out electronic messages, a type of beacon, indicating where the self-driving ice cream truck is and its specific GPS coordinates. Children and parents would be able to consult their smartphones to know when the ice cream truck is nearby. Presumably, preorders could be electronically placed, rather than waiting until the vehicle arrives.

When picking up the order, the self-driving ice cream truck might dispense the frozen goodie via some kind of robotic arm, or might make use of a set of vending machine caged slots that open when you showcase your smartphone electronic receipt.

Some are crestfallen to think that the old-fashioned ice cream truck is being turned into a seemingly vacuous experience for kids.

Well, it depends upon your point of view.

The AI system could speak with those that come up to the self-driving ice cream truck, welcoming them and offering a dialogue akin to what a human operator might have done. Via advances in Natural Language Processing (NLP), akin to Alexa and Siri, the AI could almost seem human-like in terms of focusing on the act of selling the ice cream delights.

Perhaps some enterprising operators will provide downloadable video games that enable kids to play a game on their smartphone while awaiting the arrival of the self-driving ice cream truck. Also, it could be that children will no longer have their desires shattered due to an ice cream truck that never came to their block, since the AI would be alerted whenever an electronic connection and order was placed.

Could there be as much excitement and enthusiasm sprinkled toward a conventional ice cream truck as there might be for a state-of-the-art self-driving ice cream truck?

Perhaps so, encompassing a newly formed set of traditions that those of us mired in the prior ones cannot readily discern.

Conclusion

Not all facets of self-driving ice cream trucks are necessarily rosy.

If you frighten or become startled easily, please prepare yourself for what I'm about to mention.

One aspect of self-driving cars and all such vehicles that I've repeatedly pointed out is that they will have a roving eye.

With the abundance of sensors including video cameras, radar, LIDAR, ultrasonic, thermal imaging, and the like, the self-driving driving vehicles will be able to collect massive amounts of data about our daily lives.

Imagine that as every self-driving car and self-driving truck perchance goes down your street, it is capturing a video recording of everything that is taking place.

This bodes for some handy benefits but also proffers scary privacy intrusions. In the use case of a self-driving ice cream truck, it would presumably be able to record all the comings and goings of the young children that come up to the vehicle to get their ice cream. You can then add into the equation the aspects of facial recognition. Consider how this might be adversely used, and you will get chills down your spine.

A counterargument is that the AI can do a better and more consistent job of acting friendly towards the children and the parents that make use of the ice cream dispensing capabilities. Perhaps the AI detects that little Joey or little Samantha are approaching the self-driving ice cream truck and immediately establishes their preferred snow cone or drumstick for them. No need for the kids to place an order since the AI already realizes what they usually want. The AI also calls out to them, by name, providing an ultra-personalized ice cream dispensing experience.

Here's an additional oddball twist.

Envision that the AI is so well devised that it can carry on a seemingly intelligible conversation with the children that approach the vehicle. Those kids might then tend to anthropomorphize the AI. In short, they will believe that the AI is as astute as a human, embodying human-like intelligence. This could be dangerous for those kids. Plus, it makes one wonder what those children will be like when they grow-up having been led into believing that AI is essentially sentient (it is not, and we are a long way from having such AI).

In any case, set aside that worrisome talk.

As the days and nights of winter come upon us, and the cold weather takes hold, please continue to keep friendly and warm thoughts about the coming summer and the annual revival of the ice cream truck.

Just don't be surprised if the next time you see an ice cream truck it isn't already outfitted as a self-driving vehicle and the AI is ringing the bell to welcome you all to a treasure trove of ice cream delights.

But please do keep your eye on that sneaky AI, despite those delicious snow cones and delectable popsicles.

CHAPTER 16
PARKING HEAD-IN AND SELF-DRIVING CARS

A parking lot can become a feuding landscape akin to the Old West and the infamous rivalry between the Hatfield's and the McCoy's.

Danger lurks as cars jockey to park, trolling to get that nifty open parking spot nearest to the front entrance and avoid having to park at the furthermost spaces that require a seemingly unending and endurance-busting walk across a massive-sized parking lot. Drivers eye each other warily. Civility generally seems to have gone out the window. The act of parking is a daily exhibition of the dog-eat-dog world in which we live.

There is an added twist that can really get people's goat.

Should you park your car in a head-in manner, or should you instead utilize the reverse arrangement whereby you back into a parking space?

This has become a longstanding question and an erstwhile and irksome choice, and abundantly is worthy of the Hatfield-McCoy kind of enmity. Almost any driver that you might come upon has an opinion on this fierce debate conundrum. Some drivers swear an eternal oath to the head-in parking approach and eschew the nose out as an alternative. Meanwhile, some drivers have an ironclad belief in the nose out parking, lamenting that the head-in technique is rife with problems and ought to be banned from existence.

The two camps are usually vocally adamant and diametrically opposed to each other. It can get darned ugly.

For the head-in camp, they argue that it makes obvious sense to drive your car forward into a parking spot. Doing so allows you to clearly see whether the spot is fully open and unobstructed. You can also smoothly enter into a parking space and adroitly align yourself to provide maximum distance between the cars on either side of you. The beauty too is that if you want to use your trunk, such as getting out some heavy winter jackets for the cold walk through the parking lot or to place packages into the trunk upon your return to the parked car, it is easy-peasy to do so.

They admit freely that backing out of the parking spot is a bit delicate. Nonetheless, if one carefully and slowly goes in reverse, paying attention to what is behind you, the exit-without-incident from a parking spot is relatively assured. Just stay on your toes and look over your shoulder. Plus, many of today's cars have a backup cam that provides another way to see behind the vehicle.

That covers the mainstay of the favored aspects about doing the forward first, known too as the head-in, or pull-in parking option.

The nose out camp argues that the most sensible way to park involves reversing or backing into a parking spot. They assert that it is rare that a parking spot proffers any difficulties getting into, such that if backing up is considered a dicey form of driving, best to do so when getting into a spot. Might as well take your time and back into the parking spot, which will then ease your efforts when later on exiting from the space.

When exiting from a parking space, you are now looking forward and able to use all the facilities that are associated with driving ahead. This makes indubitably good sense since the act of resuming your place into the busy lane of traffic requires the greatest precision and driving control. In addition, they point out that the driver can make eye contact with pedestrians that are walking nearby the car as you are exiting from the parking spot. This allows a driver to wave at those pedestrians or even possibly signal to a driver that is coming down the lane that they should either proceed or requesting them to temporarily halt while the car comes out of the parking space.

I believe that summarizes the back-in or so-called reverse parking, often described as the nose out positioning.

The nose out camp is apt to gleefully emphasize that most police cars and similar first responders tend to park using the back-in method. This showcases that there is an inherent advantage of being able to rapidly exit from a parking spot when the time comes to do so.

Take that, the nose outs exclaim.

The nose-in camp raises their eyebrows and asks how often a non-first-responder would ever need to screech and peel out of a parking spot, which presumably should be never. For those everyday drivers, perhaps the notion of parking via the back-in approach is tantamount to thinking that they can exit from a parking spot by putting the pedal to the floor and zooming out.

Bad idea that invites crazed driving, the head-in supporters would exhort.

Another bitter dispute is the impact on traffic and the creation of undue traffic delays. The nose-in camp claims that the back-in method causes all sorts of confusion and traffic snarling, waiting for the driver to inch their way into a parking spot, especially dicey since they often have gone past the spot and need to back-up initially to even get close to the spot. The back-in camp contends that the worst traffic woes are due to the nose-in drivers that can't seem to smoothly back out of a parking spot, often doing so in a staggered and exasperating way, starting and stopping repeatedly, as though they are at a complete loss of how to properly drive a car.

The back-in drivers tend to believe they are superior drivers altogether. This snobbishness then irks the forward-first drivers. Tempers can flare. It is one thing to have tempers emerge when simply debating the merits of either method, yet an altogether more serious matter when road rage surfaces.

You've likely seen drivers that wait patiently for a reverse parking car. Even those with grand patience are at times pushed over the brink.

You idiot, they are imploring, park your car the "right way" and it wouldn't take you so long to get into that freaking parking spot. Some of these waiting drivers get so frustrated that they begin to yell at the other car or take insidious action that ought not to be undertaken.

Of course, the same can be said of the back-in drivers that are waiting when another car is trying to back out of a parking spot. Those drivers watch as the backing out driver agonizingly moves out of the spot, for which glaciers have been known to proceed at a faster pace. It can be so exasperating that the back-in driver screams out to the other car and urges them to get a brain, ostensibly suggesting they should henceforth use the back-in method. Those words can sometimes also become undue actions such as fisticuffs, though hopefully rarely goes that far.

Cities and local parking operators have tried various experiments to see what works best.

In some locales, you are legally required to park head-in, or legally required to park nose out, depending upon what the local ordinances and driving rules state. Signs such as "Park Heading In" are placed on display, as are signs that say "If You Can't Pull Through, Please Back-In" (this is another one-off kind of parking circumstance, whereby in some parking lots they have two spaces back-to-back and you are intended to pull forward into the space at the head of the pair).

Additional complications occur when the lanes are one-way for feeding into or out of a set of parking spaces. There is also the matter of parking spots that are angled directionally versus those parking spots that are perfectly perpendicular to the lanes. In short, the design of the parking lot has a lot to do with whether one method is "best" in the given situation, wherein parking is somewhat dictated by how the parking lot maker wants you to park your car.

Going against the grain can be dangerous.

When a parking lot is designed for one of the methods, those that obstinately decide they are still going to park as they always have (assuming it isn't the approach recommended or insisted upon by the parking lot operator), they are asking for trouble. All or most of the other drivers are presumably going to abide by the parking lot rules, meanwhile, the oddball driver won't accede and therefore confounds other drivers and can spark unrest.

There is also the matter of customs or generally accepted practices. Suppose a parking lot allows for whichever parking method the drivers so prefer. If most of the drivers aim to use say head-in, the contrarian driver of the back-in method is bound to generate consternation. Likewise, if most of the drivers opt to back-in, and an occasional head-in arrives, there will be a clash of cultures.

A typical refrain involves asking the rhetorical question as to why should one drive the "stupid" way that other drivers do, simply because those dolts have the majority?

Or, if you like, just because everyone else is going to jump off a cliff or leaping off the end of a pier, does that mean you need to do so too (this is a classic line amongst parents and children, in case you've never experienced it before)?

Okay, the whole topic is quite a mess, and it would seem that the heated discourse and rampant name-calling is going to continue indefinitely.

Wait for a second, maybe it won't be an ever-present dilemma. The future of cars holds that we will inevitably have self-driving cars. Perhaps that is the answer to this frightfully unresolvable but indeed solvable problem.

Here's the question to consider: *Will AI-based true self-driving cars opt to park via the head-in approach or via the back-in method?*

If we can answer that question, perhaps we'll have dealt with this matter once and for all.

Let's unpack things and see.

Self-Driving Cars And Parking Styles

For Level 4 and Level 5 true self-driving vehicles, there won't be a human driver involved in the driving task.

All occupants will be passengers.

The AI is doing the driving.

Recall that we were perched on the edge of our seats, waiting breathlessly to find out whether self-driving cars are going to be parking via the head-in method or alternatively by the use of the back-in approach.

Is this up to the divine wisdom of some disembodied AI system that perhaps has achieved super-intelligence and therefore can utterly settle this open question?

Well, actually, there isn't such a thing as super-intelligent AI, and nor is there even AI that has reached human levels of intelligence. Anyone that tries to con you otherwise is merely either confused or seeking to mislead you as to the current state of AI. AI doesn't have common-sense reasoning and nor is it sentient. Perhaps, far in the future, this might be attained, but currently do not hold your breath.

The point is that we cannot look to AI as our seer that can resolve this question about the approach to parking.

In fact, the reality is that the AI will do whatever it has been programmed to do (assuming that the system comports with its programming and otherwise is essentially bug-free, etc.).

Even the heralded use of Machine Learning (ML) does not make-or-break the answer to the parking question. If you collected a ton of data about car parking and fed that data into a Machine Learning or Deep Learning (DL) algorithm, presumably the computationally pattern matching would identify the two types of parking, though deciding which is the better would not be especially part of the pattern identification.

If the parking data came from a parking lot or set of parking lots whereby the tendency was to park via the head-in approach, the ML/DL would tend to settle on using the head-in approach, merely because it was the more prevalent one in the data utilized. Similarly, if you collected and fed data from parking lots that had mainly nose out parkers, the ML/DL would tend to opt toward the nose out method.

You could say that there isn't any right or wrong approach per se.

Here's what that means.

If a self-driving car has been programmed or "learned" to park using either of the two methods, it would presumably use the "right" method for the appropriate circumstance. A parking lot that has established a head-in only provision would therefore be abided by and the AI would park via the forward first method. Upon encountering a parking lot that stated the nose out method must be used the AI would conform accordingly.

The AI doesn't "care" which method is to be used (I've put quotes around the word "care" because it is crucial to not anthropomorphize AI and ascribe human-like emotional qualities, which regrettably many are doing and it is misleading and inappropriate).

Just as many human drivers are switch hitters when it comes to choosing the back-in versus head-in, the AI would select the method too that is suitable for the given parking lot and the parking conditions therein.

A slight wrinkle to this ambidextrous notion is that by-and-large self-driving cars are currently devised for forward-driving purposes and less so for backing up.

The sensors on a self-driving car are usually focused on whatever is in front of the vehicle and there tend to be more such devices and of a stronger caliber aimed in that direction. Some self-driving car designers believe that ultimately the vehicles used for self-driving ought to be equally versatile in going forwards and in reverse, so much that there really should no longer be a distinction and essentially the vehicle will always be going forward, no matter whether at the presumed head or tail of the car.

In short, in today's world, similar to how human drivers are seemingly less apt at driving in reverse, so too are the existing crop of self-driving cars (generally this is the case, though there are exceptions). This raises once again the overarching question as to when is the backing up activity to be best undertaken, assuming it is the weakest link of the driving task for both humans and AI.

Another factor that needs due consideration entails the driving choices of human drivers that might be driving nearby to the self-driving car. Though some dreamily think we are going to have only self-driving cars on our roadways, the reality is that for many decades we will have a mix of both human-driven cars and self-driving cars. The advent of self-driving cars won't happen overnight and nor will the approximate 250 million conventional human-driven cars disappear suddenly.

So, the twist is the facet that a self-driving car will need to make a choice about the parking method and do so amidst human drivers that are nearby.

Should the self-driving car park in the same manner that other human-driven cars are doing?

Perhaps not, if those human drivers are not conforming to whatever the parking lot or locale has stated is the appropriate method to be used. Generally, the odds are that most self-driving cars will be programmed to drive as lawfully as possible, though I've pointed out in my columns that there will need to be exceptions allowed.

If human drivers are parking via say the back-in method, and there is no overt proclamation at the parking lot about which way to park, it would make sense for the AI to opt toward using the back-in approach. This though also assumes that the AI is able to ascertain that drivers are parking in that manner.

At this time, few self-driving cars are being crafted with software that examines how other cars are parked, and therefore the AI would not have any direct means of deciding what the parking prevalence seems to be.

Overall, most of the automakers and self-driving tech firms would suggest that the parking method selection is an edge or corner case, namely that on the list of priorities it is a quite low priority. You'll find that usually the AI developers have crafted whatever they perceive as the most common approach to parking, such as the head-in, and ergo the AI is instructed or commanded to always take that approach, regardless of any other indications that might arise.

Conclusion

We can add some flair to this discussion about the parking methods by pointing out that self-driving cars will be employing V2V (vehicle-to-vehicle) electronic communications.

This is important because it allows the AI of one self-driving car to communicate with the AI of other nearby self-driving cars. For example, suppose a self-driving car comes upon debris in the roadway, it can electronically message other self-driving cars to be watchful and avoid that debris. The V2V function is going to enable all kinds of systemic acts of vehicular coordination and collaboration, which today we get only by happenstance in a human-driving world.

Here's how the V2V comes to play in the riddle of the parking methods.

A self-driving car enters into a parking lot that it has not been in before. Another self-driving car that is already in the parking lot could be contacted, via V2V, and the AI could advise the newly entering self-driving car that it makes the most sense to park head-in. That seems to settle the matter and the AI of the self-driving car seeking to park would likely use the head-in approach.

If there are only self-driving cars allowed in the parking lot, this makes life even easier. In that case, it could be that the AI of each self-driving car can choose whatever it prefers. This is so because all of the self-driving cars are going to be able to communicate with each other whenever they are backing up, regardless of how parked, and all other of the self-driving cars can adjust and plan their routing in the parking lot accordingly.

You do not necessarily need all of the self-driving cars to park in the same manner. Their ability to coordinate allows for whichever parking method happens to have been utilized by each self-driving car.

Now, you can make an argument that things would be even smoother if they did agree to use the same method, but that's a discussion for another day.

The next time you decide to park your car, give some thought to whether you are using the head-in approach or the nose out method. Look around to see what the parking lot has stipulated or ascertained if there any local ordinances that state what parking approach is to be used. Judge too what the local custom or cultural practice seems to be.

And, when you see a self-driving car enter the parking lot, keep your eye on it. Others that haven't read this column will assume that whatever the AI chooses is seemingly the irrefutably correct approach, but you can hold your head high and be as snobbish as you want, emphasizing that just because the AI did it that way, this doesn't mean that us humans have to jump off a cliff or leap off a pier.

No AI can tell us to do that.

CHAPTER 17
BARKING COMMANDS AND SELF-DRIVING CARS

The powerful impact of the spoken word.

I was in a local park the other day and someone had let their dog off its leash, allowing the frisky pooch a chance to run around wildly and relish its newfound freedom. At one point, I saw that the canine was about to dart wantonly into the street where cars were zipping along, so I yelled out to the dog and called for it to come back towards the trees and grassy area. Thankfully, the pooch heard me and scooted away from the dangers of the busy byway.

Later that same day, I was walking along on the sidewalk in my neighborhood and saw up ahead a car that was backing out of a driveway. Meanwhile, seemingly unbeknownst to the driver, a child was riding a tricycle down the sidewalk and was inevitably going to end-up directly behind the car, for which I doubted that the driver would realize, and thus there was an imminent and painful encounter about to occur. The driver's window was slightly rolled down, so I yelled out to come to a stop, and the driver did so. Thankfully, no one was hurt, and the youngster continued peddling unabated.

What do these two incidents have in common?

Sometimes the barking out of a verbal command can make a difference, a big difference, including the possibility of choosing between life and death.

Both of the incidents became non-incidents in the sense that nobody got hurt and the world kept revolving without anyone getting injured or killed. Since these non-incidents did not produce fatalities or severities, they pretty much would be considered mundane and unworthy of any news media attention. No one would ever know that the yelling out of a type of command or instruction had saved a child and likewise saved someone's beloved pooch. Just an ordinary activity that had extraordinary and joyful outcomes.

There are some noteworthy characteristics underlying these verbal commands.

First, the command or instruction had to be short and sweet, quickly getting to the point and being abundantly clear cut as to the meaning of what was spoken. This was not the time or place to provide a lengthy soliloquy or quote eloquently from Shakespeare.

The verbalization had to be done with a semblance of strength and conviction. Doing so allows the receiver of the oral indication to realize, nearly immediately, something of great importance that requires their rapt attention. Furthermore, the vocalizing has to be directed towards the subject or target, otherwise, the intended receiver might not sense that the words are aimed at them. Imagine that if I had yelled straight up into the air the resulting confusion on the part of the receivers. They would not likely have realized that my messaging was specifically for them.

An act of this kind also tends to occur in a real-time situation whereby there can be little or no delay. If I had waited to yell out my commands there was a heightened chance that the driver would not have stopped in time, and similarly, an increased chance that the dog would have entered into the street and been in the midst of grave danger.

All told, the verbalization has to happen at the right time, in the right place, aimed at the right receiver, worded in the right way, spoken in a loud and commanding tone, and proffer a succinct and actionable warning or recommended action that will prevent a pending and looming disaster from occurring.

Wow, that's a lot of stuff jammed into a brief moment of time and without any room for error or delay. And yet it seems likely that this kind of activity happens all the time, all around us, and we do not particularly give it much notice or credit. Sure, from time to time there are stories about someone that heroically saved a life by a verbalized command, but by-and-large this is an unheralded act and one that goes on daily without fanfare or limelight.

The other side of the equation about uttering such verbal commands is that the targeted receiver has to be receptive to the utterance.

Consider the instance of the driver backing up his car. Had his driver's side window not been partially open, I doubt that he would have heard my exhortation. Most cars these days have car interiors so well-built that any noise from outside of the vehicle is essentially muted. The odds are that my yelling would have been entirely rebuffed by modern-day soundproofing. I shudder to think of what would have taken place and how chilling it would be to know that my attempts to avert calamity were for not.

Of course, the receiver of the verbalization has to also be willing to listen and react to what has been stated. The driver of the car could have completely ignored my command to stop the vehicle. He might have thought that I was referring to someone else and opted to ignore what I was saying. Or, he might have heard me and understood my instruction, yet mentally calculated that stopping is perhaps not what he should do.

Believe it or not, there have been circumstances wherein someone was told to stop, and instead they slammed their foot onto the accelerator rather than the brake pedal. This use of the accelerator might be completely unintentional and was a mistaken reaction of missing the brakes and inadvertently landing on the gas pedal. Another possibility is that the driver gets scared at someone yelling stop, perhaps worried that they are going to get robbed or mugged, and deliberately decided to use the throttle to rocket away from the predicament.

Speaking of drivers, consider the future of cars and what will occur as self-driving cars gradually become prevalent on our roadways.

For true self-driving cars, there is no need for a human driver. If you've ever seen pictures or videos of true self-driving cars, it is somewhat eerie since there isn't anyone in the driver's seat.

This brings up an interesting question: *How will the advent of AI-based true self-driving cars impact the ability to bark out commands at a car in hopes of forewarning or advising a driving action in real-time?*

Let's unpack the matter and see.

Self-Driving Cars And Spoken Exhortations

For Level 4 and Level 5 true self-driving vehicles, there won't be a human driver involved in the driving task.

All occupants will be passengers.

The AI is doing the driving.

Some people seem to believe that the AI is omniscient and able to drive a car in a miraculous manner, including being able to always avoid car crashes and avert the striking of pedestrians. Perhaps this false impression about the AI is due to science fiction movies or possibly due to self-driving proponents that either exaggerate things or outright misstate what the AI can do.

In any case, please be aware that today's AI is not sentient, it lacks entirely any semblance of common-sense reasoning and otherwise is arguably closer to a monkey-see-monkey-do than it is to the full gamut of human level of intelligence. Also, it is crucial that we prevent the misleading portrayal of AI as though it does have human qualities, which can lead to a lot of confusion and adverse consequences, so all in all let's stop anthropomorphizing the existing spate of AI.

The point herein is that you cannot expect the AI of a self-driving car to always avoid running into someone or something. I've repeatedly stated in my columns that the notion of zero fatalities due to self-driving cars is malarky and has a zero chance of happening. There will still be car crashes and sadly deaths and injuries, though the hope and expectation are that it will be a lot less than the existent annual 40,000 fatalities and some 2.3 million injuries in the United States alone from car accidents.

This emphasizes that there is still room for the use of spoken commands to alert a driver when a pending endangerment is about to happen.

Were somehow magically the AI to on its own always and perfectly be able to avoid any car collisions, presumably the providing of any external warnings would not be warranted. I'm saying and declaring that those external commands are still going to be valuable and that we should not delude ourselves into thinking that the AI is all-knowing.

Recall that earlier I had mentioned that the receiver of the verbal commands has to be receptive to hearing the spoken words, else the act of yelling or providing the instruction is null and void. For the car driver that I alerted about the toddler on the tricycle, he heard me due to his window being partially rolled down and he apparently was able to hear what I exhorted.

What about AI?

You might be pondering whether the AI of the self-driving car is going to be a willing receiver of externally urged instructions. Well, similar to the case of the human driver, some key elements have to come to play for this to happen.

One crucial aspect is whether the AI will even hear a spoken command that has been urgently barked from somewhere outside of the vehicle.

Self-driving cars are typically including *internal* audio capabilities such as microphones to be able to hear the passengers that are inside the self-driving car. The AI is using contemporary Natural Language Processing (NLP) that is slightly adapted to interact with riding passengers. Currently, this NLP is extremely crude and a bit like the stilted interaction you might have with Alexa or Siri. As such this interaction is very limited and usually focused on obvious facets such as where a passenger wants to go. In the future, it is anticipated that the AI will be much more socio-conversational and be able to engage in quite extensive dialogue related to the driving task and the wishes of the passengers.

Few of the self-driving cars are outfitting the exterior of the vehicle with audio microphones.

Doing so is currently considered relatively unnecessary and an added and unneeded cost. The use of external listening is overall ranked as an edge or corner case, suggesting that it is a matter that is a low priority and might someday rise on the list of things to do. When you are knee-deep trying to get an AI driving system to simply drive from point A to point B, doing so without hitting anything, the prospects of coping with listening to the outside world offers little added value in comparison to the other meat-and-potatoes capabilities.

Some self-driving cars are adding external audio capabilities such as speakers that will allow the AI to speak at people, such as telling pedestrians to stand away from the curb or advising them to get out of the street when in the path of moving cars. Also, these audio capabilities are including microphones. The most prominent use to-date is to listen to the sounds of sirens coming from ambulances, fire trucks, police cars, and the like. As you know, human drivers are supposed to be listening for such sirens and then are supposed to pull over, though it seems that more and more human drivers are ignoring the sirens (a quite dreadful trend).

For those self-driving cars that do not yet have any external microphones, those brands and models have little chance of hearing any externally spoken commands or instructions. There are small odds that the interior microphones might pick-up an externally uttered human command, which is kind of what happened with the human driver (he was sitting inside the vehicle at the driver's seat), but this is highly unlikely and also not being programmed with any prevalence anyway.

One supposes that a passenger riding inside a self-driving car might hear a person that yells out a command that is directed at the vehicle, and then the human passenger might repeat or attempt to relay the command to the AI system. This is fraught with difficulty. The person inside the self-driving car is bound to be startled at the externally yelled instruction and therefore not be alerted to what is happening, especially since they aren't driving the car and they naturally assume there is no need to be conscious of the driving actions.

Even if the passenger hears the spoken command, there is a significant chance of a pronounced delay between them hearing it and then opting to repeat the verbal command to the AI driving system. Keep in mind too that the passenger is not sitting at the driving controls. The rider can only implore the AI about the driving act and cannot themselves directly use the driving controls. For now, the approach of having an externally exhorted command become relayed via an internal passenger is essentially untenable and relatively unlikely.

Bottom-line: *Barking commands at a self-driving car is not going to do you any good, not today, though perhaps someday in the future this feature will be provided.*

In the instance of the human driver backing out of their driveway, if the vehicle had been among the current crop of self-driving cars, I would have been better off yelling at the toddler rather than the car.

You might also have noted that when I yelled to try and stop the dog from running into the street, I opted to call out to the dog rather than the cars. Why? I could see that the cars were all moving fast, and their windows were rolled up. Trying to yell to those drivers would have been futile. My best bet was to hope that the dog would care about a human yelling at it, despite my not being the actual owner.

All of this suggests that whenever you see a self-driving car that is about to get into trouble, the odds are that you'll have better luck at proffering a verbal command to an endangered human or animal rather than to the AI of the vehicle.

That's the current state of affairs.

Conclusion

Do not lose hope.

As mentioned, there will eventually and in my opinion *inevitably* be self-driving cars that are extensively making use of external microphones and listening to the world around them. I would anticipate that all self-driving cars will ultimately leverage such technology.

There are added twists though that need to be given due consideration.

Suppose that when I yelled to the human driver to come to a stop for avoiding the toddler, I was somehow mistaken. Perhaps it would have been better for the driver to quickly accelerate and get out of the way of the oncoming toddler (this is a bit ridiculous in this instance, but you can readily envision situations whereby the verbal command is askew of what needs to be done).

If an AI driving system hears a spoken command, should the AI obediently abide by the command?

Your initial answer might be that yes, the AI ought to always obey humans. Period, end of the story. But this belies the chances of a human that has unintentionally provided an incorrect command. Or perhaps the human is being dastardly and purposely wants the AI to drive adversely or do some other devilish act.

I believe we would all reasonably agree that we expect the AI to assess the given command, even when a command has been expressed directly by a human being. The possible downsides are just too high and risky to not evaluate whatever might perchance be spoken. We certainly expect a human driver to do so, such as the driver backing down the driveway.

I am assuming that he momentarily thought about my exhortation and then decided it made sense to come to a sudden stop. Indeed, no matter what I might have said, we generally would all concur that the driver had the final say in the matter and would be held responsible for the driving actions undertaken.

Assuming you concur that the AI would need to first assess any spoken command, you have now taken a turn into an abyss or morass. This opens a veritable can of worms.

When should the AI unquestioningly do what it is told versus possibly countermanding or ignoring a human uttered instruction?

Can we actually hold the AI responsible for the driving of the car, as though it is the legal or moral equivalent of a person responsible for the act of driving?

And so on.

One of the most fascinating aspects about self-driving cars is not merely the mobility that can be had via the use of AI driving systems, and thus no longer needing to have a human as a driver and enabling a mobility-for-all future, but this also brings up extremely important questions about AI and ethical considerations.

We might ask overall questions about AI that is being used for deciding on the granting of home loans or the AI that helps you to figure out how to invest your money, though those matters are not especially life-or-death per se. The AI for self-driving cars is in fact about life-or-death. We already know that every time a human gets behind the wheel of a car, the human is entrusted with life-or-death choices, for themselves and other nearby drivers and pedestrians. The same absolutely happens when we let AI autonomously drive a car.

Besides the excitement and delightfulness of seeing self-driving cars on our roadways, we also need to somberly consider how the AI is doing the driving and how it will be making life-or-death choices. That's a routine part of driving, yet the repercussions are far from routine.

Let's keep the AI from barking up the wrong tree, doing so by all of us listening to each other about how to best devise AI for self-driving cars.

That's verbal command or instruction that we can all live with.

CHAPTER 18
HOW AM I DRIVING AND SELF-DRIVING CARS

Sometimes bumper stickers are particularly helpful.

While out driving, you are bound to see vehicles that have the legendary "How Am I Driving?" bumper sticker that silently signals the possibility of reporting on a lousy driver. If you witness a vehicle with such a bumper sticker and it perchance cuts you off or seems to be speeding excessively, you can readily call the presented toll-free number to report on the driving transgression.

The bumper sticker is used by fleet operators that want to know how their drivers are doing and thus those owners relish the notion of getting timely feedback about their employed driving personnel. In theory, a member of the general public that spots one of their drivers going astray is in sense providing some "good news" for the firm.

How so?

The fleet owner can try to find out what is happening with that driver and hopefully forestall something even worse that might ultimately be undertaken by that designated driver. Knowing that a driver is weaving on the roads or acting callously is presumed to be a precursor to the chances of that driver causing a major accident and potentially triggering severe injuries and outright fatalities.

You could say that asking the public to tattle on their drivers is using a free resource to keep tabs on their employees and contractors. It's not as though the company paid people to be on the watch for their drivers and any foul driving behaviors. Instead, using a bumper sticker is intended to get a free watchdog, that's us all, for which the guardian is spurred simply by a kind of altruistic belief that amiss drivers ought to get what's coming to them, including being possibly taken off the roadways as a means of making us all that much safer.

Just by spending a few cents on a bumper sticker, the fleet operator is cheaply able to (essentially) sign-up an entire workforce of deputized sheriffs, serving on a widespread basis across all freeways, highways, and byways. Our eyes are locked and loaded, keenly on the look for those deficient drivers.

Of course, there is potentially a lot more cost involved to implement the driving tattling capability. A firm presumably has to set up the phone operators that will receive the calls. Those phone agents are expected to take down the info about the reported transgression. Next, the info so collected has to be analyzed by someone in the firm that needs to winnow the wheat from the chaff, as it were. Finally, communication to the manager or supervisor has to be undertaken and then a conferring with the alleged shoddy driver has to occur.

One can have doubts that all of those series of activities is really going to take place.

Maybe the bumper sticker is fakery. It is perhaps being used to suggest that the fleet is being driven by drivers that will be fearful of getting reported and therefore they will drive more carefully, merely due to the perceived threat involved. We all know how messed-up most companies are in terms of following procedures and doing paperwork, thus it is easy to naturally assume that the odds of your reporting a driver and having anything come from it is nearly nil.

Setting aside that cynical viewpoint, and certainly noting that there are firms that do not properly implement these matters, nonetheless, the bulk of those bumper sticker campaigns are given relatively serious import. Some firms are extremely quick to follow-up and do so not only because of wanting to prevent a driver from possibly wreaking havoc, but also due to the potential legal consequences that they were alerted about a driver and yet did nothing concrete and could be especially vulnerable for having skirted their presumed duty.

Oddly enough, a few firms do not adopt a bumper sticker program since they think it does make them more exposed. Generally, this seems like unwise thinking and it would be better to be proactive and implement a sound program to shore-up what they are wishing to do. A head-in-the-sand approach is not going to go over well when their drivers get embroiled in driving catastrophes.

Some companies tout the fact that they make use of a bumper sticker campaign.

They want you to know that they care about how their drivers are driving. The leadership at such a firm is aiming to get a two-for-one out of such a program. There is the fervent desire to detect and catch their drivers before disaster strikes, plus the brownie points with the general public and potential customers of their products. One can reasonably argue that the bumper stickers are reflective of a company that cares about what they do. Do not underplay the public relations enhancer that a bumper sticker approach can provide.

You might be wondering as to what do the company drivers think of those bumper stickers.

Generally, there are two main types of reaction to the bumper sticker being on their vehicle.

First, there are those drivers that consider themselves good drivers, and therefore the bumper sticker is pretty much a non-issue for them. They believe in their heart of hearts that there will never be a need for anyone to tattle on their driving. For them, always driving as courteous drivers and being adroitly civil in their driving behaviors is a reflexive habit, and the bumper sticker is ostensibly irrelevant to them.

Meanwhile, they tend to like the idea that other of their fellow drivers that are crummy drivers are going to get ensnared and drummed out via the use of the bumper sticker process. Look at it this way. You are a driver for a company and pride yourself on your driving prowess. Some fellow drivers don't give a hoot and drive wantonly. This will likely reflect poorly on all other drivers of that company. The proverbial bad apple spoils the barrel. You do not want to be cast into the same adverse light and ardently want those shabby drivers to be spotted and expelled.

Secondly, in terms of company driver reactions, there are those company drivers that despise the bumper stickers.

In their minds, those bumper stickers are a nuisance and wrongheaded. Why ask the average amateur driver to rate or tattle on the driving of a professional driver that makes a living doing the driving? It doesn't make any sense. Furthermore, those tattletales are likely to be idiots that just want to get a driver in trouble for no viable reason. Going a few miles per hour over the speed limit ought not to be a basis for calling out a driver, and likewise, an occasional maneuver that seems untoward ought not to be treated as a crime of the century.

This does bring up another facet of these bumper sticker efforts, namely the misuse and false reporting that sometimes happens.

Someone calls the toll-free number and reports on a driver. We do not know that the reporting is true and accurate. Maybe the person tattling is having a bad day and wants to share the badness with others including the innocent driver that is being busted unfairly. Perhaps the person calling out a driver is a believer in strictly driving by the book and will report on any minutiae that are not especially pertinent to the proper act of driving.

The company drivers that are doing a good job are of course hopeful that those kinds of inept reports will be weaned out by the firm and not cause undue trouble. But there is always the chance that a reported transgression could create a huge hassle for a driver that did not do what was alleged and that otherwise has a stellar driving record.

Some tattletales are quite oddballs and report on matters that have nothing to do with a driver at all. I don't like the colors of the signs on your company vehicles or I don't like the products that you sell, those are the types of outside-of-scope that some use the toll-free number to relate to the company. Assuming that those calls are without any merit, this unnecessarily increases the costs to the firm, since it means that there is more consumption of the labor time for the phone agents and the managers to deal with the absurd riffraff reporting.

All told, the bumper stickers are overall a good approach though there is a bona fide cost-benefit analysis needed as to whether any given company that operates a fleet of drivers will find it worthwhile to implement such a program. If the reporting ends-up with only a rare needle in a haystack, there is a serious question as to whether the costs to set up and continue the effort are worthwhile. Some firms even assert that by spending that same money toward picking better drivers, they can avert the bumper sticker after-the-fact usage altogether (this is somewhat argumentative, and legitimate counterarguments can be made).

Shifting gears, it is important to note that we are gradually heading toward an era of self-driving cars. In the case of true self-driving cars and true self-driving trucks, there isn't a human driver involved in the act of driving the vehicle.

This brings up an interesting question: *Are the use of bumper stickers for how one is driving inextricably a bygone anachronism that will no longer be needed for the advent of AI-based true self-driving cars?*

Let's unpack the matter and see.

Self-Driving Cars And Tattletale Bumper Stickers

For Level 4 and Level 5 true self-driving vehicles, there won't be a human driver involved in the driving task.

All occupants will be passengers.

The AI is doing the driving.

Up until recently, the public roadway tryouts of self-driving cars were being run with a human back-up driver, also referred to as the safety driver, and for which the human is supposed to take over the driving if the AI appears unable to handle a vexing situation.

The assumption has been that there would be no need for anyone in the general public to report on such a self-driving car since there was already a human operator on-board and they would presumably ensure that the self-driving car didn't do anything untoward. Even if the self-driving car did do something amiss, the human operator would report this to the company as valuable feedback for the AI developers devising the driving system.

The logic there is not impeccable.

Suppose the human back-up driver was not able to catch the self-driving car in time to prevent an undesired driving action. In theory, the human back-up driver will tattle on the AI and tattle on themselves (in terms of not having caught the AI sufficiently). We don't know that this would occur, and it is possible that the human back-up driver might not be so willing to make such a report.

You could try to argue that the sensory data being collected by the self-driving car could readily be inspected by the company and therefore easily catch that the back-up driver wasn't doing their duty. Yes, this notion has validity, but it also presumes a lot of related actions that have to be undertaken. Are the AI developers sufficiently monitoring the collected data? Are there automated tools that are also examining the collected roadway data to try and discern issues? And so on.

In short, some argue that the self-driving cars on our roadways that are in the midst of this grand experiment ought to be required to have bumper stickers that indicate how to contact the company if you witness something that you believe was an unseemly driving action.

Not many of the self-driving cars have those bumper stickers. The assumption is that you'll obviously know which company is responsible for the self-driving car, since they usually plaster their brand name all over the vehicle, and you can simply try calling the overall 800-number of that self-driving related firm.

Turns out this default approach is not a seamless means to do such reporting. First, you need to figure out what the 800-number is.

Usually, there isn't a specialized or dedicated 800-number for that purpose and thusly you would call their generic or overarching 800-number. By using their generic 800-number you are not being immediately shunted to the specific aspects underlying a roadway reporting issue (though, some do use a calling tree that allows you to select a number to be so directly routed).

Usually, a bumper sticker indicates the exact number to call for the sole purpose of reporting a roadway issue, rather than providing a bland 800-number that is used for anyone that might want to reach the firm for any purpose whatsoever. And, the phone number is right there, immediately before your eyes, rather than you have to do online research to figure out the number to be called. That extra step is likely to discourage most people from hassling about making such a call.

Another aspect of the bumper stickers is that they oftentimes showcase a unique identifier. This allows you to report the vehicle and do so by mentioning the identifier. Without any kind of identifier, you would need to explain where you witnessed the transgression, and hopefully, the company can tie together the reported location and timing with the records they have about where their numerous vehicles are riding around town.

Some of the self-driving related firms offer that you can email them if you want to report a driving transgression. This seems like a nice touch, but the reality can be less inspiring. The act of sending an email requires you to compose your message. It might or might not have the right level of details and thus could be useful or useless. Once you send the email, assuming you went to the trouble to do so, the response is either nothing at all and thus you don't know whether your email went anywhere, or you get a canned response that states they are appreciative of your feedback and have a good day. This can leave you feeling hollow and unsure that the email will ever see the light of day.

One argument by some self-driving related firms is that the general public would inundate them with crazy stuff if there were bumper stickers on their vehicles. People would call and ask questions about self-driving technology. Or people might claim that the sensors mounted on the top of the car are beaming messages to outer space and informing alien beings about our presence here on Earth. And so on.

Admittedly, there would likely be a lot more calls being made to a number listed on a self-driving vehicle versus a human-driven one. We take it for granted that human drivers are human, and we do not report them unless we likely see something quite egregious. On the other hand, for an AI driving system, the public would possibly report any of the tiniest transgressions, plus would offer a tsunami of unwarranted commentary and quackery beyond the act of driving.

For those self-driving car companies that are using the bumper sticker approach, thanks for doing so, and hopefully the results are helpful. It would be interesting to find out how many such reports are being provided and how many are relevant and sensible, though this is not currently a statutory reporting requirement per se and therefore there is no compelling reason to do so.

Once we seem to get past this experimental stage of self-driving cars, the question arises as to whether or not the bumper sticker approach would still be useful. The most apparent answer is yes, the bumper stickers would still be useful, and indeed perhaps even more so.

Why is that?

During this experimental stage, the firms are presumably being extra attentive to their self-driving cars. Once there are thousands upon thousands of self-driving cars on our roadways, there is some doubt that the same kind of extraordinary care and scrutiny will be taking place. You could argue that the bumper stickers will hence be vital for acting as a means to ascertain when self-driving cars are not performing well.

A counterargument is that self-driving cars should not be on the roadways if they aren't "perfect" in their driving actions. Via that logic, there won't be any self-driving cars on the roads that would need bumper stickers, since all of the self-driving cars on the byways will be perfect and any imperfect ones will not be on the streets.

Sorry, that logic won't hunt, as they say.

Self-driving cars are not going to be perfect drivers. There are still going to be driving transgressions. There also is going to be a mixture of self-driving cars and human-driven cars are a long time to come, especially given that there are about 250 million conventional human-driven cars today in the United States alone and those are not going to disappear overnight due to the emergence of self-driving cars.

I've also exhorted that one facet of self-driving cars that still need to be figured out involves the so-called *near-miss factor*. All in all, if you sincerely believe that self-driving cars do not need a bumper sticker because they will never drive inappropriately, you are either delusional about the matter or have fallen hook-and-sinker for quite a line.

Conclusion

The bumper sticker topic invariably is one that invites diametrically opposed viewpoints.

Some contend that putting bumper stickers of this kind onto self-driving cars would be unnecessary and counterproductive, undermining the advent of this breathtaking and moonshot innovation. Others believe that it is a necessity, and we ought to not let the AI off-the-hook while meanwhile keeping human feet to the fire, as it were.

A final thought.

Though AI is not sentient as yet and not anywhere near reaching the level of human intelligence, do you think that if AI does one day become comparable to human capacities that it would want to have a bumper sticker or not have one on the AI-driven self-driving cars?

Probably it would want the bumper stickers, since doing so would presumably showcase how much better the AI is at driving than humans and there would be the usual stream of calls about human drivers and nary a call about the AI driving systems.

Or so the AI might vainly hope:

CHAPTER 19
NO PARKING IN RED AND SELF-DRIVING CARS

You are giving a friend a lift in your car and as you approach their desired drop-off there is no apparent place to idle or park to allow them a convenient exodus from your vehicle. So, you decide to come to a brief halt at a curbside that is painted red.

Is that a right or wrong action?

More importantly, perhaps, is this a legal act or an illegal act?

In your mind, even though you acknowledge that a red zone is not to be used for this purpose (well, depending upon the state and local jurisdiction), you nonetheless feel fine about doing so since it will be only a momentary stoppage, plus you are still actively at the wheel of the car and the engine is running.

No big deal, you convince yourself, and furthermore, there are tons of people that do the same thing all the time.

In California, the official vehicle code law says this about curbs painted red: "Red indicates no stopping, standing, or parking, whether the vehicle is attended or unattended, except that a bus may stop in a red zone marked or signposted as a bus loading zone."

This seems to clearly answer the question concerning whether momentarily coming to a stop at the red curb is legal or illegal, whereby it is ostensibly illegal unless somehow you want to claim that your car is a bus (good luck on that one!). Imagine telling a judge that since you were dropping off a passenger, your car counts as being a bus and therefore you were perfectly legit in your actions. Probably this is why judges contend they have heard it all.

In any case, the law in California is seemingly and abundantly clear cut and for which you cannot stop, you cannot come to a halt or be at a standing, and nor can you park in a red zone. I realize that you are likely immediately imploring that you see people do this all the time. As such, the law is presumably stupid, ill-advised, and the will of the people seems to have decided it is not worth observing. This is reminiscent of your parents that probably used to say that just because someone else jumps off a cliff or leaps off the end of a pier it does not mean that you should do so too.

People that tend to use those red curbs are apt to claim innocence.

Your honor, I knew that you couldn't leave your car parked there while unattended, but I had absolutely no idea that it was also illegal to be inside the car and parked there. How might this plea go over? If the judge got up on the right side of the bed that morning, perhaps you'll be granted leniency. On the other hand, you might hear the famous refrain that ignorance of the law is not an excuse. Perhaps the judge will throw the book at you for your lack of driving rules awareness.

Yet another trick is to argue that the red curb was not a red curb, or that at least the red paint is so faded and chipped that it was not obviously apparent that it was a red curb. Maybe you might try too to exhort that you are colorblind and therefore the red looks to you like it isn't there are all. Akin to a magician, this is the proverbial rabbit-in-the-hat ploy of trying to convince the judge that the curb wasn't red or that nothing in this world is really red (a lofty philosophical argument).

Here's a particularly vexing curb-related case in California that especially catches the eye.

A woman parked her car in a spot wherein the curb was definitely not red. The authorities agree that she parked in a location consisting of a non-painted curb. While her car was parked there, the city came along and painted the curb red. Pictures of the car now parked in the newly painted red zone showcase that the red paint on the curb skirts around the point of her tires that were just touching the curb. There seems little dispute that the red was painted *after* she had earlier parked her car there.

Do you think she should get a ticket?

She did.

This seems egregiously unfounded, though the authorities allegedly stated that she got the ticket for being parked in that one spot for too lengthy of a time period and not due to being parked in the red. She meanwhile asserts that the ticket states that she was ticketed for parking in the red. It's all a mess.

For those that fervently believe in the red curb, they always make sure to never park, stand, or stop at a red curb. Never ever. Furthermore, those ardently faithful to the red zone are apt to indicate that scofflaws and those violating miscreants ought to get whatever is coming to them (maybe a hanging or the electric chair?).

I know one driver that recently looked in disgust at a car that was momentarily stopped at a red curb, which seemed to be only doing so to disgorge a passenger that needed extra help and could not otherwise walk a greater distance. The observing driver of the red curb stationed car spoke aloud that this was an illegal action and he frantically looked around to spot a cop that might rush to issue a ticket.

Upon not seeing any nearby police, the next comment was that perhaps it might be useful to position his car to block the vehicle that was sitting at the red curb. The logic seemed to be that this would elongate the time of the illegal procedure and give a greater chance of a ticket giver to come along. But, in the end, it became just another example to this person of how far gone we are in terms of obeying the law, allowing lawlessness to exist.

In this viewpoint, the red curb facet is a microcosm of a bigger societal problem. Letting red curb lawbreakers get away with this illegal act is tantamount to having a snowball that is rolling down a hill and becoming larger and larger as it does so. If people can commit the crime of misusing a red curb then they are bound to ultimately commit more heinous digressions.

Okay, so some people look at a red curb as simply a suggestion about what to do, while others see it as a highly visible and readily apparent indication about the exactitude of the law and a need for us all to stridently abide by our laws (or perish otherwise).

What is your viewpoint about red curbs?

Always obey? Sometimes obey? Ignore the red and do as you wish? Find a means to catch and punish all those that transgress the red? There are a dizzying variety of perspectives about those red curbs.

In thinking about the future, one aspect that comes to mind is that we will eventually and inevitably have true self-driving cars on our roadways.

This brings up an interesting question: *Will the advent of AI-based true self-driving cars imply that there will never be a violation of a red curb again, namely due to the AI aiming to always be fully legally compliant with the driving laws?*

Let's unpack the matter and see.

Self-Driving Cars And Those Red Curbs

For Level 4 and Level 5 true self-driving vehicles, there won't be a human driver involved in the driving task.

All occupants will be passengers.

The AI is doing the driving.

Some believe that the advent of AI-based driving systems means that we will have strictly legal-oriented drivers from now on. No more running of stop signs. No more zipping through red lights. No more speeding above the posted speed limit.

No more parking, standing, or stopping at a red curb.

End of story.

Maybe, maybe not.

First, keep in mind that the AI is going to presumably do whatever it has been programmed to do. In that manner, if indeed the AI developers programmed the AI to not break the law, in theory, that is what will happen. Of course, like any programming, there are potentially embedded errors or omissions and we do not know for an absolute certainty that this legally minded logic will be fully embedded and observed.

Notice that I am not suggesting that the AI is somehow sentient and will change its mind. Contrary to what you might have heard or seen on the news, there isn't any AI yet today that is sentient, and we aren't close to getting there. There isn't any AI that has common-sense reasoning and nor AI that can be said to approach the full gamut of human intelligence.

Thus, do not worry that the AI has a mind of its own and will do whatever it wants. There is no mind in the AI per se, at least not yet.

The AI can nonetheless go astray, due to errors in the code or other problems that can arise. These anomalies are not mindful ones. They are aspects that arise due to the complexity inherent in millions upon millions of lines of coding.

There is another path for the AI to opt toward illegal driving activities such as parking or idling at a red curb.

Via the use of Machine Learning (ML) and Deep Learning (DL), much of what the AI driving system is doing can at times be based on the computational patterns that it has gleaned over time. By providing lots of driving examples to the AI system, it can attempt to identify patterns of driving and then presumably seek to drive as based on those found patterns.

Here's the rub.

Suppose that the driving data consists of the efforts of human drivers and their driving actions. In a large trove of such driving-related data, there are bound to be indications of some that have opted to park or stand at a red curb. Envision that the AI finds this pattern and therefore assumes that this is an allowed driving action.

Those that are developing and testing the self-driving car might not be able to discern that the AI has a deeply embedded calculation that includes being allowed to stand or park at a red curb. The odds are that the everyday use of a self-driving car during this experimental stage of being on our roadways might not by happenstance cause the AI to park at a red curb. It could be that this golden nugget, as it were, sits deep inside the arcane AI artificial neural network and has yet to be invoked.

At some point in time, the AI might come across that embedded aspect and then choose to stand or park at a red curb. If so, would there be anyone around to tattle on the self-driving car? Would the fleet deploying the self-driving car realize this has happened?

Also, suppose that in one jurisdiction you can legally make use of a red curb for standing, as long as the vehicle is considered as being attended. Does the AI driving system count as being the attending driver? Presumably, yes, since the AI is doing the driving. On the other hand, the AI is not the same as a human, in that a human does more than simply the act of driving, and perhaps the gist of having the car be considered attended is because we expect the driver to be all-around aware of what is going on.

You might be tempted to suggest that the AI developers ought to be able to inspect their AI code and ascertain whether it has all of the properly coded legal driving rules. This is a problematic concern with the use of Machine Learning and Deep Learning.

For ML/DL, usually, the computational morass that embeds the foundations of the driving task is not readily explainable. Think of this as a bunch of numbers, piled on top of each other, out of which there is no easy way to grasp what it portends in any symbolic or logical semblance. Known commonly as the interpretability or explainability problem, there is extensive research going on to try and craft XAI, explainable AI.

What About Passengers Wants

Slightly shifting gears, consider the role of human passengers whilst inside a self-driving car.

A self-driving car is providing you with a lift to your office. Turns out there is a red painted curb directly in front of the main office entryway. Further down the street is an unpainted curb. Today there is a horrific storm and the rain is coming down in buckets. You don't have an umbrella with you.

When the self-driving car nears your destination, you speak to the AI.

As a side note, the expectation is that self-driving cars will be making use of Natural Language Processing (NLP). Similar to an Alex or Siri, the AI of the self-driving car will talk with you. You might tell the AI that you want to have the self-driving car swing through a Starbucks on the way to work so that you can get a cup of java. Some of the automakers and self-driving tech firms have been making a false assumption that there won't be much if any interaction between the AI and the passengers.

This falsehood is based on the narrow thinking that all you will do is get into a self-driving car and it will take you to your designated destination. This belies the reality of how we ride in cars and there is oftentimes a significant amount of interaction between the passenger and the human driver about driving-related matters.

In any case, back to our story about going to work on a rainy day. You tell the AI that it should drop you off directly in front of your office, which you wish to do because it is rainy and you don't want to get wet by being dropped off further down the street.

Will the AI be able to detect that the curb is red?

If it detects that the curb is red, will it determine that this is not a legally proper place to stand or park?

And, if it does all those things, what should it do about human passenger instruction?

You might wish to argue that the AI ought to do whatever the human passenger has told the AI to do. We should presumably expect that the AI will be obedient to humans. Imagine a world gone amuck if the AI won't do what humans tell it to do.

Turn out there is a slippery slope involved.

Consider the use case of a human that tells the AI to go faster than the speed limit because the person is late for work and wants to try and get to the office as soon as possible. Should the AI proceed to drive faster than the speed limit?

Worse still, imagine the use case of a human that tells the AI to run over someone. Should the AI proceed to run over a human being? Your reaction in this use case is that there is never a basis for running over a human and therefore this is obviously a verboten command.

The point of those examples is that the AI presumably should not abide by the requests or commands of human passengers without some kind of consideration about the bonafide nature of those indications. Unfortunately, trying to make decisions about those human commands is a lot harder than you think it is, and for which (as mentioned earlier) there isn't AI that has any common-sense reasoning or sentience to engage in a mindful dialogue on such topics.

For now, the answer by the automakers and the self-driving tech firms is that if a passenger wants to do something beyond the norm, the AI or the passenger will invoke a kind of OnStar-like feature that connects the rider to a fleet operator. The agent answering the connection will seemingly engage in a discussion and then potentially use a remote means to give guidance to the AI driving system.

That seems like a nifty solution, but it is not especially eloquent and at times altogether impractical.

The timing of the need of the passenger might not allow for the making of the connection and dialogue over what is to be done. Also, the remote agent might not have the capability to direct the AI driving system in the manner that the passenger hopes (plus, there are concerns about security and other facets of using a wide array of remote commands on an AI driving system). There also might not be a viable communications connection possible between the vehicle and the remote agent. And so on.

Conclusion

It might seem surprising that something as simple as coming up to a red curb could become an entire entanglement about the nature of AI and the role of self-driving cars.

We have a natural tendency to take for granted the capacity of humans to drive a car. On the surface, all that driving seems to require is the ability to press on the gas pedal or the brakes, and merely steer the wheel of the car. The reality is that there is a lot more that goes on in our minds and that ultimately drives the driving actions that we take while driving.

The next time you come up to a red curb, consider carefully what you will do.

Maybe even ask yourself, what would the AI do?

CHAPTER 20
TAILGATING AND FULL SELF-DRIVING

Let's talk about those obnoxious people that insist on driving their car as though it is an extension of the rear bumper of your car.

Those irksome tailgaters come within inches of the back of your vehicle and sit there, seemingly oblivious to the fact that they are dangerously close to your car. When this happens while on the freeway, zipping along at speeds exceeding 60 miles per hour, the odds are that those idiot drivers will not have sufficient reaction time if you have to suddenly jam on your brakes.

Some of these tailgating drivers seem to think that being on your bumper is no big deal. They do not calculate stopping distances and nor do they take into account the problems associated with driving that close to another car. For them, they are just intent on proceeding forward and are frustratedly blocked by your existence ahead of them.

Some tailgaters will try to get you to move out of the way. This might involve them flashing their headlights at you, doing so in hopes that you'll realize they want you to skedaddle. Horn honking is another favored pastime. By-and-large, they usually simply use the menacing appearance of them being in your rearview mirror and having that charging bull look about them.

Justification by tailgaters is pretty commonly expressed.

They will contend that the car ahead of them is moving too slowly. Of course, the speed-related question is a relative one. The car ahead of them might be doing the speed limit, lawfully proceeding, and yet that is insufficient for the needs of the tailgater. In their minds, no matter what speed you are going is either incorrect or not enough. The point is that anytime any car perchance is blocking the pace of another vehicle, by gosh that driver ought to expeditiously open the lane and stop bottlenecking things.

Admittedly, there are those knucklehead bottleneck drivers that are going well below the speed limit and think they own the road. In their view, it doesn't matter what speed they wish to drive at. Their viewpoint is that we should all proceed in an orderly fashion. First come, first serve, as it were. If they happen to be in front of you and want to go at a pittance of a speed, that's their right, and you should just bide your time and be properly patient to let them drive as they desire.

Sometimes the bottleneck driver does not realize they are indeed serving as a bottleneck. They are oblivious to anything happening behind their vehicle. The use of their rearview mirror is a rarity and they believe exclusively in looking ahead, not glancing backward. In that case, there are occasions wherein an entire parade of cars ends-up behind this myopic kind of driver. They don't care and they don't know what they doing to the flow of traffic.

Back to the tailgater and their view of the world, despite whatever transgression the up-ahead driver might be doing, whether purposely going too slowly or unintentionally holding things up, being glued to the bumper of another car is not warranted. Doing so is reckless. The tailgater is endangering themselves and anyone else in their vehicle. The tailgater is endangering the up-ahead driver and any passengers in their vehicle. The tailgater is undoubtedly endangering the cars next to them in adjacent lanes and likewise any stream of cars behind them.

The tailgater is apt to roll their eyes and complain that it is the up-ahead plodding driver that holds this grave responsibility and not the tailgater. That's typically a false assertion. Though there is certainly a potential for the up-ahead driver to be in the wrong, it would seem that much of the time the tailgater is the primary transgressor and the up-ahead driver is simply obeying the law. Sure, traveling at just the speed limit or going slower due to driving conditions can be irksome for tailgaters, but this valid form of driving is not justification for playing the dicey tailgating game.

For those that find themselves upset with tailgaters, they vehemently lament that there ought to be laws about such driving actions.

States indeed usually have a specific legal rule or regulation about the act of adverse tailgating. For example, here in California, the official vehicle code under section 21703 says this: "The driver of a motor vehicle shall not follow another vehicle more closely than is reasonable and prudent, having due regard for the speed of such vehicle and the traffic upon, and the condition of, the roadway."

Notice that the law does not explicitly declare what distance you should observe when behind another car. There is the old line that you ought to be at least one car length behind another vehicle for every ten miles per hour of speed. That is a handy and easily remembered rule-of-thumb, but it does not guarantee any semblance of safety.

The distance to remain behind another car is considered a judgment or driver choice, stipulated as the need to exercise reasonable and prudent care. As added clarification, the law provides a contextual indication that the otherwise amorphous notion of being reasonable and prudent encompasses the particulars of the speed, traffic, and roadway conditions at the time of the driving effort.

You might be wondering why isn't the tailgating rule more specific?

The answer is that every driving situation is different and requires using mindful reasoning about what distance you ought to follow.

Suppose the road is a weaving mountainous path and there has been a heavy drop of snow. You could presumably be tailgating even if utilizing the popular rule of the one car length per ten miles per hour. Another example would be driving on a crowded freeway in rainy weather. On and on we go, having to consider a slew of factors to arrive at what might be a proper distance to avert being a tailgater.

Having a law to go after tailgaters is essential and yet it doesn't necessarily stop the adamant tailgating driver. The odds of a tailgater getting caught doing a tailgating action is generally low. Unless we had the highway patrol or traffic police continually cruising to spot the tailgaters, most tailgaters figure they are free and clear to do their tailgating.

Sadly, many fatal car accidents can be traced to tailgating, regrettably an outcome that is akin to having already let the horse out of the barn.

To some degree, in any practical sense, the driver that is being tailgated has to be on the alert about tailgaters and opt to deal with the situation, rather than relying upon the tailgater to do what is right. Yes, this seems backward and shifts the duty from the party that appears to be in the wrong to the innocent, but that's the reality of daily driving.

What can the driver that is being tailgated do?

First, the driver should be aware of the potential for being tailgated. By watching the traffic behind you, it is oftentimes possible to anticipate those upcoming cars that might end-up trying to tailgate you. Any cars doing ninety miles per hour and fast approaching are unlikely to slow down and won't magically remain at a safe distance.

Second, the driver that might get tailgated has to detect that tailgating is about to occur or is actually underway. If you don't know that you are being tailgated there is little chance to do something about it.

Third, the driver that is being tailgated can take various actions, some that are reasonable and prudent, while other actions that are brash and perilous. The circumstances will dictate what is sensible and what might be treacherous. For example, tapping your brakes is a common ploy, attempting to signal to the tailgater that you want them to desist. Unfortunately, the mere act of tapping the brakes might not be enough to inform the tailgater, or worse still the tailgater gets angry and decides they will ride even closer to your bumper.

The actions of the tailgated driver can spark the tailgater into avid road rage. Again, it is unfair to point a finger at the tailgated driver, but that's the real-world of driving. The tailgater might in their mind become obsessed with trying to target the car being tailgated. Even if the tailgated car moves over, the tailgater might choose to follow that vehicle, persistently tailgating, in some oddball viewpoint that they are garnering revenge or somehow morally "teaching" the tailgated car a useful lesson.

Shifting gears, in the future, we will have a prevalence of self-driving cars that are not being driven by humans and instead by AI-based driving systems.

This brings up an interesting question: *Will the advent of AI-based true self-driving cars obviate any further tailgating or might tailgating still exist?*

Let's unpack the matter and see.

Self-Driving Cars And Being Tailgated

For Level 4 and Level 5 true self-driving vehicles, there won't be a human driver involved in the driving task.

All occupants will be passengers.

The AI is doing the driving.

If we had only AI-based self-driving cars on our roadways, the act of tailgating could be resolved. The AI systems of the self-driving cars could communicate with each other, using V2V (vehicle-to-vehicle) electronic communications, and coordinate their driving actions. They would be able to assess the driving conditions such as the weather, the roadway status, the amount of traffic, and ascertain what distances are safest to observe.

In theory, AI systems could optimize the distances involved. This means that the distance between cars would be the best or optimal for the given setting or conditions. Despite the seeming idealistic nature of this arrangement, there are still probabilistic facets to be considered. For example, suppose one of the self-driving cars that are involved in this collaboration suddenly has a tire blowout. Did the distance calculations assume that there are no chances of such a calamity, or did it anticipate this possibility and determine the distances accordingly?

The point is that we have a tendency to envision a Utopian world of all self-driving cars and yet this might not be especially practical and realizable.

Speaking of which, you might as well get out of your head the idea that we would have only self-driving cars on our roadway. In the United States alone, there are 250 million conventional cars, and they are not going to disappear overnight. Furthermore, there is still the open question of whether human-driving will be somehow abolished, for which some people insist you will never take away their driving (only once you pry their cold dead hands from the steering wheel).

Discussions about having only self-driving cars on the roadways are usually confined to where this might be feasible to achieve. A given locale might declare that in their downtown district the only cars allowed will be self-driving cars. Another avenue is the proposed approach of having dedicated freeway lanes that are for self-driving cars only. None of those proposals entail a widespread and across the board environment exclusively for self-driving cars.

Alright, now that we've popped the bubble about the notion of solving the tailgating issue by only allowing self-driving cars on our roadways, this means that tailgating is going to continue for quite a time to come.

We can reasonably assume that the self-driving cars won't be doing the tailgating (at least not by choice, as will be explained momentarily). Presumably, the AI systems will be programmed to avoid doing any tailgating. The automakers and self-driving tech firms are striving to have the AI be the kind of reasonable and prudent driver that is envisioned by the laws.

This is a tricky proposition.

Here's why.

A self-driving car is driving along on the freeway. It is maintaining a proper distance from the car ahead of it. Without any forewarning, a car in the adjacent lane hops into the gap between the self-driving car and the car it is trailing behind. This immediately causes the self-driving car to ostensibly be labeled as a tailgater. Though it wasn't the fault of the AI driving system, nonetheless the self-driving car is now at a shortened distance and now considered tailgating.

What should the self-driving car do?

I'm sure your immediate thought is that the self-driving car needs to quickly adjust to make-up for the momentary tailgating action. A human driver might do so, slowing down to allow for a greater gap or possibly opting to switch lanes to prevent from being too close to the interloper. We would certainly expect any AI worth its salt to do the same.

If you think about this for a second or two, you'll realize that this reaction to avoid remaining in a tailgating posture is going to have a decidedly pronounced rippling effect. Right now, when a human driver slows down or makes a lane change, we don't especially witness how this impacts all the other nearby traffic. Imagine that there were self-driving cars commonly on our roadways, and you then can envision the cascading effects of what will happen.

The disruption by that human interloper will cause the immediately impacted self-driving car to take avoidance action. Once the self-driving car does so, the odds are that other self-driving cars nearby will also then react. That's one form of cascading. Meanwhile, the interspersed human drivers will also be reacting, doing so in response to the cascading of the self-driving car's movements. The whole thing becomes like a set of dominos that were set into motion by one tiny shove.

You could try to argue that this same thing happens today. Yes, human drivers do this same kind of responsive driving, but not to the magnitude and consistency that the AI driving systems will do so. This is going to be a humongous upward scaling of this kind of traffic reacting driving.

In any case, we need to consider the other side of the coin too, namely that besides the self-driving car trying to avoid being a tailgater, there is also the use case of the self-driving car being tailgated.

What should a self-driving car do when it is being tailgated?

Well, we are all assuming that the self-driving car is presumably going to be driving in a presumptively legal way. In that case, the AI driving system is considered "in the right" and the tailgater is in the wrong. We might also reasonably assume that the tailgater is not a self-driving car, since, as just discussed, the AI driving systems are presumably going to try and avoid being a tailgater.

This means that we have a situation of a human driver that is tailgating a self-driving car.

Will that ever happen?

Yes, in fact, it happens all the time, right now.

During the experiments of the self-driving cars on our public roadways, it is exceedingly common to witness human-driven cars tailgating the self-driving cars.

Sometimes, a human driver opts to stay back from the self-driving car under a kind of fear of what the AI might do, or maybe out of respect for the AI, or perhaps due to being in awe of the AI. Generally, once the public in a given area gets used to seeing the self-driving cars on the roadways, they begin to treat self-driving cars as they would a human driver.

There is a tendency to treat self-driving cars as though they are like a newbie teenage driver. This translates into the belief by the human driver that the AI is unfamiliar with driving and going to be problematic. Newbie teenage drivers tend to strictly obey the speed limit, and stridently come to a full stop at stop signs. That is a huge source of irritation to many seasoned drivers. In our dog-eat-dog world, the moment that many drivers see a car being driven by a newbie, all bets are off and the seasoned drivers will pull all sorts of dirty tricks, including tailgating. The tailgating only makes things worse, since the newbie teenage driver gets flustered and becomes more cautious in their driving.

The emphasis overall is that we know for sure that human drivers will tailgate self-driving cars. It happens now. It is assuredly coming to happen in the future.

For most of the self-driving cars on the roadways today, the AI driving system is not specially programmed to do anything about being tailgated. In a manner of speaking, the AI is akin to those tailgated drivers that are generally oblivious to the cars behind them. Dealing with tailgaters is only significant to the degree that the AI can calculate what might happen if the self-driving car needs to come to a fast halt.

Few of the AI driving systems are currently set up to take any overt or evasive maneuvers. For example, tapping the brakes is not something that most AI systems are programmed to do, which as discussed earlier humans might do. One supposes the AI systems shouldn't be tapping their brakes, since the result might spark road rage, perhaps extraordinary road rage (what, some stupid AI thing is trying to tell me that I am tailgating, by darn that is outrageous, some human drivers might think).

The AI driving system could potentially speed-up, but this is questionable in that if it has to exceed the speed limit this then appears to cast the AI into being a lawbreaker. The more likely choice would be to switch lanes and let the tailgater go past. Unfortunately, changing lanes can be dicey, plus it might not be a viable option in all circumstances.

Conclusion

Tailgaters would seem to be with us even in an era of self-driving cars.

There is some chance though of dealing with those scofflaws.

Keep in mind that self-driving cars are chockful of sensors, including video cameras, radar, LIDAR, thermal imaging, ultrasonic, and so on. Those are what I call the "roving eye" of self-driving cars. This is worth noting because a self-driving car can readily record the actions of other drivers.

Recall that earlier I had pointed out that we cannot expect to have the highway patrol or traffic cops on the prowl and continuously trying to spot tailgaters. No need for that kind of effort in the future. The self-driving car can be the eyes and ears, as it were, and provide that data to the authorities.

In short, a human-driver might get pegged for tailgating due to a self-driving car that tattled on that human driver. By uploading the collected data to the local authorities, a ticket could be issued for tailgating. For those that are tailgated today, there would seem nothing more satisfying than to imagine the look on the face of that tailgating aggressor than for them to receive a ticket in the mail, having gotten caught red-handed in their fiendish tailgating act.

Maybe this will endear some of us to the AI systems, whilst others will rue the day that AI self-driving cars became ubiquitous."

CHAPTER 21
TULLOCK SPIKES AND SELF-DRIVING CARS

One of the most fascinating thought experiments about the safety of how we all drive our cars is the legendary "Tullock spike" idea.

Here's how it goes.

Imagine that on the steering wheel of every car there was a steel spike protruding toward the driver. Upon sitting down in the driver's seat, you would be within a fraction of an inch of the endpoint of the spike. While driving such an equipped car, you would be continually under the threat of piercing your own chest by any driving action that caused you to lurch forward in the driver's seat.

This is a crafty and yet quite simple device that would seemingly get your attention.

And presumably would be a sizable and constant reminder to drive safely.

That is the underlying crux of the thought experiment ostensibly dreamed-up by Professor Gordon Tullock of George Mason University sometime in the early 1960s (this can be found mentioned in the 1962 book entitled *Calculus of Consent* that was co-authored by Tullock and James Buchanan, which, by the way, some also believe that the idea was potentially also conceived by Armen Alchian of UCLA). In any case, the popularity of the steel spike notion has garnered Tullock's name and is typically referred to as Tullock's spike.

Would you be a safer driver if you had such a steel dagger that was always threatening your existence?

It seems patently obvious that you would be.

All of us would drive as though our lives depended upon it. Indeed, the beauty, or perhaps the ugliness of the spike concept is that you would be more conscious of the dangers involved in driving a car. The act of driving a car carries grave risks all of the time, yet we enormously downplay those risks.

Driving recklessly is easy to do.

There is a huge mental gap between thinking about how to safely drive and the potential result of driving poorly. Those drivers that zip along on the freeway, weaving in and out of lanes, do not make a mental connection between their speed and their chaotic driving actions. While inside the bubble of a car, the outside world at times appears to be a simulation as though you are playing at driving while inside a video game or maybe inside *The Matrix*.

The spike would reset that way of thinking.

Acting as a front-and-center reminder of the dangers of driving, the abstract elements of driving safely would become exceedingly tangible. Tapping the brakes with any sudden movement would likely cause your chest to take a sharp nick from the tip of the dagger. Fortunately, not enough of a bleeder to do full harm. Nonetheless, those occasional cuts and pokes would add to the reminder of what happens when you aren't driving safely.

On the surface, this steel spike seems quite telling.

Though if you try to carry this thought experiment to further mental reaches, the whole thing begins to somewhat unravel. Suppose you are a really safe driver and another car careens out of nowhere and rams into your car. There was nothing you could do to avoid the collision. No matter how attentive you were, the other vehicle mercilessly swung out of traffic and managed to steer into your car. The sad result is that you are fatally gored on the spike, albeit due to no particular cause of your own doing.

One supposes that it could be argued that you shouldn't have used a car at all. The safest way to avoid a car accident is to entirely avoid using cars.

That doesn't seem like a satisfactory way to look at things.

Perhaps you are supposed to only drive on side streets and drive slowly. Even in that context, there are still opportunities for you to get caught on the spike. A dog runs out from a wooded area onto the street, doing so without notice, and occurs in a few split seconds. Even though you were going only 15 miles per hour, and upon hitting the brakes, your body is tossed forward and once again the dagger claims a driver.

Setting aside those gruesome thoughts, there is still something useful about the steel spike concept.

Here's the deeper meaning.

This thought experiment arose during the time that seat belts were still coming into being. For those of you that perchance were around during those times, you might recall the heated debates about wearing a seat belt. Some insisted they would never wear one. One argument was that it constrained your ability to drive and thus would make you get into car accidents, rather than aiding in avoiding them. Another argument was that they were unsightly and marred the joyful experience of driving.

People came up with some real doozy of reasons to keep from putting on a seat belt. Today, we all seem to readily agree that wearing seat belts makes sense. The advent of seat belt usage control indicators served ably as a means to readily convert people into becoming seat belt wearers. Still, there were people then and likely still some people today that insist on trying to subvert the requirement by buckling the seat belt and then sitting atop it, or trying other outlandish ways to subvert a seat belt.

As they say, where there's a will, there's always a way to mess things up.

The topic of seat belts is not solely rosy.

Researchers pointed out that there was an oddball or ironic adverse consequence that undercut the safety-gaining basis of seat belts. The rub was that people would believe themselves to be safer, and therefore they would drive less safely.

Work by Sam Peltzmann had derived an economic theory of risk compensation and it was seemingly evident in the case of seat belts. He contended that attempts to increase safety measures will inexorably lead to heightened behaviors of risk-taking. This led to numerous studies that tried to figure out whether the use of seat belts by drivers was producing more car crashes and more fatalities, or whether it was reducing those numbers. The results of those studies have been mixed, sometimes making one claim and then a different study undermining that stated result.

We can seem to agree that a seat belt is an innocent device and poses no outsized threat. In theory, its primary purpose is to keep you at the wheel and in control of the car. Also, if you did get struck by another vehicle, it keeps you from flying around inside the vehicle or being ejected out onto the street.

The qualm about this added safety is that it might inspire you to drive recklessly. In your mind, you know that the seat belt allows you to stretch things to the dire edge. Without a seat belt, you would be unable to take such chances.

In short, something intended to make us safer can inadvertently spark us to be riskier in our behavior.

A one-for-one correspondence would imply that we are equally safer and equally riskier, and perhaps the net result is a balance that means the added safety measure made no difference. That would be a darned shame given the cost to implement the safety measure. Worse still, the riskiness might go off the charts, far exceeding the added safety, and ergo we become more deadly in our driving.

That's quite a dose of irony when including a new safety contraption.

If a safety measure leads to worse results, presumably the right step involves removing the added safety apparatus. Things would then go back to normal. Well, not necessarily. It could be that the genie was let out of the bottle. People got used to driving like maniacs and they do not according readjust their behavior when the safety measure is removed. You could argue that the behavior would gradually readjust, though that has some debatable contentions too.

Economist Sanford Ikeda noted in a presumed tongue-in-cheek retort that you could replace some of the steel spikes with identical-looking rubber ones. This would be randomly undertaken. When you got into a car, you (in theory) would not have any means to ascertain whether the vehicle had the relatively harmless rubber spike, or whether it had the life usurping steel spike. People would potentially be spared when they had the rubber spike, though all would presumably drive more safely since they had to assume that the steel spike was in their car.

Another twist that has been floated involves removing the brakes on cars. Yes, if brakes are a form of safety, and if safety leads to riskier driving, might as well remove any and all mechanisms of safety including the brakes. In that case, the driving behavior would no longer be as risky, or so the absurdity extremism would imply.

Shifting gears, as it were, we can ponder what the future of cars and car driving will likely consist of.

The emergence of self-driving cars would appear to eliminate the need for a steel spike at the steering wheel, for the obvious reason that there will no longer be steering wheels at all. The eventual path of self-driving cars entails removing all the driving controls from the interior and thus preventing any human attempts to drive the vehicle.

Does this imply that we put to rest the Tullock steel spike and call it a day?

Turns out that there are still some handy insights that arise by considering the vaunted steel spike, even for the revered arrival of AI-based true self-driving cars.

Let's unpack the matter and see.

Self-Driving Cars And Safety

For Level 4 and Level 5 true self-driving vehicles, there won't be a human driver involved in the driving task.

All occupants will be passengers.

The AI is doing the driving.

As mentioned earlier, the belief is that all the human accessible driving controls will ultimately be removed from true self-driving cars. Today, there are many efforts underway that have supplemented a conventional car with the self-driving suite of capabilities. In those instances, the steering wheel and pedals remain, though they are generally AI-controlled to avert a double-driver occurrence (some believe we will always keep the driving controls, while others insist that they have to be removed).

Assume for the moment that the preponderance of true self-driving cars will not have any steering wheels in them. This means there is also no steel spike either.

The underlying crux of the spike concept was that it got us to think about safety and human behavior. This was prompted too by the supposition that as a safety measure is added, there is a potential consequent reaction that drivers would become riskier in their driving.

Let's put that same overall notion into reuse.

Imagine that you are a passenger inside a self-driving car. You know that the AI is a highly safe driver, especially in comparison to a human driver (this has yet to be shown, and we might end-up with AI driving systems that are only as good as human drivers in terms of safety, perhaps worse).

Would your actions as a passenger inside a true self-driving car be less risky, equally risky, or riskier than if you were riding in a human-driven car?

Well, per the theory about safety and risk, the odds are that you would behave in a riskier manner.

Your first comment might be that it doesn't matter since you are not driving the car. That is indeed the case, namely, you aren't driving the vehicle, but you are nonetheless inside an automobile and for which you can still get injured or killed. Suppose the self-driving car is zipping along on the freeway and all of a sudden has to jam on the brakes. If you are not wearing a seat belt, due to the belief that there was no need to do so, you might go flying and end-up getting badly hurt.

Take another example.

You opt to reach outside of the self-driving car and wave at pedestrians on the sidewalk. That might be the full extent of your attempts at outreach, but since you are comfortably nestled inside a true self-driving car, you extend further out the window. About half of your body is now clinging to the outside of the car. I trust you can see where this is going. Another car comes along and perhaps sideswipes the self-driving car, crushing you, or maybe you entirely fall out of the self-driving car, doing so while the vehicle is underway.

The point is that there is a potential danger that passengers inside self-driving cars will believe themselves to be in a safer posture than when inside a conventional human-driven car, thusly leading to untoward behaviors with sad and severe consequences.

Do we need to add a kind of veritable "steel spike" to the innards of a self-driving car to remind riders that they are still inside a rolling canister that can at any time cause tremendous physical forces to adversely impact them?

Maybe.

There is another angle to the human behavior conundrum.

We have to expect that there will be both human-driven cars and self-driving cars on our roadways, both mixing together, and doing so for likely many decades to come. Keep in mind that today there are about 250 million conventional cars in the United States alone, and they will not simply disappear overnight due to the advent of self-driving cars.

I've written extensively that we are already beginning to witness human drivers that opt to play dirty tricks on self-driving cars. These roadway bullies like to force self-driving cars to make a sudden braking action, sometimes just for fun and sometimes because they (the human bully) are driving erratically. In more subtle ways, you can get ahead in traffic by rapidly switching lanes and cutting in front of a self-driving car. The AI is usually programmed to let you in, plus the AI will slow down the self-driving car to try and regain the proper driving distance between vehicles.

Why do people believe they can get away with this kind of risky driving behavior?

Because they assume that the AI self-driving car is a safe driver. Were the AI to be a rogue or rude driver, which is akin to what humans do, those human daredevils would be less likely to pull those kinds of stunts (so one would assume).

Again, the safety and risk equation rears its head. We can anticipate that as more and more self-driving cars enter into the roadway mix, and assuming they are sufficiently safe at driving, the human drivers might increase their riskiness of driving practice under the belief that it okay to do so, similar to the logic used about wearing seat belts.

Conclusion

We can add one additional example to this plateful of safety and risk heightened behavioral stew.

AI self-driving cars are ostensibly being programmed to be safe drivers. Part of this safety element involves being able to contend with human drivers. Some assert that perhaps self-driving cars should not be so gentle and therefore by being less safe (or appearing to be so), would curtail the risk increase by human drivers).

Assume that eventually there are hardly any human-driven cars and the mainstay of traffic is entirely self-driving cars.

Could the self-driving cars be amped up to take more extreme driving measures?

Sure, it seems logical, given that the other surrounding cars are all safer than before (we are so assuming), and thus the risk of driving at the edge is presumably lessened. An example would be that we could lift the existing speed limits and let the self-driving cars go as fast they so deem.

Part of the basis for speed limits was to reduce the severity of car crashes, but if there are going to be very few such car accidents, maybe we can do away with the speed limits.

This doesn't fully pencil out, so don't get overly excited. Pedestrians can still step into the street and ruin everyone's day. In any case, on freeways and open highways, there is some logic to letting those self-driving cars run with the wind.

You can imagine how elated the AI would be, asking you as a passenger whether it is okay to put the pedal to the metal. Might as well let the AI have some fun, and meanwhile, you can get to your destination in record time.

Just hope the AI keeps its steely eyes peeled on the road ahead and there aren't any steel spikes laying on the pavement.

CHAPTER 22
VACATION HOMES AND SELF-DRIVING CARS

Your vacation home awaits you.

According to the latest real estate reporting, the pandemic has spurred interest in so-called second homes, or variously known as vacation homes.

Apparently, when people realized they would be cooped up in their primary home, some decided that they would more frequently go to visit their existing vacation home as a break in the monotony. Rather than treating the vacation home as a once or twice per year visit as a special event, they opted to make their encampments on an ongoing basis. If your primary home is in a major city or similar locale, and everything is pretty much shut down, there is nothing more fulfilling than going to that vaunted vacation home to rejuvenate your spirit.

Sometimes a vacation home is a tiny shack or a simple cottage.

You've stretched your finances to squeak into getting that second home and are darned happy that you could afford anything at all. It might be tiny. It might be somewhat rundown. It might need a new coat of paint and some loving care, but all-in-all the point is that you have one and it is yours, calling to you constantly as a home away from home that beckons you to come to visit.

The mainstay of that vacation home is where it is located, rather than the size of the domicile. Perhaps your vacation home is up in the mountains, or sitting at the edge of a breathtaking bay, or perhaps overlooks a tranquil lake or resides on a sandy beach. You can brag to friends and strangers alike that you have yourself a bungalow or a retreat, conjuring images of a lovely escape from the ordinary strains of conventional living.

There are though some harsh realities that can poke through the dreamy vision of having a vacation home.

One obvious contrivance involves the act of getting to your revered vacation home.

It can be a real pain to make the journey to that out-of-the-way location and cause you a great deal of angst and effort each time you do so. Suppose you need to drive for many hours, perhaps chewing up the better part of a day to get there, and upon arrival, you are exhausted from simply being at the wheel for that length of time. You then dread the return drive and begin to think about it right away. If you are lucky, you can push those thoughts out of your head during the stay at the vacation home, and hopefully, relish the actual visit itself.

People are usually excited during the drive up to their vacation home. They have all this pent-up energy and anticipation of having a good time. Even after a half-dozen hours of driving, there is still some exuberance left, though it admittedly starts to wear thin. The drive back to your primary home is oftentimes downright sullen. Sure, there are great memories of the vacation home visit, meanwhile, the hours upon hours of mindless driving is difficult to endure and seems to take forever.

Besides the driving chore for getting up to the vacation home and to return from it, there is additional driving that needs to take place while at the wondrous locale.

You might need to drive into a local town to get provisions. Perhaps you want to drive to the other side of a lake or a mountain to visit a treasured spot that you like to see upon staying at your vacation locale. All of these driving tasks can be a blotch on the carefree nature of the vacation home visit.

Likely you are relatively unfamiliar with the local roads. When at your primary home, you know your way around like the back of your hand. At your vacation home, the territory or landscape is a faint memory and you cannot recall where things are. Indeed, some roads might have changed since your last visit and new roads might have been added.

In today's world, the use of GPS is a godsend for coping with those issues. It used to be that you would have to stop at a local supermarket or gas station to purchase a local map or ask for directions. Nowadays, a good GPS with up-to-date maps makes navigation a lot easier.

Yet, despite the advantages of those electronics, you still need to be at the wheel of the car. This means that you carry the ongoing and heavy responsibility of properly and safely carrying out the driving task. Some people love to drive, while others see driving as simply a means to an end. They would love to be free of the driving chore during a trip to their vacation home. Possibly they drive at their primary home all the time, commuting to work in crowded traffic, and are sick and tired of having to be a driver.

Okay, it might seem patently obvious that I've emphasized the driving aspects of contending with having a vacation home.

What gives?

Well, there is likely to be another boon in vacation homes when the driving duty is summarily reassigned. The advent of self-driving cars will place the burden of driving onto the shoulders of AI driving systems and free up humans from having to drive.

This brings up an interesting aspect: *How will the emergence of AI-based true self-driving cars be a spark toward the purchase and use of a second home or the celebrated vacation home?*

Let's unpack the matter and see.

Self-Driving Cars And Vacation Homes

For Level 4 and Level 5 true self-driving vehicles, there won't be a human driver involved in the driving task.

All occupants will be passengers.

The AI is doing the driving

Here's why this is going to spur people to acquire and regularly stay at vacation homes.

The act of getting to and from your vacation home, along with the burden of driving while at the desired escape, will become frictionless.

Follow me on this.

You get home from a hard day's work at the office. It is Friday night, and the workweek is over, thankfully so. Normally, there is zero chance that you would suddenly decide to head out to your vacation home. The personal exhaustion of the week has worn out any vitality needed to make that long drive.

Admittedly, you have even opened a beer or two, trying to wash down the stresses and get your mind ready for a fun weekend.

You are in no shape to be driving a car.

Voila, all you need to do is use a self-driving car to make the drive for you.

You either own a self-driving car or submit an online request to use one, akin to using any ride-sharing network via a mobile app. The self-driving car pulls up to your home, waiting outside at the curb. You grab up a few toiletries and other personal items and stridently march out to the self-driving car.

Turns out that this model of a self-driving car is one that has seats that recline.

Right now, many of the experiments with self-driving cars involve conventional vehicles. In the future, the true self-driving car will be a completely redesigned vehicle. Since there is no longer a need for a driver's seat, the likelihood is that most self-driving cars will have a set of swivel seats, allowing you to turn in any direction during a driving journey, and those seats will recline into becoming beds.

Bed usage will be handy for both short-term and long-term trips.

In the mornings, while on the way to the office, you can catch some extra winks by using the reclining capability. Upon the end of the workday, you can again use the reclining feature to grab a short nap while the self-driving car takes you home.

For a longer trip, such as a many hours long ride to your vacation home, you can completely fall asleep and get full recharging of your mind and body. Once you arrive at the vacation home, rather than suffering from the stresses of driving there, you are quite refreshed and ready to enjoy the escapades ahead.

You also know that when that marvelous stay at the vacation home comes to an end, there is no need to worry about the drive back to your primary home. Just make use of a self-driving car and you can do the sleeping thing again. Or, rather than closing your eyes, you might simply look out the windows of the car and enjoy the scenery, doing so without having to steer the car and nor be on the watch for interlopers such as perhaps deer crossing the roadway.

That's the job of the AI driving system.

There are more ways to use that seed of time while inside the self-driving car during those long trips.

The odds are that most self-driving cars will be equipped with internal LED displays, possibly even able to cover the windows of the vehicle. Those display panels can be raised or lowered, depending upon whether you'd like to watch the roadway or instead watch a movie.

You could do some pretty hefty binge-watching of your favorite cable or TV show while on the trip associated with your vacation home.

Furthermore, it is anticipated that the self-driving cars will be equipped with ultrafast high bandwidth for electronic communications. This can be used for various entertainment purposes, including streaming movies or watching a live event such as a televised football game. You can also do online interaction in a Facetime-like manner. Maybe chat with friends that are going to meet up with you at the vacation home, discussing plans of what you all will be doing together during the stay there.

This ability to interactively chat can be done from car-to-car too.

You left your primary home in a self-driving car and are about a six-hour driving distance away from the vacation home. Those friends of yours that are coming there are about four hours away. They leave once you've been on-the-road for a couple of hours. At this point, you are in a self-driving car and they are also in a self-driving car, all making a beeline toward the vacation home.

During that time in the self-driving cars, you can all be doing a pre-party, as it were (electronically, car-to-car). Talking shop and figuring out what activities to do at the vacation home. One supposes you could even have the self-driving cars coordinate their driving actions so that they both arrive at the vacation home at the same exact moment in time.

But wait, there's more.

Upon being at the vacation home, whenever you want to go over to the nearby town or take a trip to the other side of the lake, you can let the self-driving car handle the driving for you.

There is no need for you to have angst about what streets to use or where things are. The AI will look-up that info online and use its GPS and special maps to get you to your destination. You can merely sit back in your swivel seat and watch the grazing wild animals or admire the glean of the silvery lake.

In fact, there might not be a need for you to be inside the vehicle at all, such as when wanting to get provisions from the nearest supermarket or similar store. You can either call the store or use an online ordering system, and they will put your purchases into a self-driving car. The self-driving car then makes its way to your vacation home. Forget about having to drive there and back, since the self-driving car removes any of that effort on your part.

In short, if you knew that you no longer needed to hassle with the driving elements of owning and using your vacation home, this would provide an added incentive to own and use one. For some people, it would be a humongous difference and get them off the fence about whether to dive into getting a second home or not.

Conclusion

You might be wondering whether there is a catch to any of this. It seems a bit hard to believe in terms of providing all or solely benefits and no apparent downsides.

That is a good point, so let's consider some of the potholes and potential gotchas.

First, nobody knows how much it is going to cost to use a self-driving car.

One theory is that self-driving cars will be less expensive to use than using a human-driven based ride-sharing service. Some assert it will be a lot less than that, by far. If that's the case, then this use of a self-driving car for those long trips might make sense to do. On the other hand, if self-driving cars are costly to use, the dreaminess of zipping out and back from your vacation home could be expensive and prohibitive for your budget.

Second, nobody knows how available self-driving cars will be.

The ramp-up of rolling out self-driving cars in any massive way is going to be relatively gradual. This means that there might not be many self-driving cars on the roadways, for quite a while. Thus, your attempt to request a self-driving car might be unfulfilled when you use a ride-sharing network to seek one. Also, the fleet owner might prefer to keep their self-driving cars in a major city location and not be willing to have you take one on a long trip to a remote and desolate area.

Third, self-driving cars might not be familiar with the area where your vacation home resides, and thusly would be unable to drive there.

There is an ongoing debate in the industry about whether self-driving cars need to have specialized digital maps to properly make their way around. Some say yes, others argue that this is a severe limitation as it requires a mapping operation to occur before a self-driving car can presumably drive while in certain areas. Those pre-mapping efforts are likely to only be profitably undertaken in areas that have lots of people such as major cities. The odds that your vacation home sitting in a faraway and scarcely populated place will have that mapping done is seemingly unlikely.

Fourth, vacation home locales might be outside of the Operational Design Domain (ODD) of many self-driving cars.

The Level 4 self-driving cars are based on a self-restriction known as an Operational Design Domain (ODD). This means that when an automaker or self-driving tech firm makes their self-driving car, they are to stipulate the restrictions associated with where they claim their car can actually drive.

For example, a self-driving car might not be suitable for driving in snow or be unable to drive in heavy rains. If you've been wondering why a lot of the experiments seem to be concentrated in places like California, Arizona, and Florida, it is partially due to the rather bland weather and environmental conditions, allowing the self-driving cars to avoid having to deal with difficult driving climates.

It would seem likely that you have chosen a vacation home in a place that might have extraordinary weather or other unusual driving circumstances. That's a bummer as it means that you might have a difficult time finding a self-driving car able to contend with that kind of an ODD.

Fifth, few self-driving cars are currently being prepared to cope with off-road driving.

People generally seem to pick vacation homes that are accessible, meaning they are available to be reached via conventional highways and streets. Self-driving cars can usually drive on such roads.

The standard levels of autonomous driving do not address the matter of off-road driving. This is a surprise to many that are outside the industry. In any case, it means that we will likely not see self-driving cars driving off-road until most of the on-road efforts are first completed (this is due to it being somewhat easier to handle on-road driving, plus likely a lot more profitable for making money off of a self-driving car).

I hope those aforementioned caveats do not dim your enthusiasm about the possibility of self-driving cars enabling a boon in vacation homes.

Clearly, if those making self-driving cars can discern that a buck can be made by providing self-driving cars to let people reach their vacation homes, the all-mighty dollar will *drive* those pursuits in that direction.

For boisterous children that do not like the family ride up and back from a vacation home due to entrapment with their parents and being constantly under their guise in a confined space for so many endless hours, there is something that you can tell them. Namely, in theory, they could be placed into a self-driving car, by themselves, and driven by the self-driving car without any in-car adult supervision (some eschew this idea and insist they would never allow this to happen).

Remember, there isn't an adult driver needed.

Maybe those rowdy kids of yours will relish the use of self-driving cars and your vacation home.

One caveat is that though they might be alone in a self-driving car, you can likely still watch them via the internal cameras and interact with them, albeit they are being adult-like by being on their own. Of course, would that be too much of a strain on you, letting your beloved offspring be by themselves for hours upon hours in a moving vehicle?

That's a battle to be dealt with in the future and not one that you need to settle yet today.

Think instead of the dreamy vision of a vacation home that can be reached via the quiet and courteous AI driving system that will whisk you from your city-life to the joyous environs for a restful respite from the daily grind.

As I said at the beginning of this saga, your vacation home awaits you.

CHAPTER 23
CAR BUYING EXPERIENCES AND SELF-DRIVING CARS

Many people liken the act of buying a car to the same agony as going to the dentist for a root canal.

Well, maybe car buying is even worse than that.

Having to trudge down to a dealership and endure a fast-talking sales pitch is one of the trials and tribulations that has become the butt of jokes and a longstanding pilgrimage in our society. Another difficulty involves the eerie feeling that you are somehow getting snookered. Plus, there are dozens of choices to be made, and whichever selection you initially find alluring there is inevitably some cause to want something else instead. The choices are nearly overwhelming. On top of all those trepidations, there is a mountain of paperwork to be dealt with.

It is said that after the enormous magnitude of house buying comes the next largest purchase of a lifetime, namely the buying of a car. It's a big deal. You don't do it every day of your life and when it does occur, there is a mixture of apprehension and some excitement, though the dread of the process tends to undercut the elation of getting yourself a new car.

There are numerous modern-day attempts underway to disrupt the car buying process and seek to streamline and reduce the angst involved.

One approach involves undertaking the preponderance of the car buying experience online.

This allows you to avoid the exhausting walk around a dealership and having to kick those tires when trying to find the right vehicle for you. Instead, you simply pull-up pictures and videos that showcase the cars and eyeball the plethora of possibilities (even VR or Virtual Reality is being infused into these efforts). Some of the online sites allow you to customize your preferences and the system will try to find an existing car that already came off the production line or will enable you to place an order to your specifications that will be handcrafted during the automotive assembly effort.

Whether this hands-off online approach will take hold is still an open question.

Despite the potential unpleasantness of wandering into a car dealership, many people are still more comfortable with the brick-and-mortar world than they are with the online realm. This is especially the case when making such a large-scale purchase. There seems to be a need to be there physically and see and touch the cars, allowing us to make the mental leap from the frightfulness of dolling out our hard-earned dough and the tangible joy of being right there to embrace the car of your dreams.

No matter how you decide to make a car purchase in current times, you are nonetheless buying a conventional car. By conventional, I am referring to the notion that the vehicle requires a human driver. You can change up the nature of today's cars via their interior designs and by the doodads and built-in entertainment, but one thing that remains constant and seemingly unalterable is the need for a driver's seat and a set of driving controls.

That's because a human driver has to be accommodated, one way or another.

The future won't look like that.

There will eventually be self-driving cars. Those AI-based true self-driving cars will not need a human driver since the AI will be doing the driving for you. Furthermore, the interior of the vehicle no longer will need a place for a human driver to sit and operate the controls.

This vastly opens other opportunities to reimagine what the inside of a car ought to be composed of.

All in all, the hope is that with self-driving cars there will be a lot fewer roadway fatalities. Today there are a staggering 40,000 deaths per year in the United States alone due to car crashes and about 2.3 million injuries sustained. The assumption is that the AI driving system won't be driving drunk and will not drive while distracted. This added attentiveness and care in driving is anticipated to radically reduce the number of car crashes.

Some claim that the number of car crashes will drop to zero, but I've repeatedly exhorted that this is a pipe dream and there is a zero chance of zero deaths. Cars will still be bound by the laws of physics. Tires can still blowout and a vehicle can collide with other cars. A pedestrian can step into the street without any due notice and no matter what the AI can do, it cannot cause a car to miraculously and instantaneously come to a halt. And there will be a mixture of both human-driven cars and self-driving cars on our roadways, for a long time to come. This implies that there are still plenty of chances for cars to collide with other cars, including imperiling self-driving cars.

In any case, the belief is that the advent of self-driving cars will substantially reduce the number of car crashes and thereby reduce the sizable toll of annual counts of fatalities and injuries that arise today due to car accidents. We will gradually and incrementally be grateful that self-driving cars have been added to our highways and byways.

Given that background about the emergence of self-driving cars, this raises an interesting question. In particular, you might be wondering how might the car buying experience change as a result of the arrival of self-driving cars.

Ponder this: *Will the influx of AI-based true self-driving cars somehow impact the car buying experience and if so, what will it be like to purchase a self-driving car?*

Let's unpack the matter and see.

Self-Driving Cars And The Car Buying Experience

For Level 4 and Level 5 true self-driving vehicles, there won't be a human driver involved in the driving task.

All occupants will be passengers.

The AI is doing the driving

One of the first contentions to be dealt with about the car buying experience in the case of true self-driving cars is the heated debate and assertion that you won't be able to buy one.

Yes, arguments are being made that the only owners of self-driving cars will be large companies, such as automakers, car rental firms, ridesharing entities, and the like. The belief is that self-driving cars will be bought in droves, or is that herds, by companies that will have a fleet of such vehicles. No individual person will be able to buy a self-driving car.

We'll get into the basis for that argument in a moment.

Meanwhile, I'm known as a bit of a contrarian since I've all along been asserting that individuals will be able to buy self-driving cars. Of course, it will be up to the automakers and self-driving tech firms to decide, since they can presumably choose to sell their wares to whomever they wish. If they want to only sell to large companies, it would seem they can opt to do so (until or if some regulations overturn that approach, or if they realize that selling to others can be equally profitable).

So, before digging into the details, one potential answer about how the car buying experience will change is that you won't be able to buy a car. Ergo, there isn't anything anymore of a car buying experience, not at least for individuals like you and me. No need to worry about those long walks at a car dealership since you won't be able to purchase a true self-driving car there anyway (note, realize I am referring to true self-driving cars, meanwhile, the selling of conventional cars and semi-autonomous cars will presumably continue unabated).

If your belief is dogmatic that self-driving cars will not be sold to the public at large, the question about the car buying experience is no longer relevant and the simple answer is that there won't be any such car buying to experience.

I am going to override that assumption and proceed under the guise that there will nonetheless still be a car buying experience for the public, even in the case of true self-driving cars, and thus we can fruitfully consider what that future will look like.

Stay with me, if you brave to do so.

Just like any customer journey or so-called customer experience lifecycle, there are a series of stages that will be involved in buying a self-driving car.

The key stages or steps can be briefly summarized as follows:

1) Identifying the right self-driving car for your needs
2) Doing a test drive of the self-driving car
3) Figuring out the financials
4) Making the needed arrangements
5) Getting the self-driving car
6) Starting use and ensuring dutiful care

In many respects, the stages on a surface level appear to be quite similar to the actions entailing the purchase of a conventional car. When we get *under-the-hood* about each stage (yeah, that was a planted pun), you'll see that there are some notable differences, mainly in degree and diligence.

First, consider the aspect that you'll need to figure out what type of self-driving car is best suited to your needs.

This is somewhat surprising to many since they assume that all self-driving cars will be the same.

That's just not so.

There will be numerous brands and models to choose from. You might want a self-driving car that has bench-style seating, two seats facing two seats, as is commonly emerging for the classic robo-taxi style of a car. Or, you might prefer a self-driving car that has four swivel seats, allowing the passengers to face in whatever direction they prefer. There are larger sized self-driving cars that resemble an SUV or a van and proffer more seating. And there will be smaller sized cars that can only accommodate one or two people but might instead have set aside space for the carrying of packages or goods.

I've even predicted that we will have high horsepower sports cars that are self-driving. Some doubt that people will enjoy a sports car if they cannot be at the wheel, but I disagree and contend that the sports car that drives itself will still be exhilarating and exciting to ride in and possibly own.

The twist to the first step or stage of the car buying experience is that you will no longer be making the decision based solely on your own interests per se, and will need to consider the money-making element too.

Here's what that means.

The odds are that if you buy a self-driving car, you are doing so to provide yourself with transportation, and, you are simultaneously aiming to leverage the self-driving capability by ridesharing out your prized vehicle.

This is rarely done today.

Certainly, some people rent out their privately owned cars, but it is a still quite minuscule portion of car owners. There are a lot of people that have gone the route of becoming a ridesharing driver, making use of their owned vehicle, and thus in that sense they are renting out their car (though, they are also driving it too).

For the bulk of today's car owners, they own an asset that sits idly for most of the time. Some estimates suggest that a car is parked and unused for perhaps 95% to possibly 99% of the time. This means that you have all these costly assets that do nothing for the predominance of their existence. It is a waste of an asset, but this is well-accepted and abundantly understandable due to a severely limiting factor, namely, a human driver is needed.

Self-driving cars do not need a human driver. The AI driving system is available whenever and for however long needed. Most are expecting those self-driving cars will be operating nearly 24x7, continually being on the go. This makes a lot of sense because you can be making money whenever a self-driving car is on the roadways (well, maybe, as will be explained shortly).

The notion is that a person, a normal everyday person, will buy a self-driving car and then use it for their own personal use, along with listing the vehicle onto a ridesharing network. Imagine that you go to work, having your self-driving car take you to the office and while at work the self-driving car then proceeds to provide lifts. This continues throughout your workday. You are making money at work and your self-driving car is making money on top of your normal salary or wages.

The same can happen when you are at home for the evening. Your self-driving car might have given you a ride home, and then you sent it along to be used throughout the night. In fact, while you are nestled in your bed, the self-driving car is making money all night long.

In essence, the ownership of a self-driving car becomes a miniature business, for which there is money to be made.

Whether it is profitable depends upon numerous factors, such as the cost to keep the self-driving car in proper shape and the continual upkeep that will be required. The money won't necessarily be pouring in, since you have to consider how much of the time your available self-driving car will be called upon to provide rides. The money-making will be conditioned on how many other self-driving cars and other mobility options exist wherever you live or have decided to deploy your self-driving car. Heavy competition could dramatically reduce your potential earnings.

All in all, though some think that owning a self-driving car will be a goldmine, it all depends upon a slew of factors and you could end up not making any money. That would be a tough pill to swallow, especially if the cost of purchasing a self-driving car is going to be relatively high (some think so). In that sense, buying a self-driving car might be akin to purchasing stock in the stock market. There is a chance of big profits and also a risk of losing your shirt.

That's why not everyone will clamor to buy a self-driving car.

On the other hand, I've predicted an expanding cottage industry of people buying self-driving cars to try and make a living, or at least substantially supplement their existing means of making money. In a manner similar to how people today are at times leaping into ride-sharing their vehicle and doing the driving, we will witness people deciding to purchase a self-driving car and put it into the ride-sharing arena.

As a quick aside, you might also be making this decision as a group, wherein I've predicted that there will be small-sized consortia or pods that are put together of people jointly seeking to buy and invest in a self-driving car for their separate and joint benefits.

Let's get back to the stages or steps of the car buying experience now that we've gotten the aforementioned context in mind.

When identifying the type of self-driving car for your needs, you'll need to think about your personal existence, such as whether you have a family and want to have a vehicle that accommodates a bunch of people, and also how you hope to make your self-driving car be appealing as a ride-sharing vehicle. Maybe in your area of deployment, there is a greater need for smaller sized self-driving cars and not larger ones. Or, perhaps the opposite, which means that if you get a smaller-sized self-driving car it will not do well in terms of ridesharing opportunities.

Another factor is the Operational Design Domain (ODD) of the self-driving cars being considered for purchase. The ODD is the conditions or restrictions under which a self-driving car has been devised to operate, such as some self-driving cars might not be able to safely function in heavy rains or when there is snowfall. For both personal use and the deployment on a ridesharing basis, it will be crucial to select a self-driving car brand and model that befits the target driving environment.

The point is that the car selection activity will have changed markedly in that you'll need to deliberately consider two audiences at the same time

- What do you want for your personal purposes?
- What will be the most appealing and optimally money-making choice for ridesharing purposes?

This is a dualism that today is less important and rarely considered.

Assuming you are serious about getting a self-driving car, you can likely have the candidates come to your home so that you can try them out. This will be easy for a dealership to arrange. They just send the self-driving car over to you. When your time is up, perhaps an hour to go for a test drive (not per se a *test drive*, as it were, more like a test ride), the self-driving car will return to the dealership, on its own. Dealerships are likely to optionally provide a ride-along companion, a salesperson if you want to have one come along and tell you why their self-driving car is the best of all of them.

Figuring out the financials is going to be the complex side of things. If you thought that financing a car is complicated, wait until you get into the realm of buying a car as an asset that will be considered an investment. The good news is that there will be various tax advantages in buying a self-driving car. The rougher news is that it is akin to suddenly overnight becoming a small business owner. For those that have never run a business, they will either learn to do so right away or might be quick to fail in this kind of startup endeavor.

Making the arrangements for a self-driving car are definitely more involved than those of a conventional car.

You'll need to ensure that the self-driving car is kept in tiptop shape. This means that the sensors are always working and kept clean and free to do their job. Since you are ridesharing out your vehicle, you'll want to make sure it is clean both on the outside and the inside. There will be specialized cleaning services that arise during the self-driving car era, and you'll likely make a deal with one of those.

Once all the proper arrangements have been made, your self-driving car will show up at your doorstep and you are now the proud owner of a brand-new and sparkling self-driving car. Envision the excitement as you and the family pile into the self-driving car to go for those first rides. Undoubtedly, you'll be equally excited when the cash register starts ringing due to your self-driving car making big bucks for you. The last step or stage is to realize that you cannot do a purchase-and-forget kind of buying action.

Today, you buy a car and it is up to you as to what you do with it. If you are going to be using your self-driving car on a 24x7 ridesharing basis, it will be the squeaky wheel that always needs the grease, meaning that you'll need to devote a sizable chunk of your time and attention to keeping your invested asset in good and money-making shape.

One of the major reasons that self-driving cars might *not* be sold to consumers is the concern by the automakers and self-driving tech firms that those individual owners will not do the proper upkeep. This could lead to self-driving cars getting into car crashes and essentially become the bad apples that spoil the barrel. Presumably, large companies having self-driving cars in fleets would be a safer and more sensible bet.

There are undoubtedly going to be some that buy a self-driving car and decide not to make it into a new venture. Instead, they will treat the self-driving car as though it is a *commoner*, akin to contemporary cars. They will use the vehicle themselves and not rideshare it out to the world. Whether you think that is a shame depends upon your perspective, wherein some believe that all self-driving cars will owe a duty to society to aid in achieving a mobility-for-all goal.

CHAPTER 24
ASIMOV'S LAWS AND SELF-DRIVING CARS

Those robots and their wild and crazy ways.

Advances in Artificial Intelligence (AI) will continue to spur widespread adoption of robots into our everyday lives. Robots that once seemed so expensive that they could only be afforded for heavy-duty manufacturing purposes have gradually come down in cost and equally been reduced in size. You can consider that Roomba vacuum cleaner in your home to be a type of robot, though we still do not have the ever-promised home butler robot that was supposed to take care of our daily routine chores.

Perhaps one of the most well-known facets about robots is the legendary set of three rules proffered by writer Isaac Asimov. His science fiction tale entitled *The Three Laws* was published in 1942 and has seemingly been unstoppable in terms of ongoing interest and embrace.

Here are the three rules that he cleverly devised:

1) A robot may not injure a human being or, through inaction, allow a human being to come to harm,
2) A robot must obey the orders given it by human beings except where such orders would conflict with the First Law,
3) A robot must protect its own existence as long as such protection does not conflict with the First or Second Law.

Though he referred to these as laws, please know that they are ostensibly are not actual laws per se.

One viewpoint about laws is the notion of laws of nature. Those three rules are not laws of nature as there is nothing about them that somehow is determinable as being inexorably imbued via nature or required by the course of nature. Those rules are manmade and humanity discretionary. They can be observed and obeyed, or they can be completely disregarded, whichever we might choose to so abide.

Another perspective on laws is the aspect of mankind derived regulations and stipulations. Our revered Constitution is an indication of laws, something that we as a society have opted to try and live within. In that way of consideration, you could argue that Asimov was proposing laws that we ought to put onto our legal books as sensible to have in an era of robots that might be wandering amongst us.

His three rules are not yet embodied directly into our laws and we'll have to see whether it eventually makes sense to codify them explicitly accordingly. You might find of interest that there is a great deal of angst and attention right now on how to best govern the latest AI systems and we might find ourselves leaning heavily into Asimov's three rules.

When you read Asimov's remarks about robots, you might want to substitute the word "robot" for simply the overarching moniker of AI. I say this because you are likely to otherwise narrowly interpret his three rules as though they apply only to a robot that happens to look like us, conventionally having legs, arms, a head, a body, and so on.

Not all robots are necessarily so arranged.

Some of the latest robots look like animals. Perhaps you've seen the popular online videos of robots that are four-legged and appear to be a dog or a similar kind of creature. There are even robots that resemble insects. They look kind of creepy but nonetheless are important as a means to figure out how we might utilize robotics in all manner of possibilities.

A robot doesn't have to be biologically inspired. A robotic vacuum cleaner does not particularly look like any customary animal or insect. You can expect that we will have all sorts of robots that look quite unusual and do not appear to be based solely on any living organism.

Anyway, amongst the variety of robots that we are going to see emerging, the Asimov three rules are quite helpful, regardless of what kind of robot it is and what it might look like. I know it seems perhaps a bit of a stretch of the imagination, but the lowly robotic vacuum can be a candidate for abiding by the three rules. Yes, presumably, your swirling robotic vacuum in your home should not try to harm you and ought to do what it can to avoid doing so.

Some robots are readily in front of our eyes and yet we do not think of them as robots.

One such example is the advent of AI-based true self-driving cars.

A car that is being driven by an AI system can be said to be a type of robot. The reason you might not think of a self-driving car as a robot is that it does not have that walking-talking robot sitting in the driver's seat. Instead, the computer system hidden in the underbody or trunk of the car is doing the driving. This seems to escape our attention and thus the vehicle doesn't readily appear to be a kind of robot, though indeed it is.

In case you are wondering, there are encouraging efforts underway to create walking-talking robots that would be able to drive a car.

Imagine how that would shake-up our world.

Right now, the crafting of a self-driving car involves modifying the car to be self-driving. If we had robots that could walk around, sit down in a car, and drive the vehicle, this would mean that *all* existing cars could essentially be considered self-driving cars (meaning that they could be driven by such robots, rather than having a human drive the car). Instead of gradually junking conventional cars for the arrival of self-driving cars, there would be no need to devise a wholly-contained self-driving car and we would rely upon those meandering robots to be our drivers.

At this time, the fastest or soonest path to having self-driving cars is the build-it into the vehicle approach. Some believe there is a bitter irony in this approach. They contend that these emergent self-driving cars are going to inevitably be usurped by those walking-talking robots. In that sense, the self-driving car of today will become outdated and outmoded, giving way to once again having conventional driving controls so that either the vehicle can be driven by a human or be driven by a driving robot.

As an added twist, there are some that hope we will be so far along on adopting self-driving cars that we will not use independent robots to drive our cars.

Here's the logic.

If a robot driver is sitting at the wheel, this suggests that the conventional driving controls are still going to be available inside a car. This also implies that humans will still be able to drive a car, whenever they wish to do so. But the belief is that the AI driving systems, whether built-in or as part of a walking-talking robot, will be better drivers and reduce the incidences of drunk driving and other adverse driving behaviors. In short, a true self-driving car will not have any driving controls, precluding a walking-talking robot from driving (presumably) and precluding (thankfully, some assert) a human from driving.

This leads to the thinking that maybe the world will have completely switched to true self-driving cars and though a walking-talking driving robot might become feasible, things will be so far along that no one will turn back the clock and reintroduce conventional cars.

That seems somewhat like wishful (or possibly wistful) thinking.

One way or another, the central goal seems to be to take the human driver out of the equation.

This brings up another crucial and sometimes overlooked point about robots, namely that they can be put into positions of effort that entail life or death activities. Your home robotic vacuum cleaner is unlikely to be a life-or-death decision-maker. Meanwhile, a self-driving car, one that has the AI driving system built-in, or even a robot driver, would undeniably be in a life-or-death posture of ascertaining the fate of humans.

Each day that you get behind the wheel of a car, you are a life-or-death decision-maker, whether you realize it or recognize that this is so. With a bad turn of the steering wheel, you can get killed. Plus, you can end-up killing others, whether by veering into another car or possibly hitting pedestrians. There is life-or-death entirely surrounding the act of driving.

That might seem rather doom-and-gloom, but it is a harsh reality that needs to be emphasized.

This is also why the moment when you help your teenager learn to drive is more than just some simple bonding time. The instant that you put your beloved newbie driver at the driving controls, the specter of life-or-death suddenly becomes quite pronounced. The teenage driver usually also senses this heavy-duty, and you can see that some are reluctant to take on such a hefty burden.

Since it is life-or-death on the line, it is conceivable that we should consider applying Asimov's three rules in the use case of self-driving cars (it would seem inconceivable to not do so, as suggested by *The Princess Bride*).

Here is today's intriguing question: *Do the Asimov three laws of robots apply to AI-based true self-driving cars, and if so, what should be done about it?*

Let's unpack the matter and see.

Self-Driving Cars And Asimov's Laws

For Level 4 and Level 5 true self-driving vehicles, there won't be a human driver involved in the driving task.

All occupants will be passengers.

The AI is doing the driving

Let's briefly take a look at each of Asimov's three rules and see how they might apply to true self-driving cars.

First, there is the rule that a robot or AI driving system (in this case) shall not injure a human, either doing so by overt action and nor by its inaction.

That's a tall order when sitting at the wheel of a car.

Here's why.

A self-driving car is driving down a street and keenly sensing the surroundings. Unbeknownst to the AI driving system, a small child is standing between two parked cars, hidden from view and hidden from the sensory range and depth of the self-driving car. The AI is driving at the posted speed limit. All of a sudden, the child steps out into the street.

Some people assume that a self-driving car will never run into anyone since the AI has those state-of-the-art sensory capabilities and won't be a drunk driver. Unfortunately, in the kind of scenario that I've just posited, the self-driving car is going to ram into that child. I say this because the law of physics is paramount over any dreamy notions of what an AI driving system can do.

If the child has appeared seemingly out of nowhere and now is say a distance of 15 feet from the moving car, and the self-driving car is going at 30 miles per hour, the stopping distance is around 50 to 75 feet, which means that the child could readily get struck.

No two ways about that.

And this would mean that the AI driving system has just violated Asimov's first rule.

The AI has injured a human being. Keep in mind that I'm

stipulating that the AI would indeed invoke the brakes of the self-driving car and do whatever it could to avoid the ramming of the child. Nonetheless, there is insufficient time and distance for the AI to avoid the collision.

Now that we've shown the impossibility of always abiding by Asimov's first rule in terms of strictly adhering to the rule, you could at least argue that the AI driving system *attempted* to obey the rule. By having used the brakes, it would seem that the AI driving system tried to keep from hitting the child, plus the impact might be somewhat less severe if the vehicle was nearly stopped at the time of impact.

What about the other part of the first rule that states there should be no inaction that could lead to the harm of a human?

One supposes that if the self-driving car did not try to stop, this kind of inaction might fall within that realm, namely once again being unsuccessful at observing the rule. We can add a twist to this. Suppose the AI driving system was able to swerve the car, doing so sufficiently to avoid striking the child, but meanwhile, the self-driving car goes smack dab into a redwood tree. There is a passenger inside the self-driving car and this person gets whiplash due to the crashing action.

Okay, the child on the street was saved, but the passenger inside the self-driving car is now injured. You can ponder whether the action to save the child was worthy in comparison to the result of injuring the passenger. Also, you can contemplate whether the AI failed to take proper action to avoid the injury to the passenger. This kind of ethical dilemma is often depicted via the infamous Trolley Problem, an aspect that I have vehemently argued is very applicable to self-driving cars and deserves much more rapt attention as the advent of self-driving cars continues.

All told, we can seemingly agree that the first rule of Asimov's triad is a helpful aspirational goal for an AI-based true self-driving car, though the fulfillment of that aspiration is going to be pretty tough to achieve and will forever likely remain a conundrum for society to wrestle with.

The second of Asimov's laws is that the robot or in this case the AI driving system is supposed to obey the orders given to it by a human, excluding situations whereby such a human-issued command conflicts with the first rule (i.e., don't harm humans).

This seems straightforward and altogether agreeable.

Yet, even this rule has its problems.

I covered the story of a man that used a car to run over a shooter on a bridge that was randomly shooting and killing people (see my discussion posted June 1, 2020). According to authorities, the driver was heroic by having stopped that shooter.

If the Asimov second law was programmed into the AI driving system of a self-driving car, and suppose a passenger ordered the AI to run over a shooter, presumably the AI would refuse to do so. This is amply obvious because the instruction would harm a human. But, we know that this was a case that seems to override the hard-and-fast always-to-be-obeyed convention that you should not use your car to ram into people.

You might be complaining that this is a rare exception, which I totally concur is absolutely an oddity.

Furthermore, if we were to open the door to allowing passengers in self-driving cars to tell the AI to run over someone, the resulting chaos and mayhem would be untenable. In short, there is certainly a basis for arguing that the second rule ought to be enforced, even if it means that on those rare occasions it would lead to harm due to inaction.

The thing is, you don't have to reach that far beyond the everyday world to find situations that would be nonsensical for an AI driving system to unquestionably obey a passenger. A rider in a self-driving car tells the AI to drive up onto the sidewalk. There are no pedestrians on the sidewalk, thus no one will get hurt.

I ask you, should the AI driving system obey this human uttered command?

No, the AI should not, and we are ultimately going to have to cope with what types of utterances from human passengers the AI driving systems will consider, and which commands will be rejected (see my analysis of the barking of commands problem posted on December 13, 2020).

The third law that Asimov has postulated is that the robot or in this case the AI driving system must protect its own existence, doing so as long as the first and second rules are not countermanded.

Should a self-driving car attempt to preserve its existence?

In a prior column, I mentioned that some believe that self-driving cars will have about a four-year existence, ultimately succumbing to wear-and-tear in just four years of driving (see my posting on September 3, 2019). This seems surprising since we expect cars to last much longer, but the difference with self-driving cars is that they will presumably be operating nearly 24x7 and gain a lot more miles than a conventional car (a conventional car sits unused about 95% to 99% of the time).

Okay, so assume that a self-driving car is nearing its useful end. The vehicle is scheduled to drive itself to the junk heap for recycling.

Is it acceptable that the AI driving system might decide to avoid going to the recycling center and thus try to preserve its existence?

I suppose if a human told it to go there, the second rule wins out and the self-driving car has to obey. The AI might tricky and find some sneaky means to abide by the first and second rule, and nonetheless find a bona fide basis to seek its continued existence (I leave this as a mindful exercise for you to mull over).

Conclusion

Based on the aforementioned logic, it would seem that Asimov's three rules have to be taken with a grain of salt.

The AI driving systems can generally be devised with those rules as part of the overarching architecture, but as might be abundantly evident from this discussion, the rules are aspirations and not ironclad irrefutable and immutable laws.

Perhaps the most important point of this mental workout about Asimov's rules is to shed light on something that few are giving due diligence toward. In the case of AI-based true self-driving cars, there is a lot more to devising and deploying these autonomous vehicles than merely the mechanical facets of driving a car.

Driving a car is a huge ethical dilemma that humans oftentimes take for granted. We need to sort out the reality of how AI driving systems are going to render life-or-death decisions. This must be done before we start flooding our streets and byways with self-driving cars.

Asimov said it best when he lamented a remark that still applies today, some eighty years or so after he implored us with this: "The saddest aspect of life right now is that science gathers knowledge faster than society gathers wisdom."

True words that are greatly worth revisiting.

CHAPTER 25
KNOWING VS TELLING AND SELF-DRIVING CARS

We know more than we can tell.

That's an assertion made by philosopher Michael Polanyi in his 1966 book entitled *The Tacit Dimension.*

Later on, an economist named David Autor wrote: "At a practical level, Polanyi's paradox means that many familiar tasks, ranging from the quotidian to the sublime, cannot currently be computerized because we don't know the rules" (as mentioned in his research paper *Polanyi's Paradox and the Shape of Employment Growth*). This economist, therefore, crowned Polanyi's statements with the anointing of the now-famous moniker of Polanyi's Paradox.

What exactly is the paradox, you might be wondering?

Presumably, the fact that we know more than we can tell is a paradox due to the conundrum that if you know something then apparently you ought to be able to explain it. If you cannot explain it, this begs the question of how you know that you know it. Meanwhile, if you can explain it, this seems to showcase that you do indeed know it.

In short, it is purportedly paradoxical to know something and not be able to tell or explain the thing that you seemingly know.

A bit of a wild carriage ride and not an aspect that all agree makes indubitable sense. Let's take a close look at the question of knowing versus telling, doing so as it relates to humans, and then consider how this pertains to AI systems.

For those interested in the topic of knowing versus telling, there is an allied discussion that can be had about the capability of animals in similar regards.

Does your beloved pet cat know things, and can it potentially tell or explain those things that the feline knows?

Based upon watching the inordinate volume of online cat videos, it might seem to be the case that cats know more than we think they do, and they might be able to "tell" what they know in ways that aren't so apparent to us (yet might be evident to their fellow felines). The same can be said likewise about dogs, birds, and all manner of creatures..

Humans seem to provide an easier means of ferreting out the knowing versus telling puzzle, so we shall begin this analysis with an assessment of humanoids. My cat probably knows quite a bit about humans, but I've grabbed the keyboard from the mischievous kitten and will opt to proceed accordingly.

First, let's consider whether knowing something and being able to explain it are intertwined brethren.

Many people can utter a spoken language and craft reasonably grammatically correct sentences and stories. Yet if you ask them to explain the semantic and syntax rules of their fluent language, they might be stumped at doing so. How many times have you heard someone able to well-articulate the difference between verbs and adverbs? Unless you happen to be an English major, much of how the English language works in any technical details is rather foreign to you.

Nonetheless, you can speak and write fluently.

The point being that just because you might not be able to explain the underlying process or procedure that you use to undertake a task or make a decision, this does not axiomatically imply that you must therefore not fully comprehend the task or the decision-making chore. It could be that you are simply unable to articulate how you do what you do. And this doesn't sizably and nor necessarily lessen your ability to do what you do.

An oft-cited example of this gap between knowing and telling is claimed as pertinent to the act of driving a car, and also the same qualm is said to be associated with self-driving cars, which I'll get to in a moment.

Return for now to the presumed mystery of knowing versus telling, there really isn't any gleaming paradox about not being able to tell what you know. Sometimes you are able to explain what you know, while sometimes you are not able to do so.

For the example of language fluency, if we taught such a person the various rules of English, they would be able to henceforth explain how they compose their words. Either way, whether they know the explanation or not, they remain fluent in their language nonetheless.

As an added aside, do not mix the facet of telling to be an assured indication of the knowing, since it is quite possible to be able to explain something and yet not be able to do the something that you can explain.

Hope that doesn't give anyone a headache.

Yet another key concern on this knowing-versus-telling riddle is the glaring and wide-open question as to whether telling about what you know is even the same thing as what it is that you know.

Here's the rub on that.

You ask someone why they decided to eat a pastrami sandwich for lunch today. The person tells you that they determined that their biological hunger would be satiated via the consumption of pastrami. They also figured out the number of calories and the types of nutrients involved. By making a calculated and overtly conscious effort, they came to the rightful conclusion that pastrami had to be the meal of choice for today's lunch.

Do you believe this explanation?

Maybe yes, maybe no.

The odds are that it is more so an after-the-fact concocted justification.

You wanted to get an explanation, and by gosh, you got one. Whether this is what really went through the person's mind when they settled on having pastrami for lunch is likely quite unknown. Perhaps an office mate got pastrami and the smell induced the urge to get a pastrami sandwich. Or the hunger was sparked by a billboard outside their office window that touted the local sandwich shop and its prized pastrami sandwiches.

There ostensibly isn't any means to open a person's brain and see what happened when they made a choice or have some bit of knowledge about something. Any explanation is always a second-hand indication. To some degree, we are taught to provide cogent explanations for our behaviors. In that manner, you seem to be doing things sensibly and in an orderly fashion. Whether that is what transpired in your noggin is a completely different matter altogether.

Bringing us back to the facet of knowing more than you can tell, the emphasis on this second point is that the things you tell are not necessarily a true introspection to the things that you know. The telling or explanation can be a separate signal that might or might not have much to do with the actual rendering inside your head.

You could argue that it is utterly true that we know more than we can tell since the things that we tell are offshoots of whatever it is that we know. The telling is a sort of fictional account. It might tie to what we truly know, or it might be tangential to what we know.

This brings us to the most worrisome of the contentions in this portrayal of knowing more than we can tell.

The suggestion or allegation that we cannot computerize things that we might know but that we cannot tell is the blot upon this whole house of cards. Such an exhortation makes it seem that unless you can fully explain how something works, it is not amenable to being implemented via a computer system.

That's a darned shame of an assertion and would be unlikely voiced by anyone fully versed in the computer field itself. This is something that those outside the field of computer science might think is sensible, but in the end, it is just not the case. Those people were probably taught to write computer programs by writing out every line of code and starting from scratch to do so. They probably found the task laborious and tired of it. This left them with the impression that this is the only way to program a computer.

Not so.

You could readily make the argument that the widespread popularity of today's Machine Learning (ML) and Deep Learning (DL) is to a great extent based partially on the focus of being able to program computers without necessarily knowing what the system is precisely doing in any logically intelligible way (for more about how this works and why it pertains to this discussion, see my analysis at **this link here).**

That's both a good thing and a not so good thing.

The use of Machine Learning and Deep Learning makes use of mathematical approaches to pattern matching and relies upon a computational means of carrying out pattern detection. Upon the discovery of said patterns, the system can attempt to find those patterns in newly acquired data and then act as per the responses established when being trained on the initial set of patterns.

In some cases, the pattern matching is so densely arcane in a computational and mathematically detailed way that it defies any ready means of being logically explained. Sure, you can trace the system and see that this calculation and that calculation took place. But, trying to raise that to a level of human understandability and logically grasp the telling, can be very hard to do, possibly not feasible at all.

The not so good aspect of that lack of telling means we are left with the hope that the system is doing things appropriately. I've written repeatedly about the dangers of AI systems that might latch onto unfair, inequitable, and discriminatory practices, such as deciding on loan applicants based on say their gender, yet we as a society might not generally know this is taking place under-the-hood.

There is a big push from the AI Ethics front to get XAI (an acronym for Explainable AI) so that we can all have a clearer understanding of what the innards of these AI systems are doing.

For those trying to craft XAI, one of the questions that arise is akin to the points made earlier about the telling versus the knowing of something, specifically this: Does the explanation that is crafted about what is going on inside the AI system have to be aligned with what the AI is truly calculating, or can the explanation be something perhaps easier for humans to understand and yet does not track specifically to what the AI is internally performing?

You are welcome to ponder that thorny question.

We now can turn to the topic of key focus herein: *Are AI-based true self-driving cars vulnerable to the alleged Polanyi Paradox and if so, what does this foretell?*

Let's unpack the matter and see.

Self-Driving Cars And Telling What They Know

For Level 4 and Level 5 true self-driving vehicles, there won't be a human driver involved in the driving task.

All occupants will be passengers.

The AI is doing the driving

We can reconsider the knowing-versus-telling (alleged) paradox when it comes to driving a car.

Can humans drive a car?

The answer is obviously yes, though we can certainly carp about how some people drive, albeit they are still considered a car driver.

Can humans explain how they drive a car?

By-and-large, you would pretty much have to answer yes to that question.

If you ask someone why they made a left turn and then swung into the outer lane, they would likely provide an explanation. The driver might say they made the left turn because they were trying to get to a destination on that block. There was a place to make a left turn onto that block, so they did so. They might then tell you that they quickly swung into the outer lane to position their car closer to the curbside, which is where they intended to park the car once they got further down the block.

You might not be completely satisfied with this answer and seek more details.

Okay, the person explains, they sat in the driver's seat and had the engine running. They made the left turn by pushing down on the accelerator pedal, which gave gas to the engine, and caused the car to roll forward. They then maneuvered the car by using the steering wheel. After making the left turn, they steered into the outer lane and then applied their brakes in anticipation of stopping and parking the vehicle.

One supposes you could keep asking for greater and greater details, maybe asking them to explain the molecular elements of their bodies and the car.

Anyway, you've got yourself an explanation, being done at various levels of granularity.

The driver told what they knew, or so it seems.

Perhaps the explanation is a concoction, and it does not directly proffer what went through the person's mind at the time of making the left turn. On the other hand, it is a rather logical and seemingly on-target explanation. In that sense, we'll probably make a reasonable assumption that the explanation does match what they know.

Shifting gears, can we get an AI system to drive a car?

The answer is a tentative yes, in the sense that we can certainly devise an AI system to drive a car, though we don't yet know whether the driving can be done in the same manner and range of circumstances that a human can drive a car. We also don't know if the AI will drive as safely as humans, for which the desire is yes, and indeed the hope is that the AI driving systems will be much safer than human drivers.

Can the AI explain how it drives a car?

That one is a bit of a head-scratcher since it depends upon what you mean by the AI providing an explanation.

The AI that we are referring to in today's era is not sentient, and not even close to being sentient. Some believe that we can only have satisfactory AI driving systems whence AI is sentient, but that seems a dubious precondition and so far, the progress to-date seems to belie that bone of contention.

The more disconcerting and practical omission right now would seem to be the lack of AI-based common-sense reasoning. Assuming that common-sense is not solely viable due to the existence of sentience, we could use a bona fide semblance of articulated common-sense reasoning to boost AI driving systems into the driver's seat more aptly.

In any case, yes, the AI can be devised to provide an explanation of what it is doing while driving a car.

Some portions of the AI driving system are written in a conventional programming kind of way, making use of millions of lines of programming code. You could claim that the code itself is the explanation, but I don't think most people are envisioning that as the explanation they are seeking. There would presumably need to be a higher-level logical explanation for people to readily consume.

Other portions of the AI driving system are using Machine Learning and Deep Learning. This takes us back to the earlier discussion that the ML/DL might be readily explainable or it might not be, and the role of XAI. The arcane mathematical and computational calculations do not especially proffer a logical and nor readily comprehensible explanation.

We have returned once again to the potential gap between what the knowing is, and what the telling is.

You might have heartburn that the "knowing" is the conglomeration of the program code and the ML/DL, which some would argue is not the same as human knowledge. They would assert that the ascribing of a "knowing" to the computer system is an anthropomorphic overplay. Humans can do knowing, but computers cannot, they would emphasize.

I've tackled that heated discourse in my prior columns and won't revisit the rancor here.

For the alleged paradox about knowing versus telling, it would seem that the AI can be made to tell, and it can be made to "know" (at least to the degree of what we consider to be a knowing within a computer system of today's caliber).

In that sense, the AI can tell what it knows, though with the caveat that we have to be careful in using both the word "tell" and the word "knows" since those are laden with all kinds of hidden meaning.

Conclusion

Some have asked a related question, namely, they wonder whether we even need to have the AI driving system be able to explain itself.

If you get into an AI-based true self-driving car, and it whisks you to your destination, there would seem to be little need for an explanation. You might say that having an explanation is quite unnecessary. All the AI needs to do is the driving job, and we can be happy in our potential ignorance or unawareness of how this task was accomplished.

Perhaps that makes sense at an initial glance and in a fairytale world, but the odds are that the AI driving systems are not going to be so lucky as to never be in a car crash or otherwise avoid doing things we find untoward as a driving act.

For those of you clinging to the notion that the advent of AI self-driving cars will lead to zero fatalities on our roadways, I've stated over and over again that this is a zero chance. There are still going to be car crashes and human fatalities, along with human injuries, in an era of self-driving cars. This is partially due to the likely ongoing mix of human-driven cars and self-driving cars, plus the physics involved in the driving of a car.

You can bet your bottom dollar that there are going to be inquiries seeking explanations of what the AI was doing. These might be sought during lawsuits about self-driving cars that have gotten into car accidents and might also be expected by regulatory authorities.

Many of the automakers and self-driving tech firms have placed any kind of XAI onto the backburner for now, since they have their hands full just trying to get a self-driving car to drive safely from point A to point B. The capability of providing an explanation of the AI, by the AI, sits on an edge or corner case list, awaiting its turn to be considered high enough in priority to figure out.

As a quick recap:

- As humans, we inarguably know more than we can tell.

- The lack of telling does not axiomatically negate or undercut per se the knowing, though it has that strong possibility and can cause queasiness about the depth or nature of our knowing.

- We can also tell, yet the telling might have little or no bearing on the knowing, thus, you could smarmily say that we at times tell more than we know.

Adding to these precepts is the aspect that the AI can be of a knowing (of a kind), and can do a telling (of a kind, if so devised), and the telling might also have little or no bearing on the knowing (depending upon how the telling is constructed).

Someday, we might end-up with AI that does have a knowing, and it might or might not wish to do a telling, for which the telling might be concocted to placate humans, and the AI holds dear the secrets of its knowing.

Of course, inevitably, cats will rule the world, which begs the question of whether they will opt to make use of AI.

My cat knows but smugly refuses to tell.

We might not know this when it happens, but I assure you, I'll tell you when I spot it.

That's my promise on the knowing *and* the telling.

CHAPTER 26
SNOW BURIED AND SELF-DRIVING CARS

Snowstorms aplenty are upon us as the winter decides it is time to let loose.

A recent news report about a snowfall calamity that luckily had a happy ending is both surprising, an eyecatcher for sure, and helpful to ponder and mindfully reflect upon.

Here's the story.

A man in upstate New York inadvertently drove off an icy roadway, plowed into a bank of snow, and while inside the car, he became entrapped when an abundance of accumulating snow engulfed his vehicle. As if that wasn't already unnerving enough, apparently snowplows might have shoveled snowy buildup onto his trapped automobile when attempting to clear the adjacent roadway of the rapidly falling snow (reportedly, the local area got about four feet of snow).

Let's do a quick recap.

Imagine yourself stuck inside a car, buried under by snow, and having no ready means of escape. It seems like one of those wild stunts that a Houdini-inspired prankster might try to pull.

But this was deadly serious business.

Freezing cold temperatures were underway. He had gone off-the-road at about midnight. It was dark with arctic-like weather conditions.

Inside the car, the bitter cold was taking its toll on the man. His body temperature began to wane, and the looming possibility of hypothermia and frostbite became a frightening reality.

I'm sure that we all have had our own worries that we might one day be driving and do a slip-and-slide off an icy and snowy road, but the worst-case scenario was that your car might get wrecked and you'd need to hoof your way to the nearest point of civilization. In this case, he was in the midst of civilization, wherein his car was embedded into a snowy embankment that was amid a series of homes and mailboxes. In other words, this didn't happen in some remote off-the-beaten-path and instead occurred in the middle of a relatively populated area.

It seems impossible to envisage that you could be buried inside a snow-covered car while nearby are people inside their homes, sitting in front of cozy fires in their fireplaces, perhaps lazily looking out their windows at the fluttering snowflakes and enjoying steaming mugs of hot cocoa.

As they say, reality is sometimes stranger than fiction.

Well, your first thought might be that he must have had a cell phone, since everyone has a cell phone nowadays, and all he would need to do is call 911 to have someone come and rescue him. According to the media reports, he did try calling 911, repeatedly, but his cell phone reception was extremely weak, and he was, unfortunately, unable to get a solid signal. As a side note, I suppose that if you've ever cursed the phone companies about their cell coverage, this is an instance whereby you really would have a bona fide beef about it.

Eventually, around 8:30 a.m. in the morning, his cell phone managed to finally get sufficiently connected with 911. This good luck was undercut by the bad luck that the geolocation of where he was had troubles being determined, and the best guess was that he probably was somewhere along a 3-mile stretch of roadway. Presumably, he either did not know where he exactly was or might have been unable to convey his position via the spotty cell phone connection.

The local police drove along the expected roadway to search for the snow-covered car. One policeman stated that he stopped at numerous snowbanks to dig into the snow to see if the vehicle was buried within. Finally, after the search had been underway for quite a while, and at around 10 a.m. or so, the policeman that was periodically digging into snowbanks noticed a large clump of snow that was in front of a house. It was not considered a suspected place for the car to be.

Thinking that the snow was covering mailboxes, the cop opted to plunge his arm deep into the snow to clear a hole to spot the address on the mailbox. Turns out, he startlingly realized that he had just punched the side of a car window.

The policeman was standing atop the snow buried car.

With the help of a passerby, the policeman pulled the nearly frozen man out of the car and then loaded him into the police car. The icy man was taken quickly to a nearby ambulance and then transported to a local hospital. The man managed to survive this oddball "snow buried car" dilemma and reportedly was doing okay at the hospital.

That's the gist of the story, now here's some after-the-fact couch-based quarterbacking going on.

Some have already criticized the man for not having snow-related gear in his car such as perhaps having the kind of stuff you'd wear when going skiing or camping in the snow. Sure, we all ought to be always prepared, but it seems a bit farfetched and one of those hindsight-is-always-right exhortations to unduly ding him for not being packed to the gills with cold-weather gear.

Note to self: Go right now and put my winterized insulated goose-down filled sleeping bag in my car as a future scenario precaution.

Another criticism in our smarmy world of today is that he should have broken a car window and dug his way out.

First, you'd need some viable means to break out one of the car windows, which it turns out are a lot more resilient than you might assume. The retort there is that we should all be riding around with one of those specialized tools that can smack and smash a car window.

Second, if you did somehow get through a window, what would you use to dig or tunnel your way out of the snow cave that you are immersed in? The flippant answer is that you ought to be carrying a hiker's collapsible shovel with you at all times, presumably in the trunk of your car (which, you'd need to presumably reach into from the backseat of the car, assuming this was feasible to undertake).

Or, all in all, you might do a MacGyver, perhaps by tearing apart a car seat, and then cleverly using the various metal and plastic components as both a window smasher and then as a digger to burrow your way through the snow.

It is stunningly amazing the number of snippy comments that people can come up with on these grim occasions. Some say he shouldn't have driven off-the-road, to begin with, and implied he deserved whatever happened next. Really? That's a pretty tough outlook on life. Others wondered why he didn't just run the car engine and use the car heater to keep warm. Reportedly, the car was no longer functioning after going off the roadway.

Yes, we can come up with dozens of questions and zillions of variations. One supposes that if nothing else, this tale of survival maybe gets people thinking about the topic overall and might prepare any of us for the day that some similar untoward scenario happens in our daily lives.

Speaking of thinking contemplatively about these dire situations, consider that the future of cars is that we will inevitably be using self-driving cars.

Here's an interesting question: *What would happen if an AI-based true self-driving car were to slide off a road and end up in a snowy embankment, and what about a riding-along passenger inside the vehicle?*

Let's unpack the matter and see.

Self-Driving Cars And Being Snowbound

For Level 4 and Level 5 true self-driving vehicles, there won't be a human driver involved in the driving task.

All occupants will be passengers.

The AI is doing the driving

This means that if there is a passenger inside the self-driving car, they would be innocent of driving the car off the roadway, and thus those that were earlier tossing acrid barbs at the man that drove off the road in the snowy conditions could no longer blame a human driver for such a transgression.

In turn, this might get you wondering whether the AI would somehow inadvertently drive off the road.

Some seem to think that AI driving systems will always be driving in a perfect manner. By perfection, they seem to suggest that the car will defy the laws of physics and otherwise be acting as though operating in a fairytale world.

Let's be clear about this, a car is a car. And, the AI is not omniscient, nor able to avoid all possibilities of calamity and roadway problems.

We are going to have car accidents in an era of self-driving cars.

Forget those hollow slogans that say we are going to have zero fatalities, which I've repeatedly proffered has a zero chance of happening. The hope is that we'll have a lot less crashing and colliding of cars, which I agree should so occur, but it will not magically eliminate all car-related fatalities and injuries (it's a big number right now, amounting to about 40,000 human fatalities per year and approximately 2.3 million injuries, that's only in the United States and the numbers are much higher on a global basis).

In short, the AI driving system could indeed end up in a predicament such that the AI was unable to keep the self-driving car from sliding off the roadway. You could in fact have a self-driving car that goes into a snowy embankment.

It can happen.

It will happen.

Envision that the self-driving car is making its way in snowy and icy conditions. The roadway is super slick. Despite all the state-of-the-art sensors, including video cameras, radar, LIDAR, thermal imaging, ultrasonic, and so on, the roadway status can still be murky and not fully detectable. The car comes upon an especially bad patch, and the wheels and the vehicle begin to skid.

What will the AI do?

I've previously described that some of the AI driving systems are being infused with specialized driving capabilities for these snowy and icy buildup driving situations. In that case, the AI would invoke the driving skillset for this particular circumstance. That will certainly help but still does not provide a guarantee that the vehicle won't nonetheless go off the road.

If you've been following along about the progress of self-driving cars, you might have noticed that most of the self-driving car experiments on our public streets are being done in warm weather climates, such as California, Arizona, and Florida. This is partly because the driving efforts in those locales don't have an abundance of snow and seldom have ice, thus they are a lot easier to deal with. In that sense, many of the existing self-driving cars are not yet fully prepared to drive in those freezing cold temperatures that embody adverse roadway conditions.

In the self-driving car industry, there is specialized parlance that refers to the Operational Design Domain (ODD) for a vehicle. The ODD is an indication of the stipulated conditions that the AI driving system can handle.

For example, an automaker and self-driving tech firm might specify that their existing AI driving system can cope with warm weather and sunny days but is not yet capable of driving in cold weather and darkness. Meanwhile, some other AI driving system by another maker might be trained for nighttime driving and daytime driving, but only is capable in city environs and not ready for outlier locations. And so on.

Having an ODD that encompasses the extremes of driving situations, such as driving in snowy conditions, generally is considered a lower priority and placed onto the edge or corner case list. This means that this type of driving will be dealt with later on. Right now, the belief overall is that it is timelier and more sensible to focus on day-to-day driving in the city and suburbs, which is where the money is most likely to be made by providing a so-called robo-taxi service.

The AI driving system is supposed to figure out when its ODD is being exceeded.

Let's say that you get into a self-driving car and it starts on a journey to your grandmother's house. During the driving trip, the weather goes afoul. If this bad weather is considered outside the scope of the ODD, the AI driving system is intended to detect this aspect and then gradually and safely bring the car to a halt.

I've pointed out that this will be quite disturbing for people that are riding in self-driving cars. You might be inside a self driving car, and if it had a human driver the vehicle could have kept going, but since the AI is in-charge, and the vehicle has reached its ODD boundaries, the AI will refuse to continue driving and park you on the side of the roadway or in some such considered "safe" place.

Before you start to carp about this functionality, it does bring up an interesting point related to the story of the man that went into the snowbank.

If AI had been driving the car, perhaps it might have earlier determined that the roadway conditions were overly dangerous, or the conditions were outside the defined ODD for that AI driving system, and ergo it would have not kept driving. By not driving, it would have presumably avoided sliding off the roadway.

Problem solved by never getting into the problem per se. Of course, that was one of the unctuous comments that some had already uttered, namely blaming the driver for driving in conditions that he should (apparently) not have been driving in.

This is somewhat easy to assert as a broad statement, but the devil is in the details.

Suppose that you are heading to your grandmother's house because you have her pills and she is in bad health, desperately needing her latest batch of medicine. You probably are willing to take a heightened chance at driving in adverse conditions. We all make such decisions. When it comes to an AI-based self-driving car, you as a passenger will essentially no longer be in the driver's seat and therefore cannot make those kinds of tough decisions.

It will be quite fascinating to see how this works out.

People will presumably no longer be able to make high-risk driving journeys, at least with respect to whatever ODD falls within that high-risk category. On the other hand, even for moderate risk trips, the AI is presumably going to be a better driver, ostensibly because it won't drink and drive, nor will it drive distracted, and therefore we ought to have fewer fatalities accordingly.

On the balance, how will society perceive the benefits of self-driving cars versus the "costs" associated with perhaps not being able to use a car whenever you wish to do so?

This might also be a basis for some people clinging to keeping human-driven cars around and argued as a basis to avert any movement toward having only self-driving cars on our roadways. There is a contingent that insists we need to eventually and inexorably get rid of all human driving, though this is quite a radical proposition and opponents often say that you will only get them out of the driver's seat whence you have pried their cold dead hands from the steering wheel.

Conclusion

The point of the aforementioned context about self-driving cars is that there will still be a possibility of even a self-driving car going off the roadway and into a snowy embankment.

There's more to consider on this matter.

It is assumed that by-and-large self-driving cars will be deployed in fleets by large companies on a ridesharing basis.

As such, those fleet operators are going to be keeping close tabs on where their self-driving cars are at all times (doing so to know when the vehicle is available for its next money-making ridesharing requested ride). The odds are that if a self-driving car did slide into a snowbank, the fleet operator would likely know where this happened, and be aware that the vehicle had stopped moving. In that case, presumably, the fleet would send out a rescue mission or contact 911, right away.

Another facet of self-driving cars is their OTA (Over-The-Air) electronic communications capabilities. This allows the fleet operator to push updates into the AI software and allows the uploading of the driving data from the vehicle. It is likely that if an AI driving system got itself into a bad spot, it would do the classic "phone home" to alert the fleet operator.

There is also the use of V2V (vehicle-to-vehicle) electronic communication.

We are going to have self-driving cars that convey electronic messages to each other. A self-driving car that detects debris on the roadway could alert any nearby self-driving cars to be watchful. In that same manner, a self-driving car that has encountered a slick roadway could warn other self-driving cars. And, if a self-driving car perchance got into a pile of snow, it could try using the V2V to send an alarm to other nearby self-driving cars, which they could then take appropriate rescue actions.

Here's a final twist that you might find poignant.

The existing standard about the levels of self-driving cars does not cover the aspects of off-road driving.

In essence, there isn't an explicit requirement to be able to drive in an off-roading situation. Some automakers aren't dealing with the off-road facets as yet, since it seems apparent that making money from self-driving cars is first going to come from driving on-roads rather than when off-road in deserts, pastures, the mountains, or similar.

Once an AI self-driving car ends up in a snowbank, it would presumably not have the capability included to cope with trying to drive out of it. Of course, a human driver might not be able to do so either.

Eventually, the odds are that AI driving systems will include off-roading provisions, which will be somewhat curious to see. I say this because some believe that the fun of going off-roading is being at the wheel and having to contend with the challenges of the driving experience. Will we equally enjoy an off-roading jaunt when the AI is doing all the driving?

Anyway, please be watchful of those snowy and icy roads that are increasingly appearing as the winter embrace strengthens, and if you see a car completely covered in snow, I guess you cannot assume it is empty. There might be a human in there.

In the future, there might not be a human at all in the vehicle, but there might be AI, although the AI won't be worried about the snowy entrapment, other than that it ostensibly wants to perform its duty of driving a car and cannot do so until the vehicle is released from its snowed-in confinement. Help me, the AI might be decrying, help me to help you, by getting back onto the roadway and driving people wherever they want to go.

Well, within reasonable limits, one might say.

CHAPTER 27
CYBER HACK AND SELF-DRIVING CARS

They say it is the largest ever cyber hack.

Unless you are living under a rock or inside an Internet-disconnected cave, you've undoubtedly heard about the recent cyber-attack encompassing an estimated 18,000 or more U.S. companies and governmental agencies, including notables such as a preponderance of Fortune 500 businesses, most of the top accounting firms, many of the top telecommunications entities, and a wide swath of federal departments such as Homeland Security, Treasury, Commerce, and the military branches.

Some have referred to this sly cybersecurity breach as the most insidious and widespread in history (for my prior coverage about cyber-attacks, see **the link here**).

It is breathtaking in its scope and devilishly clever in its approach, and as a result, has caught many by utter surprise. On the one hand, it is not particularly a surprise that a massive scaled cyberattack has occurred since cyber protection experts have been warning about these possibilities for years on end. The surprise is that we didn't know it was underway and that by size alone it presumably should have earlier been somehow detected. An itsy-bitsy cyber-attack might squeak through under the radar, while one that cuts across hundreds or thousands of organizations ought to have been sniffed out by either happenstance or by watchful oversight.

The real twist, some exhort, might be that this is only the tip of the iceberg. Perhaps there are other similar cyber-attacks already underway and we just haven't ferreted those out as yet. Or new cyber breaches are being devised and for which when they are unleashed will be beyond breathtaking and veer into the full borne calamity and cyber catastrophic sphere.

In brief, here's how the recent cyber trickery worked.

A tech company called SolarWinds provides networking-related software that is immensely popular and used by thousands upon thousands of companies and governmental agencies. The networking software in this case is known as Orion. To update the Orion software from time-to-time, SolarWinds pushes out various patches that are sent electronically, which then automatically get downloaded and installed into computers loaded with the Orion system.

I'm sure you've experienced the same kind of automatic updates that occur on your smartphone or your home computer. They happen usually behind-the-scenes. Sure, you might see a notification telling you that an update is happening, and you might be annoyed that the device is possibly unavailable during the updating process, nonetheless, you really do not know for sure what in the heck the patching is doing and can only hope that all is well and that you are in good hands.

Unfortunately, there is no guarantee that you are in good hands, and likewise, the Orion updates were surreptitiously in bad hands, as it were.

The cyber hackers had infused some dastardly instructions or coding into the Orion updates. According to news reports, the hacked insertions and distributions took place between March and June of 2020. Besides the insertions, the hacking provided additional means for the cyber crooks to gain additional access to the computers that had downloaded the patches. For example, in some cases, this allowed access to emails and other data and systems that were within the company or governmental agency that was ensnared.

This cyber breaching technique is commonly known as a Trojan Horse, reminiscent of the famous story involving the Greeks using subterfuge to sneak into the city of Troy.

You likely recall from your history lessons that the Greeks had pretended to sail away from Troy and had left behind a large wooden statue that looked like a horse. The Trojans decided to keep the statue and dragged it into the city and thus readily brought it through the heavily fortified and guarded gates. Lo and behold, Greek soldiers were hiding in the statue and upon nightfall opted to make their way out of the statue and opened the city gates. Meanwhile, the Greek army had unobtrusively sailed back and when the gates were opened by their insider crew, the warriors poured into the city and took over the city of Troy.

I realize that nearly everyone knows the story of the Trojan Horse and thus telling the legendary tale once again seems perhaps excessive, but I've retold it here for an important reason. Let's briefly consider how the Trojan Horse might have been defeated and not been such an overwhelming success.

First, the Trojans brought the statue behind the city defenses and ergo made life easier for the attackers. The same can be said of the SolarWinds situation. Companies and federal agencies willingly allowed the Orion software updates to come straight into their computer systems and readily avoid the likely zillions of firewalls and other expensive and continually vigilant cybersecurity protections.

Second, for the Greeks, once they had luckily gotten the Trojans to take the bait, their hidden Greek soldiers were able to get out of the statue and sneak around. The same can be said about the cyber crook insertions into the Orion patches. Once those patches got installed into the inner sanctum of the companies and federal agencies, this allowed the hackers to start looking around.

Third, the Greek hidden soldiers were able to provide a means for the Greek army to readily pour into the city of Troy, doing so by opening the gates. As far as we know today, the Orion patches might have similarly created openings for the hackers to otherwise enter into those companies and governmental agencies, providing added avenues for attack.

Unlike the Trojan Horse tale, the cyber hackers had not yet made a wholescale outright attack that would have gotten all the bells and gongs to start ringing.

It is conceivable that they might have not ever gone the route of pouring an entire army of cyber attackers into the realms they were able to penetrate. Instead, the chances are that they would have continued to quietly hunt and peck their way into more and more secrets. That's not to say that at some point they might have decided enough is enough, or possibly chosen to pull the kill-switch if caught redhanded, and then attempted to do colossal damage. For all we know, the endpoint might have been to first get as much secretive stuff as they could, and then do a scorched earth approach of wreaking havoc, which doubles as both a means of harming those they attacked and potentially covering up the attacker footprints too.

There is a well-worn motto among cybersecurity specialists that the protector has to be right all of the time, while the attacker only has to get it right one time. In this case, despite the aspect that many of those companies and agencies spend bucko bucks on cybersecurity and are stridently diligent in protecting their computers, the cyber hack nonetheless got in.

This brings up another lesson from the Trojan Horse tale, namely that the Trojans could have potentially caught the hidden Greek soldiers, even after having voluntarily bringing the statue into the city and thus have prevented those implanted spies from opening the gates. In that sense, having guards inside are oftentimes as important as having guards at the perimeter. The problem with the internal guarding is that it can be disruptive to those innocents that are inside and become overly oppressive and onerous.

You might have experienced this same consternation when trying to do something on your home computer and the anti-malware software stops you from doing so.

Now that we've covered the gist of the largest ever cyber hack, recall that I had earlier mentioned that this SolarWinds and Orion matter might be a taste of what the future will hold. There is always the specter hanging over our heads that an equally sinister and large-scale cyber attack is being planned and will once more catch us flatfooted.

Where might this arise?

Using a crystal ball, let's envision what the future will contain. We know that the advent of self-driving cars is going to eventually occur and we will be utilizing those autonomous vehicles on a daily basis.

Here's an interesting question: *Will a large-scale cyber hack potentially confront the emergence of AI-based true self-driving cars, and if so, how might it take place?*

Time to unpack the matter and see.

Self-Driving Cars And Cyber Attacks

For Level 4 and Level 5 true self-driving vehicles, there won't be a human driver involved in the driving task.

All occupants will be passengers.

The AI is doing the driving.

As a society, we are all hoping that the advent of true self-driving cars will be immensely beneficial.

One touted benefit will be a reduction in the annual 40,000 fatalities due to car crashes in the U.S. alone, and likewise a substantive lessening of the estimated 2.3 million injuries associated with car accidents. The belief is that the AI driving systems will be safer drivers than humans due to the lack of DUI for the AI (the AI won't be drinking and driving) and being able to avoid other human foibles such as distracted driving. Another anticipated benefit is that a kind of mobility-for-all will arise, wherein those that today are mobility constrained or mobility disadvantaged will finally have ready access to mobility via self-driving cars.

These benefits are not going to be entirely friction-free (see my column at **this link here** for a myriad of ways that there are potentially adverse "unexpected" consequences that I've predicted).

A noteworthy concern that has to be at the top of any such list includes the potential for evildoer cyber hacking associated with self-driving cars.

We can readily use the recent SolarWinds and Orion instance as a type of template.

Self-driving cars will be outfitted with OTA (Over-The-Air) updating capabilities. The automaker or self-driving tech maker will have access to the in-car on-board computer systems and the AI driving system, doing so via the OTA electronic connection. Whenever a new patch needs to be installed into the self-driving car computers, the OTA is activated, and the patches are downloaded and installed.

Indeed, this act is considered one of the most uplifting aspects of self-driving cars. Rather than having to take your car to a dealership to get something updated, by-and-large the assumption is that you can have changes made remotely. While your car is sitting in the garage or parked outside your house, the OTA can be activated and used to make sure you have the most recent updates. Perhaps the updates include improvements to the braking capabilities of the vehicle. Or suppose the AI has been enhanced to do a better job at making left turns or being able to swiftly change lanes on highways.

You might already be sensing where I am taking you on this journey about self-driving cars.

Suppose a cyber hacker is somehow able to place a cyber hack into the downloaded patches to a self-driving car. Imagine that this is done at the cloud of the automaker or self-driving tech firm. Unbeknownst to those guardians, a surreptitious cyber piece of code has been snuck into their patches. The next thing that happens is that those sneaky elements are carried down into your self-driving car.

No one is the wiser.

The use of the vaunted Trojan Horse upon those unsuspecting self-driving cars.

What might the cyber-attack do?

One possibility is that it will sit quietly, trying to be unobtrusive in hopes of not getting detected. There might be something else that gets it sparked, or possibly is using a timer to become active, or might be active in relatively mundane and less apparent ways.

Keep in mind that a self-driving car has a slew of specialized sensory devices such as video cameras, radar, LIDAR, ultrasonic, thermal imaging, and the like. Those sensors can collect a ton of data about everything they spot around the vehicle and can also capture what is going on inside the vehicle too (via cameras pointed inward, see my discussion at **this link here** of the "roving eye" of self-driving cars).

In short, the cyber attack could be seeking to get private info, about you and what you do.

Each time you go for a ride in the self-driving car, it will be tracking where you have gone, how long you were there before riding again in a self-driving car, etc. This privacy intrusion can include too what you did while inside the vehicle, including whom else was with you, what you discussed, and so on.

If a sinister plot involved trying to track the whereabouts of someone, this is a handy means to do so.

There is also the concern that the cyber hack might attempt to override the AI driving system, getting access to the driving controls of the self-driving car. This might be directly undertaken or could utilize the AI driving system itself, merely nudging the AI driving system to do something possibly untoward.

I won't spell out what this might achieve, other than to hint that this could range from having the vehicle become a robo-jacking incident (akin to a carjacking but as led by the AI), or might get the vehicle into a car crash scenario.

Some insist that this kind of speculation about cyber-attacks and self-driving cars is hogwash and will never happen. They claim that this is like griping about the sky falling.

I'm not sure what world they live in that there is a one-hundred percent guarantee that none of those actions could ever happen. Though I certainly agree that there are ways to reduce the odds of such calamities, anybody clinging to the assertion that it will never happen would seem to be reliant upon a false assumption that is probably going to do more harm than good. Staying on the edge of concern has advantages for being inspired toward permanent vigilance.

I am sympathetic to the complaints about any unwarranted exaggeration of this happening, yet to flatly deny the possibility is seemingly also a foul move.

Anyway, let's take a moment and see if we can glean some insightful lessons from the SolarWinds and Orion cyberattack that has now become famously the purported largest ever such breach.

Here are some vital lessons to contemplate:

- **Didn't know the hack existed for quite a while** – this is especially disconcerting since the cybersecurity goal ought to be that even if you can't stop something, at least catch it soonest feasible. The same goes for any untoward infiltrations of self-driving cars.

- **No apparent hunt for Red October** – one wonders how the internal cybersecurity of this many companies and entities was not seemingly scrutinizing the patches and the resultant behaviors, which yes, you can argue that the assumption was that SolarWinds was trusted, but there is always the need to "trust but verify" in these settings. Systems onboard the self-driving car need to also take a look inside the wooden horse and make sure there aren't hidden Greek soldiers if you get what I mean.

- **Run silent, run deep** – as emphasized earlier, the added cleverness was that the cyberattack was subtle and relatively well-hidden, whereas much of today's cybersecurity protections are looking for the bold and the brash. Self-driving cars must look for the noisy intrusions and the (potentially) deadly silent ones.

- **The chain gang and leveraging the software supply chain** – There is a vast software supply chain that is involved in the software used by all of us, meaning that at any point in the chain there is an opportunity (threat) that something diabolic will be inserted. Everyone else in the chain makes the assumption of trust throughout the chain. When you consider the millions upon millions of lines of code and hundreds or thousands of software modules that go into these immensely complex AI driving systems, there are potentially a lot of software supply chain intrusions that can readily occur. Keep your eyes open.

- **OTA opens the gate, hoorah, and yet opens the gate, yikes** – the use of OTA for modern-day cars is fantastic and offers substantial benefits, but this should not blind us to the downsides that go along with this handy portal. Your self-driving car will be getting patches just like your smartphone or home computer, wherein you won't know what the patches actually contain. If a Windows laptop freezes, it can be discomforting, while if the OTA for a self-driving car lets in a fiend the result can be shudderingly quite severe.

- **Go big or go home** – this cyberattack was impressively wide, stoked by the number of customers that SolarWind had. We can assume that an automaker X or self-driving car tech firm Y will inevitably have thousands if not millions of their self-driving cars on the roadways, gradually over time (there are 250 million conventional cars in the U.S. today). The scale is going to be alluring to cyber hackers. They might not especially care about self-driving cars right now, since there are so few on the roadways, but once the self-driving car boon takes hold, you can bet that the cyber attackers will be fighting over each other (or collaborating) to get at this revered innovation.

Conclusion

For those that might misinterpret these remarks, do not somehow think that I am suggesting we ought to curtail or prevent self-driving cars from reaching fruition. That's decidedly not what is being stated. What I am saying is that we can assiduously learn from this SolarWinds and Orion cyber attack and make sure to apply what we can to the advent of AI-based true self-driving cars.

Most of what is taking place in the self-driving car development world are pretty much under wraps and hidden from view. We cannot know for sure how much of a cybersecurity effort is being undertaken by each of the self-driving car development teams and their respective leadership (well, there are always platitudes, but this does not necessarily equate to real-world on-the-ground bona fide in-depth and well-funded cybersecurity efforts).

It is generally well-known in the cybersecurity field that companies often do not provide sufficient resources for cybersecurity precautions and only do so once an incident occurs and makes the headlines. This is similar to the reaction to earthquakes. Most people do not prepare for earthquakes, and when one happens, they suddenly awaken to the need for earthquake preparedness. After a while, they become lulled into complacency, letting their guard down and their attention goes lax until the next big earthquake happens.

Let's all stay awake in the self-driving car field and make sure to fully invest in cybersecurity. The last thing anyone wants is an earthquake-like cybersecurity outsized break-in into self-driving cars, regardless of which brand or model, for which the resulting fallout could be an outcry to stop all self-driving car efforts (the proverbial bad apple in the barrel mindset). Please learn something substantive from the SolarWinds instance, along with the historical lessons of the fabled Trojan Horse, so that we can hopefully stave off those dastardly evildoers that are eyeing those shiny new and altogether alluring self-driving cars.

CHAPTER 28
MURDER CASES AND SELF-DRIVING CARS

The nationwide murder rate is heading in the wrong direction.

It is decidedly on the rise, rather than on the decline.

According to the latest news reports, the number of murders in the U.S. rose last year, increasing by about 40% in the country's ten largest police districts over the prior year. Resources to investigate those murders are being stretched tenuously thin. Meanwhile, family and friends of the murdered victims become overtly frustrated and extremely exasperated over the delays in solving these homicides. The public at large also remains on edge as to whether a murderer is still loose within their community and ought to have already been captured and detained.

One potential new gizmo in the detective toolkit for undertaking murder investigations is something only now starting to appear. It is an innovation of technology that has already been predicted as a wide benefit for society in many ways, though few have considered the potential role in solving crimes. This new technology has still a long way to go before being fully ready for active use, and will undoubtedly take many years to be widely deployed, yet nonetheless has a multitude of uses for the betterment of us all.

What is that new technology?

Surprisingly, for some, the means of aiding the catching of criminals such as murderers could be spurred via the advent of true self-driving cars.

Yes, that's right, the emergence of self-driving cars has all the makings of being a kind of modern-day gumshoe that can be a devout crime fighter. Note that self-driving cars aren't going to leap tall buildings and nor do they need to drive faster than a speeding bullet. There are other ways in which a plethora of self-driving cars will be part of the law enforcement kit and caboodle.

The future of a world with self-driving cars is supposed to reduce the annual number of car crashes and car accidents, both large and small, dramatically ratcheting down the count of those yearly 40,000 fatalities and 2.3 million injuries that occur in the United States alone. Furthermore, the hope is that self-driving cars will spark a mobility-for-all era. Those that are currently mobility constrained or disadvantaged will finally have ready access to mobility at a presumed low cost and plentiful availability.

Seldom considered is the fact that self-driving cars can also be a vehicle toward serving justice, truth, and the American way (well, got a few puns in there, but anyway, the point is hopefully well-taken).

Here is the question worthy of rapt attention: *Will the advent of AI-based true self-driving cars aid in solving murders and other crimes, acting on behalf of the law, and in pursuit of justice?*

Let's unpack the matter and see.

Self-Driving Cars As The Detective On The Beat

For Level 4 and Level 5 true self-driving vehicles, there won't be a human driver involved in the driving task.

All occupants will be passengers.

The AI is doing the driving.

Your first thought might be that other than the nicety of not having to yourself be at the wheel of a car anymore, there doesn't seem to be much in the way of crime-fighting skills as part of an AI-based driving system. In that respect, you would be correct that the AI itself is not going to be wearing a badge and will not be the local on-the-beat detective per se.

Here's how self-driving cars are going to become a roadway warrior in the war on crime.

Imagine that a murder has just taken place on a street corner in the downtown area. A lone gunman opted to shoot someone. The murderer rushes off.

Normally, by the time that the authorities arrive, the perpetrator is long gone. One of the first actions to undertake involves trying to find witnesses that can attest to what happened. What did the murderer look like? Which way did the murderer go? Did anyone recognize the brazen killer? And so on.

Shift gears and envision a future whereby there are self-driving cars aplenty on our byways and highways.

First, keep in mind that true self-driving cars are chockful of specialized sensory devices, such as video cameras, radar, LIDAR, ultrasonic units, thermal imaging, and the like. These highly tuned sensors are used as the eyes and ears of the vehicle. The AI collects data about the driving environment surrounding the car via these sensors and plots out the means to navigate and operate the driving controls to safely proceed.

There is a somewhat unexpected byproduct to all that sensory equipment which bodes for both great advantages and sadly also great consternation. Besides the sensory data being used to drive the vehicle, there is also the possibility of using that collected data for other purposes. I've referred in my columns to this ancillary usage as the "roving eye" and discussed the merits and drawbacks accordingly.

Here's what this data allows.

When a self-driving car drives down a city block, the sensory devices are voluminously capturing everything within their designated range. The video cameras are collecting visual sightings of the street, people on the sidewalk, buildings adjacent to the street, and so on. All of the sensors are doing their thing, soaking up whatever they scan. This data gets stored on-board the self-driving car and can be kept inside the in-car computers and various electronic storage capabilities.

At some point, the self-driving car can perform an OTA (Over-The-Air) electronic communication, typically connecting with the cloud of the automaker or self-driving tech firm that devised the AI system. The most widely known use of the OTA involves pushing down patches or updates to the AI driving system of the vehicle. This can allow for example the capability to remotely update aspects of the vehicle such as the braking facility or perhaps used to tune the AI to improve making tricky left turns.

As they say, what comes down can also go up (not everyone says it that way, but you know what I mean).

The data that has been collected by the self-driving car during its travels can be uploaded into the cloud during the OTA process. If so desired, this could include every nook and cranny of whatever the sensors captured during the driving journey. Assume that the self-driving car was driving around for several hours. This implies that there are hours of a roving eye that has been like a souped-up video camera, one that has been moving around and not just planted in one spot. Also, besides the video data, there is the radar, LIDAR, ultrasonic, thermal images, and a slew of other assorted stuff.

Suppose a self-driving car drove down your neighborhood street, perhaps doing so on its way to pick-up someone that had requested a ridesharing lift. You were outside of your house, standing on the front lawn, perhaps playing kickball with your son and daughter. Without you directly realizing that you were being viewed, the self-driving car managed to record a video of you and your kids, doing so as the vehicle simply drove down the street.

This video gets uploaded into the cloud.

You might be thinking that you don't care and cannot envision why you should.

Realize that at this point, the OTA has uploaded the video and other sensory data, including the GPS positioning indications, as part of the upload. Inspection of the cloud-based data would tie together that at that street address there was an adult and two children. If you then correlate that data with other demographic info, it sure might be interesting to firm selling toys to know that possibly someone living at that particular house has two small children and they like to play kickball.

This data could be a goldmine for the automaker or self-driving tech firm that is collecting it from the self-driving cars.

Amp this up.

Over a period of a week, each time a self-driving car goes down your block, this data gets uploaded. One day you were out mowing your lawn. Another day you were planting pretty flowers. By examining the uploaded data over time, a fuller semblance of what you do, how you live your life, begins to become more apparent.

That's based on just one self-driving car that perchance comes down your street on an occasional basis.

Imagine that there are hundreds, perhaps thousands, or eventually millions of self-driving cars on our streets (there are about 250 million conventional cars in the U.S. today, and the expectation is that by-and-large they will inevitably be replaced with self driving cars). The odds are that throughout the day and night, there are going to be self-driving cars all around us, and relatively continuously cruising down your street and other streets.

By stitching together this data from those zillions of self-driving cars, it would be possible to piece together an overall semblance of what takes place daily in our world.

The good news is that this is how crime-fighting comes to the fore.

Return to the earlier scenario about the murder that took place on a street corner in the downtown area.

Rather than trying to find a happenstance of a video camera that was perched on a nearby building, an astute place to look for any captured data about the incident would be in the uploaded data from self-driving cars.

Assuming that self-driving cars are going to be always on the go, rolling around 24x7, which makes sense since they are potential money makers and only able to make money once they are transporting someone or something, the odds are high that the murder scene came within the purview of a self-driving car during the murderous act.

It could be that several self-driving cars wandered past that murder scene and caught the whole act from multiple angles. If you piece it all together, this could offer an uncanny portrayal of the murder from start to finish, and from a multitude of perspectives. One perspective might only show the back of the murderer, while another self-driving car got a glimpse of the front and the face of the killer. Think of those video editing special effects these days that can rotate in a 3D fashion around a fictional portrayal of a fight or other action and think about how this can be done for real-life incidents.

Okay, let's switch into a crime-fighter mode.

We would check the uploaded data to stitch together the crime scene at the moment of the murder. This could likely showcase how the murder took place, along with providing an exact timestamp of when it happened.

Essentially, we have an electronic eyewitness to the murder.

Next, we could inspect the cloud data to see if we can trace where the murderer came from, before reaching the street corner and committing the crime. This might help figure out where the killer lives or maybe was at a restaurant or other place that they tend to frequent and might be known by others.

Remember that the murderer fled the scene.

We can inspect the collected cloud data to see where the murderer went. If he ran to another block and went into an apartment complex, there is a solid chance that this was also seen or detected via a multitude of self-driving cars that were perchance roaming around or making trips in that area.

It might also be useful to use the data to trace where the victim came from and how they arrived at the point of the murderous act.

In this instance, we are assuming that the victim fell right there, upon being killed, but suppose the murderer dragged the body or tried to do some kind of cover-up. Again, the data from a multitude of passing self-driving cars might reveal this aspect of the crime.

So far, we have been using the data solely to figure out the crime and sought to take a look at the killer and the victim.

Let's expand our approach.

In the collected video, there were other people on the sidewalk and they seemed to have witnessed the killing. A person inside a store nearby was looking straight out the store window and appeared to see the murder take place.

These are all potential witnesses that can further help in solving the crime, including finding the murderer.

We can invoke facial recognition software to see if we can figure out who those people are. It is conceivable they are already posted somewhere on the Internet via social media or in other databases. This provides us with their names and contact information.

You could go to the scene and try to talk with these witnesses. Another possibility would be to contact them and ask if they would be willing to come to the police station to share what they know about the murder and what they saw happen.

Some of them might be willing and eager to help, but might not readily have transportation available to come to the police station. No problem. You send them a self-driving car that picks them up and provides them a lift to the police station, and will likewise give them a ride home afterward.

You decide that it would make sense to go to the crime scene and then go throughout the nearby area to do a canvas. Using a self-driving car, you head over to the scene. There is no need for you to be driving the vehicle and therefore can use the time while inside the self-driving car to be further analyzing the case. Driving is otherwise a distraction and instead, you can devote your full attention to the murder case.

Here's the final tipping point on solving the murder.

From the data collected, you have an image of the killer that is relatively unobscured. Attempts to use facial recognition did not identify who the person is and apparently, they have not been previously spotted or otherwise posted their image anywhere online.

No problem.

All those self-driving cars that are crisscrossing the city on a moment-to-moment basis are now deputized as part of your murder investigation. You merely indicate that at any time, if any of those zillions of continually on-the-go vehicles spot that person, the face of the apparent murderer, the AI driving system should immediately send an alert to 911.

If that person meanders anywhere in the city, they are going to get nabbed.

For the moment, we can have pleasant thoughts that those that heinously wish to commit murders are going to have self-driving cars on their case. Those roving Sherlock Holmes will make it harder for murderers and other criminals to escape the hands of justice.

Conclusion

There are a bunch of caveats to keep in mind on this gumshoe self-driving car scenario.

Ponder these thorny questions:

- Will the automakers and self-driving tech firms allow law enforcement to have access to the data being collected?
- Will laws be enacted to force the data to be made available to law enforcement?
- Will the data on-board the vehicles be uploaded, or will the data instead be kept only inside the self-driving car and not uploaded?
- Will only some of the data be uploaded, selectively, diminishing the opportunity to use it in the fashion depicted herein?
- Will the data be deleted immediately upon use for the act of driving the self-driving car and otherwise not be accessible beyond the moment that it was needed?
- Etc.

Realize too that there are going to be a multitude of self-driving car brands and models.

This suggests that trying to tie together the disparate data and formats of data is going to be somewhat arduous. Yes, that's a bit of a hurdle, but in the end, if the data is made available across these differing clouds, it will be technologically feasible to do the needed conversions and matchings. Of course, the computational costs to do so might be rather prohibitive, so we'll need to see if this is the kind of usage that will get the financial backing needed to bring it to fruition.

As a final thought, we certainly should look beyond the assumed altruistic use of this data for exclusively undertaking the virtuous notion of fighting crime. You probably got chills up your spine since this facility has a dual-edged sword to it. Though it can be used as a crime fighter, there is an equally looming possibility of using it to invade our privacy and pursue those that are innocents.

We are in the midst of bringing to fruition self-driving cars, ostensibly a great asset that can benefit humanity and that will simultaneously provide a means to undercut humanity. Darned if this always seems to be the case with most innovations.

I realize this all seems like some bizarre future world of unimaginable nature, but do realize that everything described herein can be done with today's technology.

That being said, as mentioned at the start, there aren't enough self-driving cars on the roadways today to make this especially viable. On the other hand, once self-driving cars start to become viable, you can anticipate that a huge and frenetic race of sorts will take place to deploy as many of them as possible, as rapidly as possible (under the presumption that they are money makers on wheels, plus these vehicles offer the societal benefits of lessened lives lost and might fulfill the mobility-for-all potential).

Is this advent of self-driving cars and their use as amateur sleuths going to really happen?

Please take a moment and carefully put on your detective's cap.

As a great fictional detective once emphasized, when you have eliminated the impossible, whatever remains, however improbable, must be the truth.

CHAPTER 29
PEDESTRIAN MISCLASSIFICATION AND SELF-DRIVING CARS

Have you ever eaten a papple?

Probably not, and the odds are that you might not have even heard of one before either.

It is a type of pear that resembles an apple in appearance and texture, though once you take a bite out of this juicy fruit, you would realize right away that it tastes quite different from an apple. From the looks of things, a papple is usually round like an apple, reddish-orange like an apple, crunchy feeling like an apple, and yet it is decidedly not an apple. It is a member of the pear family.

Suppose you were reaching to grab an apple and by mistake grabbed a papple.

This could easily happen if you were not paying close attention, perhaps looking intently at your smartphone at some important cat video and meanwhile absentmindedly reaching over to a nearby plate that seemed to be filled with apples. If you shifted your otherwise diverted attention to the fruit that was now in your hand, the chances are that upon closer inspection you might suspect that this delicious-looking item was not an apple.

Of course, those cat videos are so mesmerizing that you likely would simply bring the fruit up to your mouth and start chomping down on the assuredly tasty item.

Imagine the look on your face when your tastebuds registered that something was amiss.

The problem would not be an especially harmful or disastrous issue and merely would be a mismatch of expectations. Your brain was expecting an apple, and your mouth got something else. The taste would be familiar, akin to the taste of other pears you've had before. Perhaps your mind would contemplate that this was an apple that just so happened to somehow have a taste reminiscent of a pear. You might take a startled glance at the fruit, trying to calculate what was going on.

Imagine that by a bad stroke of luck that it turns out you are allergic to pears. You've spent your life avoiding pears. Now, unbeknownst to you, by your own hand, you have inflicted yourself with a pear that you'll now have an allergic reaction to.

Admittedly, that would seem like a pretty remote chance, namely that you happen to have an allergy to pears and mistakenly thought a pear that looked like an apple was readily edible as an apple. Maybe this is the same chance of winning the lottery or finding yourself taking a flight to the moon.

Stepping back for a moment, the crux to this whole apple-versus-pear conundrum arose due to a misclassification.

You misclassified a pear as an apple. No need to be especially hard on your self about this misclassification since this special kind of pear does have a notable resemblance to an apple, especially by visual examination alone.

We misclassify a lot of things, all the time, daily, and at any moment.

You are waiting in a restaurant for a friend to come and have lunch with you. Your eyes are scanning the people that are entering the busy eatery. Assume that it is a cold day and raining or snowing, which means that most of those coming into the restaurant are wearing heavy clothes and generally covered up. It would be quite easy to spot someone that appeared to be your friend, based perhaps on their height and overall shape, yet once they removed their coat and hat, presumably by now seeing clearly the face of the person, you would realize it is not the person you were waiting for.

No harm, no foul.

Consider another example of a misclassification, though one with greater consequences.

You are driving your car on a winding road. It is hard to see very far ahead. As you come around a sharp curve, there is something in the middle of the roadway. What is it? Your mind races to quickly assess the nature of the object. Time is a key factor. You need to decide whether to try and swerve around the object, which is going to be dangerous to perform, or directly plow into the object, another potentially dangerous act.

In a split second of available attention, your mind decides it is a tumbleweed.

Usually, it is feasible to ram into a tumbleweed and do so without any notably adverse results. Sure, your car paint might get scratched, but at least you stayed in your lane and did not incur the dangers of swerving, especially on this winding road that was (let's say) rounding on sheer cliffs. So, you drive immediately ahead, and the tumbleweed lightly smacks your car. You are still thankfully safe and sound, able to continue the driving journey unabated.

But imagine that in that brief moment of classification, you inadvertently misclassified the object.

Turns out it was a meshy ball of steel cables that had come from a construction site and fallen off the back of a truck on this same winding road. The mesh was rolling and bobbling, just like a tumbleweed, and happened to be painted white and resembled a tumbleweed in both looks and actions on the roadway. Yikes, your decision to proceed ahead based on the belief that this was a tumbleweed is now quite problematic. You strike the object and it smashes your left headlight and gets entangled with your tires. A tire blows out. The car is now difficult to control.

That's an example of how misclassification can ruin your day (let's assume, for sake of discussion, you, fortunately, survive the incident and live to tell the tale of the misclassified tumbleweed, so go ahead and let out a sigh of relief, and continue reading herein).

Why bring up this discussion about classifications and misclassifications?

Besides humans making classifications, there is an expectation that AI systems will be making classifications. Consider the use case of AI-based true self-driving cars that routinely need to classify the roadway objects that are encountered during a driving journey.

The sensors of a self-driving car are collecting voluminous data about the world surrounding the vehicle. This includes data from the on-board video cameras, radar, LIDAR, ultrasonic units, and the like. As the data gets collected by the sensors, the AI system has to discern what is out there in the world and thus inspects the data mathematically accordingly. Various computational pattern matching techniques are often utilized, including the employment of Machine Learning and Deep Learning (ML/DL).

Some people seem to think that AI is amazingly infallible and an idealistic form of mechanized perfection.

Please toss that absurd notion out of your mind.

You already would seemingly agree that humans can misclassify things, and as such, you need to realize and expect that AI systems can and will also misclassify things too (I'm not suggesting that humans and AI of today are equivalent, and do not wish to somehow anthropomorphize current AI, thus merely pointing out that AI can misclassify, in the same semblance of a notion of misclassification as that which befalls humans).

Per the driving example of the human driver that was on the winding road, a misclassification while at the wheel of a car can be life-threatening. We can presumably allow some slack about misclassifying a pear as an apple, based on the logic that this is rarely a life-or-death kind of classification, but providing latitude toward misclassifying objects that are in a driving environment can have quite serious and sobering consequences.

A recent social media post by Oliver Cameron, CEO of Voyage, brought up an interesting question about the classification and misclassification aspects of self-driving cars. In particular, I'm referring to a posted indication of a snowman that was misclassified as a pedestrian by an AI driving system.

I'll give you a moment to ponder the ramifications of that type of misclassification.

Almost as though you were playing a chess game, consider what kind of moves and countermoves that specific misclassification portends.

Is it more akin to the misclassifying of a pear as an apple, or closer to the misclassification of the tumbleweed?

Before we get into the details, first let's clarify what I mean when referring to AI-based true self-driving cars.

Let's unpack that and see.

Self-Driving Cars And Misclassifications

For Level 4 and Level 5 true self driving vehicles, there won't be a human driver involved in the driving task.

All occupants will be passengers.

The AI is doing the driving.

Here's our scenario: A self-driving car is going for a jaunt, doing so in an area that had a recent snowfall. Assume that the self-driving car is either heading to pick-up a ridesharing passenger or maybe is simply roaming and awaiting a request for a lift.

Imagine that a snowman has been assembled on a somewhat snow-covered grassy area that is adjacent to the roadway.

This happens all the time and we can certainly expect that once the snow season arrives, there will be lots of bustling children (and adults) that opt to craft a snowman. Perhaps this amounts to one of the most delightful aspects of living in an area that gets snow. You might carp about having to shovel snow from your driveway or complain bitterly about how treacherous the streets become when coated with snow and ice, but by gosh, you can make snowmen!

As the self-driving car comes up on the road that has the snowman, the sensors of the vehicle are all doing their thing, such as visual imagery pouring in from the cameras, radar data being obtained, LIDAR data being collected, etc.

This data is assessed computationally to classify the objects that are in the driving environment. A properly devised AI driving system makes use of Multi-Sensor Data Fusion (MSDF), meaning that the interpretations that are being derived via each of the types of sensory data are being aligned and compared, aiding in trying to discern and classify objects (think of this as though you might use your eyes *and* your ears, in combination, when trying to decide what an object is, thus, a multi-sensory form of classification.

Upon collecting the sensory data, the AI driving system determines that a thing consisting of puffy white balls (of snow) and that has a hat and some seeming arms (made of sticks) might be a pedestrian.

Most people do not realize that these kinds of AI-based classifications are usually assigned a probability or, if you will, an uncertainty value. Perhaps the AI classifier has computed a 90% chance that this is a pedestrian or maybe only a 5% chance. Depending upon the threshold devised for the AI driving system, and the nature of the object as it is estimated to be, the result can be that the AI stipulates that the object is a pedestrian, though with an assigned chance that it is and an assigned chance that it is not.

Anyway, let's assume that the snowman has been classified, or more worrisome, misclassified as a pedestrian.

Your first thought is that this is funny and not at all a concern. It is seemingly a lot better to misclassify a snowman as a pedestrian than to do the opposite of misclassifying a pedestrian as a snowman. If an AI-based classifier mistook a pedestrian to be a snowman, and if the AI system was devised to assume that snowmen do not move and otherwise are not to be a matter of attention, this could lead to some rather unfortunate and possibly ugly consequences.

Hopefully, even in this reversal of a misclassification, once the pedestrian ("snowman") started to walk or move, the sensors would detect the action, and the AI classifier would reclassify the object to be considered a pedestrian. That doesn't quite solve the issue though. Perhaps, if the AI had correctly classified the pedestrian at the start of the process, it would have maybe slowed down the self-driving car since there appeared to a pedestrian near the roadway. Now, somewhat after-the-fact, having reclassified, the available time to take an avoiding driving action might be diminished and thus increase the risks associated with the existing driving scene.

Back to the situation of misclassifying the snowman as a pedestrian.

You are perhaps now thinking that it is "safest" to have made the misclassification in that direction rather than somehow doing the reverse misclassification. All told, this would seem to be a "get out of jail free" card, namely that it is better to misclassify (if misclassification is inevitable) toward being a human than being a non-human (i.e., a pedestrian in lieu of a snowman).

Yes and no.

It partially depends upon what actions the AI driving system has either prior devised via the use of ML/DL or been explicitly programmed to do when encountering a pedestrian.

Suppose the AI determines that since this does seem to be a

pedestrian, the self-driving car should slow down. This seems quite prudent. The pedestrian is standing near the curb. There is a possibility that the pedestrian might opt to suddenly leap into the street or dart across the road. Jaywalking happens all the time.

Admittedly, this pedestrian is not moving around, and nor crouched as though about to lunge into the street. By all appearances, the pedestrian seems to be at a standstill and not an immediate threat to the path of the self-driving car. But, better to be safe than sorry, as they say in self-driving cars.

The self-driving car slows down.

Meanwhile, the sensors continue to feed data about the object (and the other myriad of objects in the scene), just in case this particular object (which is now assumed to be a pedestrian), makes any sudden moves.

You could argue that the act of slowing down, when slowing isn't required, would be a somewhat unintended and possibly adverse consequence of this misclassification. Perhaps a human driver in a car behind the self-driving car is caught off-guard. There doesn't seem to be any reason whatsoever to be surprisingly slowing down. The human driver wouldn't even imagine that the snowman is the culprit in this case. Human drivers see snowmen all the time and realize right away that it is a snowman, mindfully classifying the snowman as indeed being a snowman.

You can still assert that the slowing down is fine, and though perhaps disturbing to the human driver in the car behind, nonetheless not a big deal.

Let me take you on a slippery slope about this. Assume that there are lots and lots of self-driving cars on the roadways. Envision that they are all using the same AI-based classifiers (at least for a given brand and model). Whenever they spot a snowman, they each of their own accord will slowdown. This happens by the thousands upon thousands of those self-driving cars. None of them classifying a snowman as indeed a snowman (well, in some instances), and always opting to slow down under the misclassification of the snowman-as-pedestrian.

If the world only consisted of self-driving cars, perhaps this would be dandy. But, the reality is that there will be a mix of self-driving cars and human-driven cars for quite a while, likely decades (there are about 250 million conventional cars in the U.S. alone, and they are not going to overnight be replaced by self-driving cars). These "safety first" self-driving cars are going to disrupt on a large-scale the human-driving population. In theory, this could end-up leading to human drivers rear-ending those self-driving cars (being caught off-guard by the slowing action) or lead to road rage against self-driving cars (we'll get in a moment to the counterargument about the nature of human drivers, hold on).

I don't want to extend that futuristic vision very far since it does fall apart rather quickly.

Presumably, the automakers and self-driving tech firms would get feedback about the exasperating misclassifications and take action to enhance the classifier for dealing with the "snowman apocalypse" if you will.

And, for those seeking to ultimately ban human driving, under the assumption that AI driving systems will be safer as drivers (not drinking and driving, not driving distracted, etc.), they would undoubtedly use this snowman-as-pedestrian reaction by human drivers as yet additional evidence that human drivers need to go (which, some human drivers insist you will only take away their driving whence you pry their dead cold hands from the wheel).

Conclusion

There is a slew of other considerations on this rather simple but telling snowman-as-pedestrian dilemma.

Someone opts to purposely build a snowman in the street as a joke or prank on self-driving cars, which is distinctly not a good idea, and I've discussed repeatedly in my columns that people pranking self-driving cars ought to not do so. By the way, in case you are worried that I've just let the cat out of the bag, please know that people do sometimes build snowmen in the street just for fun, not due to self-driving cars, and hence this is something that self-driving cars need to be prepared for.

What does the self-driving car do?

Human drivers would presumably ascertain that it is a snowman, and in a civil manner drive slowly around the obstruction. Some self-driving cars of today would do the same, while other brands or models might get logically jammed-up about what to do and send an alert to the fleet operator. And so on.

One argument is that self-driving cars ought to not be on our public roadways until they have been taught or "learned" how to deal with all these various roadway aspects. Others argue that the only viable way for the AI driving systems to be readied involves being on public roadways, rather than relying solely on simulations and special closed training tracks. This is an ongoing and at times acrimonious debate.

Here's another twist on the snowman-as-pedestrian.

Even if you believe that defaulting to the snowman-as-pedestrian is a safer way to treat the matter, nonetheless the public at large might become concerned that self-driving cars cannot seem to differentiate between the likes of a snowman and a pedestrian.

Say what?

This to most humans is a rather obvious and ordinary form of classification. If self-driving cars cannot figure this out, it bodes for some grave concern.

Furthermore, those same qualms might be extended further, leading to the trepidation that maybe there are lots of other misclassification going on. Maybe fire hydrants are being classified as pedestrians. Maybe small trees are being classified as pedestrians. Where does this end? Indeed, maybe the AI-based classifier is classifying *all* objects as pedestrians.

For those in the self-driving car industry, they would say that kind of thinking is misguided and outright hysteria. Maybe so, but it is useful to keep in mind that the public at large is the determiner of whether self-driving cars will be on our roadways, doing so via their elected officials and the regulations that are ultimately put in place or as laws are adjusted based on public opinion.

There is also the ever-present specter of lawsuits that might one day be launched against those that make self-driving cars. Suppose a self-driving car gets into a car accident, one that the AI ought to arguably have avoided. An astute attorney during the trial might cleverly undertake a showy indication to the jury that this AI was (by implication) so bad that it couldn't even identify a snowman. Unfair, you say? Well, the counterargument is that it is true, though perhaps meanwhile your side is counterarguing that it is a misleading and poisoning alliteration, depending upon the court case issues at hand.

All because of a normally joyous and completely uneventful snowman.

Despite all of that bit of an icy tale about snowmen, one might say that we ought to not take this instance and turn it into a snowball that runs down a snow hill and becomes a larger issue than it deserves (let's avoid making a mountain out of a molehill, one would contend).

Wait for a second, here's another viewpoint, maybe tell children they can no longer make snowmen near the street anymore. This comports with the belief by some that the real-world will need to conform to what self-driving cars can do, rather than self-driving cars being sufficiently improved to handle the real-world that there are immersed in.

One shudders to think that kids would no longer be able to make snowmen out in front of their homes, and assuredly is not the spirit of the snowy season and an absurdly upside-down way of solving things.

As they say, snowmen aren't forever, but their memories are.

CHAPTER 30
SCAVENGER HUNTS AND SELF-DRIVING CARS

You might have fond memories from childhood about going on neighborhood scavenger hunts.

Usually, these were fun-filled treasure hunts involving a list of unusual items to be found and then going door-to-door to ask whether any of your neighbors happen to have the peculiar object. Perhaps the list included something relatively commonplace such as a red crayon or a copper penny. The oddball items such as a receipt from a local grocery store or a slightly used baseball game ticket were usually discovered on a happenstance basis.

If the scavenger hunt was more challenging it might consist of riddles that had to be solved. Either the riddle would be used to indicate what items were to be found (imagine a riddle for which the answer is a red crayon, that kind of thing), or the riddle could only be solved if you also had obtained the designated item from a neighbor. These kinds of scavenger hunts were typically reserved for older children since the whole aspect of figuring out riddles could be quite frustrating to toddlers and seemingly ruin the joy and excitement associated with the cherished hunt.

Here's something that perhaps you might not have tried.

When I was in college, I'd go on scavenger hunts with my college-age buddies and do so via professionally organized driving-based scavenger hunts. Not many people have done this, and likewise not many are even familiar with the concept altogether.

The way it worked was that you would sign-up and pay a modest fee to participate in the scavenger hunt. Besides the fun of participating, there was usually a prize of some kind for whoever completed the scavenger hunt the soonest and had the most items correctly obtained. The prize might be cash or a gift card or merely a trophy. In any case, you would start the timed activity by arriving at a designated parking lot on a certain day and time. There would be lots of other cars there too, all waiting for the event to get underway.

An organizer of the event would come to your car, provide you with the list for the scavenger hunt, and then markdown your starting time. This allowed for everyone to get underway on a staggered basis and not be jockeying crazily to get underway. Despite this notion of separating out the vehicles, the reality was that once you got partway through the scavenger hunt, the odds were that you would encounter other cars that were circling in the same places as they desperately attempted to find the items on the list.

Unlike going door-to-door, the driving-oriented scavenger hunt usually consisted of merely eyeing things and writing down what you saw.

For example, the list might ask how many fire hydrants there are on a particular street. You would need to drive to that street, cruise down the street, and count the number of fire hydrants. This might be tricky because the list could subtly state that you were to spy only yellow fire hydrants, thus if you weren't paying close attention you might miscount by including a red fire hydrant that just so happened to be on the street too (the organizers intentionally tried to mess you up by providing those kinds of conditions or criteria, knowing full well that some players would be inattentive and ultimately mess-up accordingly).

To properly undertake a driving scavenger hunt, the most common approach consisted of having a driver and several passengers that were supposed to be the eyes and ears for spotting the items.

The passengers would be responsible for inspecting the list, marking the answers, and being the mainstay of solving the clues. In some cases, teams decided to have each passenger inside their car be responsible for looking out their particular side window, doing so on an assigned basis, and thus averting having all the passenger's strain from looking wildly back and forth. Others thought that was a stupid tactic and just had everyone look whichever way they wanted.

Though this was supposed to be a joyful experience, some people took things a bit far and made the trek into a do-or-die kind of affair. You could see people inside other cars that were yelling and screaming at each other. They weren't having fun, they were threatening each other with bodily harm. Indeed, sometimes at the endpoint of the scavenger hunt that had all the cars come to a parking lot to see who won, the driver and passengers would oftentimes no longer be speaking to each other. I knew of some friendships that completely fell apart due to a scavenger hunt that got quite ugly and a team decided they never would be around the other person ever again.

That was quite sad and not at all in the spirit of the matter.

I assure you that I have fond memories of those driving-based scavenger hunts. If you had a team that perceived the event as a chance to be with friends and have a good time, the likelihood was that win-or-lose the point was well-taken that you were just having a grand old time.

There was something else though that was a bit disconcerting about these events, beyond the possibility of friendship splitting.

The off-putting aspect involved the task of driving.

In theory, the driver for each car would be fully concentrating on the driving task. They would not be distracted by figuring out the riddles and nor be sidetracked by counting fire hydrants (they would let their passengers do this). Of course, that's not how things actually worked.

The drivers wanted to partake in the whole process. This meant they were not entirely focused on the road ahead. That's a recipe for disaster. There were numerous occasions of near misses with other vehicles. If pedestrians happened to be on a street that was being used for the scavenger hunt, heaven help them. A jaywalker was likely to get poked.

It was rumored that some of the drivers would have a few drinks before starting the scavenger hunt. We didn't do this, but it isn't surprising to think that others did so. The outlaw brazen teams would have liquor inside the car and be drinking during the scavenger hunt. Most of the contests usually stipulated that no drinking while driving was allowed, but this was not especially monitored, and unless someone tattled there was little chance that the organizers would know that the rules were being broken.

I don't know how everyone ended up surviving these madcap activities.

You had drivers that were wildly distracted and driving like maniacs (recall that the scavenger hunt was being timed, so being speedy was a near necessity). There were tons of near-misses and yet I never heard of anyone actually colliding. Some idiots drank beforehand or were drinking while driving. Again, amazingly no one got into a car crash though I cannot say why that lucky streak occurred.

Let's be abundantly clear, do not drink and drive, and do not drive while drunk.

Shifting gears, consider the notion of a driving-based scavenger hunt in the future, and ponder what it might be like.

Here's a question to contemplate: *Will people potentially use AI-based true self-driving cars to carryout driving-based scavenger hunts, and if so how might it be undertaken?*

Let's unpack the matter and see.

Self-Driving Cars And Scavenger Hunts

For Level 4 and Level 5 true self-driving vehicles, there won't be a human driver involved in the driving task.

All occupants will be passengers.

The AI is doing the driving.

An obvious advantage of undertaking a driving-based scavenger hunt via a self-driving car is that you don't need to have a human driver. No need to worry that the driver is going to be driving while intoxicated. No concerns about the driver being distracted by the treasure hunt riddles or by the spying of the road to find the clues and answers.

Instead, the passengers can have all the fun and do so without the worries of a human driver at the wheel. This also means that everyone inside the car can partake in the same manner and none of you has to take on the arduous chore of watching the road. Presumably, your self-driving car is not going to ram into other cars, it won't strike pedestrians, and otherwise, the last thing on the minds of the passengers is anything whatsoever involving the driving of the vehicle.

Party time!

There are several other twists and turns involved too.

One aspect would be the surprisingly difficult aspect of getting the AI driving system to drive where you need to go.

Allow me a moment to explain this.

Most of today's self-driving car efforts are assuming that people will use self-driving cars to simply go from point A to point B. In a ridesharing kind of way, you will request a lift, the self-driving car will arrive at wherever you are, and you will have stated where you want to go. Perhaps you need a lift from your home to the grocery store. In that sense, you are going from point A to point B.

I've previously emphasized that people are not going to like being constrained in such a manner. Sure, if you are using a conventional ridesharing service, you expect that you can only go from point A to point B. But, if you owned a car and took it for a drive, the odds are that you would not restrict yourself in that same fashion.

Think of the number of times that you were driving your car and suddenly decided that you wanted to swing through a drive-thru fast-food eatery, or maybe opted to drive to a Starbucks to get a cup of java. Furthermore, you might be driving along and see something that catches your attention, maybe an interesting looking house that looks like the kind of house one day that you'd like to live in. Even though you are ostensibly driving from point A to point B, you decide to take a bit of an offshoot so you can drive past that noteworthy home.

The emphasis being that though most of the self-driving cars are aiming right now for the straight-ahead idea of going from point A to point B, you can bet your bottom dollar that people are going to want to have much more latitude in the driving navigation and direction.

For the scavenger hunts that I've described, there was never any specific point B that we were trying to reach. The clues might have said something like drive forward three blocks, make a left turn, go down two blocks, and now you are to start counting the number of fire hydrants. There wasn't a specific address that we could have merely entered into a self-driving car ridesharing system.

This brings up another salient topic.

Self-driving cars are likely to be using Natural Language Processing (NLP) to interact with passengers.

This is important since the riders will want to discuss with the AI driving system the facets of the driving journey. Maybe someone in the car has gotten car sick and urgently wants the AI to bring the car to a halt so they can get out of the vehicle and find some momentary relief. NLP is not quite yet at the proficiency level on the driving nuances and adjustments that people are going to express.

The NLP will gradually be getting better and better at having discourse with the riders.

Meanwhile, the back-up posture is that the passenger will invoke an OnStar-like capability in the vehicle that will connect them with a remote human agent, for which the remote agent might then instruct the vehicle about what to do.

Few of today's NLP for AI driving systems could cope with a scavenger hunt.

The ambiguity of where you want to go is beyond the realm of a typical NLP system. The beauty, as it were, of human drivers is that they can tolerate ambiguous or open-ended instructions while driving a car. You might tell someone to just start driving and focus on watching the road, while you are figuring out when the next turn should be undertaken. AI driving systems aren't ready for that kind of haziness.

I'm not saying that human drivers don't get upset at such ambiguity, and I'm sure you've been in a car whereby you told your friendly driver to wait for instructions, and they gave you the evil eye. People are people and when driving a car it can be exasperating to not know where you are driving to. With a scavenger hunt, the drivers realized this was a free-for-all and they were ready for the nuttiest of instructions and those last moment "turn here!" exclamations.

Another aspect to consider deals with illegal driving.

Admittedly, there were driving efforts underway during the scavenger hunts that either verged on the cusp of being illegal or were without question absolutely illegal. Making a sudden U-turn was the norm, trying to quickly go back and recount those fire hydrants. Going faster than the posted speed limit was going to happen. In many respects, this was a car race, and when that happens, there is a temptation to cut corners.

Again, I don't condone that kind of driving and anyone that crossed over into illegal driving during the scavenger hunts should have gotten busted.

Well, that's water under the bridge now.

For AI-based true self-driving cars, the base assumption is that the AI driving systems are going to drive strictly by the book. No illegal driving. Speed limits will be completely observed. And so on. I've indicated in my columns that this is not quite a realistic perspective and there will be times that self-driving cars might need to break the law (suppose a medical emergency happens, such as a passenger having a heart attack while inside a self-driving car, does this allow the AI to drive faster than the speed limit to reach the nearest hospital).

In the case of scavenger hunts, you can readily argue that it is fantastic that the AI driving systems won't drive illegally. This makes the playing field equal for all. With human drivers, at times there was a chance that some other driver was willing to despicably break the law to win the scavenger hunt. That was unfair to those that abided by the driving laws. With an AI driving system at the wheel, the assumption is that all of the scavenger hunt participants are playing by the same driving rules.

In recap, it might be hard to use a self-driving car for a scavenger hunt since the AI driving system is not fluid enough to cope with the uncertainty and ambiguity of where you are going. This could be perhaps mitigated by shaping the scavenger hunt into a series of waypoints and thus the hunt would be made into a set of destinations. It isn't quite the way things used to be done, but nonetheless, a means to still have the essence of a scavenger hunt via the use of a modern-day self-driving car.

The nicest changes will be that there is no longer a crazed human driver, nor a drunk one, and not even a distracted one. All the riders can be comforted in the belief that they are being safely driven. Plus, all the riders can join in the festivities of the hunt.

Conclusion

One criticism that undoubtedly would be launched is that this seems like a rather foolhardy use of self-driving cars.

People used to complain that using conventional cars for scavenger hunts was wrong because you were using up precious gasoline needlessly and you were polluting unnecessarily by running a car that was not serving a serious purpose. Driving to work, that's serious, and driving to get groceries is likewise, but using a car to simply go for a kind of joyride hunting expedition is decidedly not, they would exhort.

The good news for the use of self-driving cars is that they are most likely going to be EV's, and you can therefore counterargue that there is little if any pollution involved (a controversial topic that I won't wade into here), plus they aren't using petrol and instead are using electrical power.

Given such counterarguments, those that are opposed to the use of self-driving cars for a scavenger hunt are bound to take an altogether different tack and bring up the point that there is better use to be had. Some assert that the advent of self-driving cars is going to finally open the door for a mobility-for-all in our society. Those today that are mobility limited or disadvantaged will be able to get around and the self-driving car will be a kind of a godsend to bring that dream to fruition.

That being the case, they would likely be disheartened and quite dismayed to think that those wonderous self-driving cars are going to be used for scavenger hunts. Put those state-of-the-art contraptions to better and higher use, they would exclaim. This contention is not so easy to address since it has to do with supply and demand. We do not know how plentiful self-driving cars will be. If they are essentially a scarce resource (likely so, especially at first emergence), the argument that they should be used judiciously becomes much more paramount.

One last comment and then let's call this topic sufficiently hunted down for now.

Would there even need to be passengers inside the self-driving car during a scavenger hunt?

This might catch you by surprise.

Here's the logic.

The self-driving car is chockful of sensors such as video cameras, radar, LIDAR, ultrasonic units, thermal imaging, and the like. These are used by the AI driving system to serve as the eyes and ears, as it were, providing the data that indicates what is taking place in the driving environment.

If a driving-based scavenger hunt is going to occur that does not require getting out of the vehicle and solely has to do with what you see as a passenger, the aspect of using a self-driving car ergo portends that you do not need to be inside the vehicle at all. You could be sitting at home, maybe assembled with friends, and merely remotely watch what the self-driving car sees, and similarly, remotely instruct the AI driving system as to which way to go.

An eerie idea, I realize.

For those that didn't like the notion of using a self-driving car for a scavenger hunt, this last point will certainly put them over the edge. If you aren't even going to be riding in the darned thing, it for sure makes no sense to be running a self-driving car on our streets and highways when there isn't anyone inside the thing.

As some might say, that dog just don't hunt.

Time will tell.

APPENDIX

APPENDIX A
TEACHING WITH THIS MATERIAL

The material in this book can be readily used either as a supplemental to other content for a class, or it can also be used as a core set of textbook material for a specialized class. Classes where this material is most likely used include any classes at the college or university level that want to augment the class by offering thought provoking and educational essays about AI and self-driving cars.

In particular, here are some aspects for class use:

- Computer Science. Studying AI, autonomous vehicles, etc.
- Business. Exploring technology and it adoption for business.
- Sociology. Sociological views on the adoption and advancement of technology.

Specialized classes at the undergraduate and graduate level can also make use of this material.

For each chapter, consider whether you think the chapter provides material relevant to your course topic. There is plenty of opportunity to get the students thinking about the topic and force them to decide whether they agree or disagree with the points offered and positions taken. I would also encourage you to have the students do additional research beyond the chapter material presented (I provide next some suggested assignments they can do).

RESEARCH ASSIGNMENTS ON THESE TOPICS

Your students can find background material on these topics, doing so in various business and technical publications. I list below the top ranked AI related journals. For business publications, I would suggest the usual culprits such as the Harvard Business Review, Forbes, Fortune, WSJ, and the like.

Here are some suggestions of homework or projects that you could assign to students:

a) Assignment for foundational AI research topic: Research and prepare a paper and a presentation on a specific aspect of Deep AI, Machine Learning, ANN, etc. The paper should cite at least 3 reputable sources. Compare and contrast to what has been stated in this book.

b) Assignment for the Self-Driving Car topic: Research and prepare a paper and Self-Driving Cars. Cite at least 3 reputable sources and analyze the characterizations. Compare and contrast to what has been stated in this book.

c) Assignment for a Business topic: Research and prepare a paper and a presentation on businesses and advanced technology. What is hot, and what is not? Cite at least 3 reputable sources. Compare and contrast to the depictions in this book.

d) Assignment to do a Startup: Have the students prepare a paper about how they might startup a business in this realm. They must submit a sound Business Plan for the startup. They could also be asked to present their Business Plan and so should also have a presentation deck to coincide with it.

You can certainly adjust the aforementioned assignments to fit to your particular needs and the class structure. You'll notice that I ask for 3 reputable cited sources for the paper writing based assignments. I usually steer students toward "reputable" publications, since otherwise they will cite some oddball source that has no credentials other than that they happened to write something and post it onto the Internet. You can define "reputable" in whatever way you prefer, for example some faculty think Wikipedia is not reputable while others believe it is reputable and allow students to cite it.

The reason that I usually ask for at least 3 citations is that if the student only does one or two citations they usually settle on whatever they happened to find the fastest. By requiring three citations, it usually seems to force them to look around, explore, and end-up probably finding five or more, and then whittling it down to 3 that they will actually use.

I have not specified the length of their papers, and leave that to you to tell the students what you prefer. For each of those assignments, you could end-up with a short one to two pager, or you could do a dissertation length paper. Base the length on whatever best fits for your class, and the credit amount of the assignment within the context of the other grading metrics you'll be using for the class.

I mention in the assignments that they are to do a paper and prepare a presentation. I usually try to get students to present their work. This is a good practice for what they will do in the business world. Most of the time, they will be required to prepare an analysis and present it. If you don't have the class time or inclination to have the students present, then you can of course cut out the aspect of them putting together a presentation.

If you want to point students toward highly ranked journals in AI, here's a list of the top journals as reported by *various citation counts sources* (this list changes year to year):

- Communications of the ACM
- Artificial Intelligence
- Cognitive Science
- IEEE Transactions on Pattern Analysis and Machine Intelligence
- Foundations and Trends in Machine Learning
- Journal of Memory and Language
- Cognitive Psychology
- Neural Networks
- IEEE Transactions on Neural Networks and Learning Systems
- IEEE Intelligent Systems
- Knowledge-based Systems

GUIDE TO USING THE CHAPTERS

For each of the chapters, I provide next some various ways to use the chapter material. You can assign the tasks as individual homework assignments, or the tasks can be used with team projects for the class. You can easily layout a series of assignments, such as indicating that the students are to do item "a" below for say Chapter 1, then "b" for the next chapter of the book, and so on.

a) What is the main point of the chapter and describe in your own words the significance of the topic,

b) Identify at least two aspects in the chapter that you agree with, and support your concurrence by providing at least one other outside researched item as support; make sure to explain your basis for disagreeing with the aspects,

c) Identify at least two aspects in the chapter that you disagree with, and support your disagreement by providing at least one other outside researched item as support; make sure to explain your basis for disagreeing with the aspects,

d) Find an aspect that was not covered in the chapter, doing so by conducting outside research, and then explain how that aspect ties into the chapter and what significance it brings to the topic,

e) Interview a specialist in industry about the topic of the chapter, collect from them their thoughts and opinions, and readdress the chapter by citing your source and how they compared and contrasted to the material,

f) Interview a relevant academic professor or researcher in a college or university about the topic of the chapter, collect from them their thoughts and opinions, and readdress the chapter by citing your source and how they compared and contrasted to the material,

g) Try to update a chapter by finding out the latest on the topic, and ascertain whether the issue or topic has now been solved or whether it is still being addressed, explain what you come up with.

The above are all ways in which you can get the students of your class involved in considering the material of a given chapter. You could mix things up by having one of those above assignments per each week, covering the chapters over the course of the semester or quarter.

As a reminder, here are the chapters of the book and you can select whichever chapters you find most valued for your particular class:

Companion Book By This Author

Advances in AI and Autonomous Vehicles: Cybernetic Self-Driving Cars

Practical Advances in Artificial Intelligence (AI) and Machine Learning

by

Dr. Lance B. Eliot, MBA, PhD

Chapter Title

1 Genetic Algorithms for Self-Driving Cars
2 Blockchain for Self-Driving Cars
3 Machine Learning and Data for Self-Driving Cars
4 Edge Problems at Core of True Self-Driving Cars
5 Solving the Roundabout Traversal Problem for SD Cars
6 Parallel Parking Mindless Task for SD Cars: Step It Up
7 Caveats of Open Source for Self-Driving Cars
8 Catastrophic Cyber Hacking of Self-Driving Cars
9 Conspicuity for Self-Driving Cars
10 Accident Scene Traversal for Self-Driving Cars
11 Emergency Vehicle Awareness for Self-Driving Cars
12 Are Left Turns Right for Self-Driving Cars
13 Going Blind: When Sensors Fail on Self-Driving Cars
14 Roadway Debris Cognition for Self-Driving Cars
15 Avoiding Pedestrian Roadkill by Self-Driving Cars
16 When Accidents Happen to Self-Driving Cars
17 Illegal Driving for Self-Driving Cars
18 Making AI Sense of Road Signs
19 Parking Your Car the AI Way
20 Not Fast Enough: Human Factors in Self-Driving Cars
21 State of Government Reporting on Self-Driving Cars
22 The Head Nod Problem for Self-Driving Cars
23 CES Reveals Self-Driving Car Differences

This title is available via Amazon and other book sellers

Companion Book By This Author

Self-Driving Cars:
"The Mother of All AI Projects"

by Dr. Lance B. Eliot, MBA, PhD

Chapter Title

This title is available via Amazon and other book seller

Companion Book By This Author

Innovation and Thought Leadership on Self-Driving Driverless Cars

by Dr. Lance B. Eliot, MBA, PhD

Chapter Title

This title is available via Amazon and other book sellers

Companion Book By This Author

New Advances in AI Autonomous Driverless Cars Self-Driving Cars

by Dr. Lance B. Eliot, MBA, PhD

Chapter Title

This title is available via Amazon and other book sellers

Companion Book By This Author

Introduction to
Driverless Self-Driving Cars

by Dr. Lance B. Eliot, MBA, PhD

Chapter Title

This title is available via Amazon and other book sellers

Companion Book By This Author

Autonomous Vehicle Driverless Self-Driving Cars and Artificial Intelligence

by Dr. Lance B. Eliot, MBA, PhD

Chapter Title

This title is available via Amazon and other book sellers

Companion Book By This Author

Transformative Artificial Intelligence Driverless Self-Driving Cars

by Dr. Lance B. Eliot, MBA, PhD

Chapter Title

This title is available via Amazon and other book sellers

Companion Book By This Author

Disruptive Artificial Intelligence and Driverless Self-Driving Cars

by Dr. Lance B. Eliot, MBA, PhD

Chapter Title

This title is available via Amazon and other book sellers

Companion Book By This Author

State-of-the-Art
AI Driverless Self-Driving Cars

by Dr. Lance B. Eliot, MBA, PhD

Chapter Title

This title is available via Amazon and other book sellers

Companion Book By This Author

Top Trends in AI Self-Driving Cars

by Dr. Lance B. Eliot, MBA, PhD

Chapter Title

This title is available via Amazon and other book sellers

Companion Book By This Author

AI Innovations and Self-Driving Cars

by Dr. Lance B. Eliot, MBA, PhD

Chapter Title

This title is available via Amazon and other book sellers

Companion Book By This Author

Crucial Advances for AI Self-Driving Cars

by Dr. Lance B. Eliot, MBA, PhD

Chapter Title

This title is available via Amazon and other book sellers

Companion Book By This Author

Sociotechnical Insights and AI Driverless Cars

by Dr. Lance B. Eliot, MBA, PhD

Chapter Title

This title is available via Amazon and other book sellers

Companion Book By This Author

Pioneering Advances for AI Driverless Cars

by Dr. Lance B. Eliot, MBA, PhD

This title is available via Amazon and other book sellers

Companion Book By This Author

Leading Edge Trends for AI Driverless Cars

by Dr. Lance B. Eliot, MBA, PhD

Chapter Title

This title is available via Amazon and other book sellers

Companion Book By This Author

The Cutting Edge of AI Autonomous Cars

by Dr. Lance B. Eliot, MBA, PhD

Chapter Title

This title is available via Amazon and other book sellers

Companion Book By This Author

The Next Wave of AI Self-Driving Cars

by Dr. Lance B. Eliot, MBA, PhD

Chapter Title

1 Eliot Framework for AI Self-Driving Cars

2 Productivity and AI Self-Driving Cars

3 Blind Pedestrians and AI Self-Driving Cars

4 Fail-Safe AI and AI Self-Driving Cars

5 Anomaly Detection and AI Self-Driving Cars

6 Running Out of Gas and AI Self-Driving Cars

7 Deep Personalization and AI Self-Driving Cars

8 Reframing the Levels of AI Self-Driving Cars

9 Cryptojacking and AI Self-Driving Cars

This title is available via Amazon and other book sellers

Companion Book By This Author

Revolutionary Innovations of AI Self-Driving Cars

by Dr. Lance B. Eliot, MBA, PhD

Chapter Title

This title is available via Amazon and other book sellers

Companion Book By This Author

AI Self-Driving Cars
Breakthroughs

by Dr. Lance B. Eliot, MBA, PhD

Chapter Title

This title is available via Amazon and other book sellers

Companion Book By This Author

Trailblazing Trends for
AI Self-Driving Cars

by Dr. Lance B. Eliot, MBA, PhD

Chapter Title

This title is available via Amazon and other book sellers

Companion Book By This Author

Ingenious Strides for
AI Driverless Cars

by Dr. Lance B. Eliot, MBA, PhD

Chapter Title

This title is available via Amazon and other book sellers

Companion Book By This Author

AI Self-Driving Cars
Inventiveness

by Dr. Lance B. Eliot, MBA, PhD

Chapter Title

This title is available via Amazon and other book sellers

Companion Book By This Author

Visionary Secrets of AI Driverless Cars

by Dr. Lance B. Eliot, MBA, PhD

Chapter Title

This title is available via Amazon and other book sellers

Companion Book By This Author

Spearheading AI Self-Driving Cars

by Dr. Lance B. Eliot, MBA, PhD

Chapter Title

This title is available via Amazon and other book sellers

Companion Book By This Author

Spurring
AI Self-Driving Cars

by Dr. Lance B. Eliot, MBA, PhD

Chapter Title

This title is available via Amazon and other book sellers

Companion Book By This Author

Avant-Garde
AI Driverless Cars

by Dr. Lance B. Eliot, MBA, PhD

Chapter Title

This title is available via Amazon and other book sellers

Companion Book By This Author

AI Self-Driving Cars Evolvement

by Dr. Lance B. Eliot, MBA, PhD

Chapter Title

This title is available via Amazon and other book sellers

Companion Book By This Author

AI Driverless Cars Chrysalis

by Dr. Lance B. Eliot, MBA, PhD

Chapter Title

Companion Book By This Author

Boosting
AI Autonomous Cars

by Dr. Lance B. Eliot, MBA, PhD

Chapter Title

This title is available via Amazon and other book sellers

Companion Book By This Author

AI Self-Driving Cars Trendsetting

by Dr. Lance B. Eliot, MBA, PhD

Chapter Title

1 Eliot Framework for AI Self-Driving Cars
2 OTA Myths and AI Self-Driving Cars
3 Surveys and AI Self-Driving Cars
4 Tech Spies and AI Self-Driving Cars
5 Anxieties and AI Self-Driving Cars
6 Achilles Heel and AI Self-Driving Cars
7 Kids Alone and AI Self-Driving Cars
8 Infrastructure and AI Self-Driving Cars
9 Distracted Driving and AI Self-Driving Cars
10 Human Drivers and AI Self-Driving Cars
11 Anti-LIDAR Stance and AI Self-Driving Cars
12 Autopilot Team and AI Self-Driving Cars
13 Rigged Videos and AI Self-Driving Cars
14 Stalled Cars and AI Self-Driving Cars
15 Princeton Summit and AI Self-Driving Cars
16 Brittleness and AI Self-Driving Cars
17 Mergers and AI Self-Driving Cars

This title is available via Amazon and other book sellers

Companion Book By This Author

AI Autonomous Cars
Forefront

by Dr. Lance B. Eliot, MBA, PhD

Chapter Title

This title is available via Amazon and other book sellers

Companion Book By This Author

AI Autonomous Cars Emergence

by Dr. Lance B. Eliot, MBA, PhD

Chapter Title

This title is available via Amazon and other book sellers

Companion Book By This Author

AI Autonomous Cars
Progress

by Dr. Lance B. Eliot, MBA, PhD

Chapter Title

Companion Book By This Author

AI Self-Driving Cars Prognosis

by Dr. Lance B. Eliot, MBA, PhD

Chapter Title

This title is available via Amazon and other book sellers

Companion Book By This Author

AI Self-Driving Cars
Momentum

by Dr. Lance B. Eliot, MBA, PhD

Chapter Title

This title is available via Amazon and other book sellers

Companion Book By This Author

AI Self-Driving Cars Headway

by Dr. Lance B. Eliot, MBA, PhD

Chapter Title

This title is available via Amazon and other book sellers

Companion Book By This Author

AI Self-Driving Cars
Vicissitude

by Dr. Lance B. Eliot, MBA, PhD

Chapter Title

1 Eliot Framework for AI Self-Driving Cars

2 Leaving A Tip and AI Self-Driving Cars

3 Digital Nudging and AI Self-Driving Cars

4 Carpool Lanes and AI Self-Driving Cars

5 Sleep Solving and AI Self-Driving Cars

6 Nostradamus and AI Self-Driving Cars

7 Advanced Driving and AI Self-Driving Cars

8 Cybertruck Windows Shattered Mystery

9 Artificial Stupidity and AI Self-Driving Cars

10 Revenue Estimates Of AI Self-Driving Cars

11 Survivalists and AI Self-Driving Cars

This title is available via Amazon and other book sellers

Companion Book By This Author

AI Self-Driving Cars Autonomy

by Dr. Lance B. Eliot, MBA, PhD

Chapter Title

1 Eliot Framework for AI Self-Driving Cars

2 Your Bucket List and AI Self-Driving Cars

3 Highway Stunts and AI Self-Driving Cars

4 Future Wonderment and AI Self-Driving Cars

5 AI On-The-Fly Learning and AI Self-Driving Cars

6 Level 4 and Level 5 of AI Self-Driving Cars

7 Explaining Key Acronyms of AI Self-Driving Cars

8 Walmart Edge Computing and AI Self-Driving Cars

9 Stonehenge Lessons and AI Self-Driving Cars

10 Levels of Autonomy Feud and AI Self-Driving Cars

11 Hide and Escape Via AI Self-Driving Cars

This title is available via Amazon and other book sellers

Companion Book By This Author

AI Driverless Cars Transmutation

by Dr. Lance B. Eliot, MBA, PhD

Chapter Title

This title is available via Amazon and other book sellers

Companion Book By This Author

AI Driverless Cars Potentiality

by Dr. Lance B. Eliot, MBA, PhD

Chapter Title

This title is available via Amazon and other book sellers

Companion Book By This Author

AI Driverless Cars Realities

by Dr. Lance B. Eliot, MBA, PhD

Chapter Title

This title is available via Amazon and other book sellers

Companion Book By This Author

AI Self-Driving Cars
Materiality

by Dr. Lance B. Eliot, MBA, PhD

Chapter Title

This title is available via Amazon and other book sellers

Companion Book By This Author

AI Self-Driving Cars Accordance

by Dr. Lance B. Eliot, MBA, PhD

Chapter Title

This title is available via Amazon and other book sellers

Companion Book By This Author

AI Self-Driving Cars
Equanimity

by Dr. Lance B. Eliot, MBA, PhD

Chapter Title

This title is available via Amazon and other book sellers

Companion Book By This Author

AI Self-Driving Cars Divulgement

by Dr. Lance B. Eliot, MBA, PhD

Chapter Title

This title is available via Amazon and other book sellers

Companion Book By This Author

AI Self-Driving Cars Consonance

by Dr. Lance B. Eliot, MBA, PhD

Chapter Title

1 Eliot Framework for AI Self-Driving Cars

2 Baby Yoda on Hoods Life and AI Self-Driving Cars

3 Ugliest Cars Looks and AI Self-Driving Cars

4 MacGyver Shrewdness and AI Self-Driving Cars

5 Strong vs Weak AI and AI Self-Driving Cars

6 Trolley Problem and AI Self-Driving Cars

7 Evasive Maneuvering and AI Self-Driving Cars

8 Movie Miscasting AI and AI Self-Driving Cars

9 Snakes In A Car and AI Self-Driving Cars

10 Cognitive Tests and AI Self-Driving Cars

11 Lightning Strikes and AI Self-Driving Cars

12 Neanderthal DNA and AI Self-Driving Cars

13 Plane Lands on Highway and AI Self-Driving Cars

14 Turing Test and AI Self-Driving Cars

This title is available via Amazon and other book sellers

Companion Book By This Author

Revelatory AI Self-Driving Cars

by Dr. Lance B. Eliot, MBA, PhD

This title is available via Amazon and other book sellers

Companion Book By This Author

Edifying AI Self-Driving Cars

by Dr. Lance B. Eliot, MBA, PhD

This title is available via Amazon and other book sellers

Companion Book By This Author

Edifying AI Self-Driving Cars

by Dr. Lance B. Eliot, MBA, PhD

This title is available via Amazon and other book sellers

ABOUT THE AUTHOR

Dr. Lance B. Eliot, Ph.D., MBA is a Stanford Fellow and a globally recognized AI expert and thought leader, an experienced executive and leader, a successful serial entrepreneur, and a noted scholar on AI, including that his Forbes and AI Trends columns have amassed over 4.5+ million views, his books on AI are frequently ranked in the Top 10 of all-time AI books, his articles are widely cited, and he has developed dozens of advanced AI systems.

He currently serves as the CEO of Techbruim, Inc. and has over twenty years of industry experience including serving as a corporate officer in billion-dollar sized firms and was a partner in a major consulting firm. He is also a successful entrepreneur having founded, ran, and sold several high-tech firms.

Dr. Eliot previously hosted the popular radio show *Technotrends* that was also available on American Airlines flights via their in-flight audio program, he has made appearances on CNN, has been a frequent speaker at industry conferences, and his podcasts have been downloaded over 100,000 times.

A former professor at the University of Southern California (USC), he founded and led an innovative research lab on Artificial Intelligence. He also previously served on the faculty of the University of California Los Angeles (UCLA) and was a visiting professor at other major universities. He was elected to the International Board of the Society for Information Management (SIM), a prestigious association of over 3,000 high-tech executives worldwide.

He has performed extensive community service, including serving as Senior Science Adviser to the Congressional Vice-Chair of the Congressional Committee on Science & Technology. He has served on the Board of the OC Science & Engineering Fair (OCSEF), where he is also has been a Grand Sweepstakes judge, and likewise served as a judge for the Intel International SEF (ISEF). He served as the Vice-Chair of the Association for Computing Machinery (ACM) Chapter, a prestigious association of computer scientists. Dr. Eliot has been a shark tank judge for the USC Mark Stevens Center for Innovation on start-up pitch competitions and served as a mentor for several incubators and accelerators in Silicon Valley and in Silicon Beach.

Dr. Eliot holds a Ph.D. from USC, MBA, and Bachelor's in Computer Science, and earned the CDP, CCP, CSP, CDE, and CISA certifications.

ADDENDUM

Edifying AI Self-Driving Cars

Practical Advances in Artificial Intelligence (AI) and Machine Learning

By
Dr. Lance B. Eliot, MBA, PhD

For supplemental materials of this book, visit:

www.ai-selfdriving-cars.guru

For special orders of this book, contact:

LBE Press Publishing

Email: LBE.Press.Publishing@gmail.com

Made in the USA
Coppell, TX
05 November 2026

11292670R00208